ALL ABOUT
UPHOLSTERING

By John Bergen

Illustrated by Lou Burrows and Eldon Shiel

HAWTHORN BOOKS, INC.

New York

Library of Congress Catalog Card Number: 77–85359
ISBN: 0-8015-0169-5
1 2 3 4 5 6 7 8 9 10

This book is written primarily for the home craftsman, the homemaker, the student and apprentice upholsterer, to acquaint them with the tools, materials and basic principles used in upholstery. Long a neglected hobby, upholstering furniture with the help and guidance given in this book can be a source of great satisfaction to the home craftsman. The student and apprentice will find the information in this book a practical supplement to their current training.

The beginning upholsterer will find it best to read this book carefully from cover to cover before actually starting his project. This study will reveal the three basic forms of upholstery work from which he may choose and should prepare him to be able to overcome any difficulties that he may encounter.

Upholstery-supply houses and the large mail-order houses can furnish the materials needed for upholstery.

The author wishes to thank the following firms for their assistance and help in supplying information and photographs for use in compiling this book:

C. S. Osborne and Co.
Fred Frank and Co.
Bostitch, Inc.
The Seng Co.
Singer Sewing Machine Co.
Cripe Equipment Co.
Ascot Products Co., Inc.
The Turner and Seymour Mfg. Co.
Phoenix Trimming Co.

John Bergen

CONTENTS

PART ONE

Introduction to Upholstery

Lesson One — THE PAD SEAT

THERE ARE three basic forms into which upholstered work may be classified. The first part of this book illustrates these forms and their basic construction procedures.

Upholstered furniture built without springs have what are called *pad seats*. These seats are the easiest to build. The pad seat is generally used on pieces of furniture not designed to include the added resilience of spring construction. Basically all pad surfaces are built the same—a base is padded with loose stuffing and overlaid with felted cotton, or the base is padded with cotton alone. The comfort of a pad seat depends upon the quality and amount of stuffing used in padding. A seat made with cotton only is harder than a seat stuffed with hair or moss covered with cotton.

The base or foundation on which to build a pad seat can be an open frame or a closed, solid area. A webbed, open frame is more comfortable than a solid base. It must be webbed before a pad can be built.

Figs. 1 to 9 inclusive show the general procedure in upholstering a pad seat. Fig. 1 shows the frame to be upholstered; Fig. 2, the frame with webbing in place. Notice that the webbing is tacked to the top side of the frame. Fig. 3 illustrates the burlap over the webbing and shows how the rolled edge is built up around the outer edge to prevent loose stuffing from working over the edges. The work shown in Figs. 4, 5 and 6 should be done first on the seat, then the back. Fig. 4 shows loose stuffing placed level with the top of the edge roll and stitched in place to reduce shifting. In Fig. 5, felted cotton is placed over the stuffing, and Fig. 6 shows the muslin cover used to compress the stuffing and cotton and hold it in the planned shape. Fig. 7 shows the chair with the final cover placed. In Fig. 8 the cover is being applied to the back side of the chair back. In Fig. 9, cambric is tacked to the chair bottom to prevent stuffing from falling to the floor when the chair is in use.

SPRINGS ARE USED between the webbing foundation and the stuffing in a tight-spring seat. This seat is more comfortable than a padded seat because spring construction naturally produces a more resilient seat than even the best pad-type construction.

Here padded backs are used, for the backs of these chairs have too shallow a frame to take springs. On pad-seat chairs the top edge of the front rail of the frame is from 14 to 16½ inches above the floor, while on chair frames that are to have springs, the top of the front rail is less than 13½ inches above the floor. The minimum depth of the rails should not be less than 3 inches in a spring seat.

Figs. 10 through 21 show procedure for tight-spring upholstery. Fig. 10 shows the frame. Fig. 11 shows the frame webbed; note that the webbing is tacked to the bottom side of the seat frame. In Fig. 12 seat springs are sewn to the webbing at the bottom and tied four ways across the top of the springs. In Fig. 13 seat springs have been covered with burlap sewn to them, and burlap is tacked over the webbing of the back and inside arms. The burlap overhangs the sides of the back over the arms and across the top rail where an edge roll is formed. Fig. 14 shows the stuffing stitched in place. In Fig. 15, cotton has been placed over the stuffing. Fig. 16 shows the muslin cover.

In the operations shown in Figs. 14, 15 and 16, the materials are applied first to the seat, then to the back and last to the arms. Fig. 17 illustrates how to cut and sew covers for seat, inside back and arms. Fig. 18 shows how covers are applied to the seat and arms. In Fig. 19, the back and arms are covered. Fig. 20 illustrates how to cover the outside of arms and back. Cambric is tacked to the bottom of the chair in Fig. 21.

A spring edge, described in the next lesson, Fig. 24, may also be used in tight-spring construction.

Lesson Three — **THE OVERSTUFFED SEAT**

WHERE EXTRA SOFTNESS in the seating is desired, such as on sofas, love seats, easy chairs, lounging chairs and wing chairs, overstuffed upholstering is used.

The overstuffed seat varies from the tight-spring seat in that it uses two sets of springs. Here the seats and backs both have springs. The lower springs are the same as those used in a tight-spring seat. The top seat springs are individual springs sewn into separate cloth pockets and tied together to form a single piece called a marshall unit. The lower set of seat springs, with the tops of the springs built up with stuffing, is called a deck or platform. The marshall unit can be built in over this deck and upholstered as a single unit. However, in most cases the lower springs are up-

(Continued on page 24)

TIGHT-PAD CHAIR FRAME

14"
TO
16½"

1

FRAME WEBBED

2

BURLAP OVER WEBBING

3

STUFFING STITCHED
TO BURLAP

After this stitching, more loose
stuffing is added in the center
of the seat and back to build up
a crown. The cover fabric cannot be drawn uniformly taut
over surface lacking this crown

4

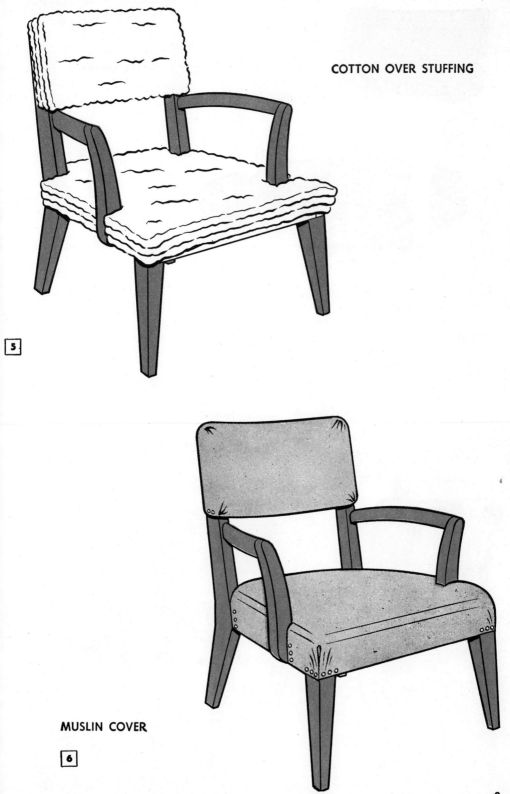

COTTON OVER STUFFING

5

MUSLIN COVER

6

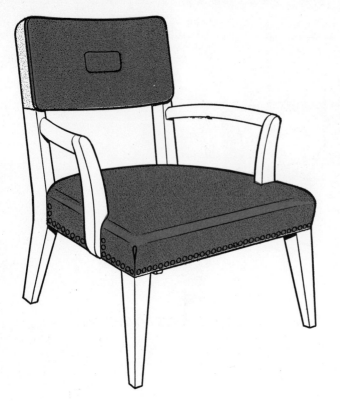

FINAL COVER

7

APPLYING BACK COVER

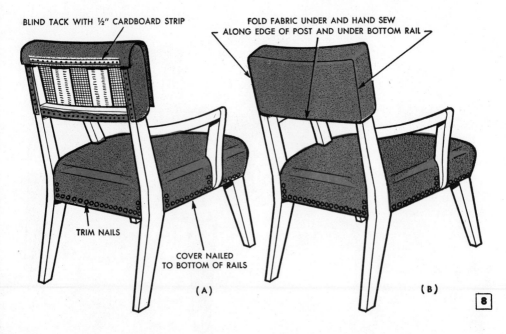

BLIND TACK WITH ½" CARDBOARD STRIP

FOLD FABRIC UNDER AND HAND SEW
ALONG EDGE OF POST AND UNDER BOTTOM RAIL

TRIM NAILS

COVER NAILED
TO BOTTOM OF RAILS

(A)

(B)

8

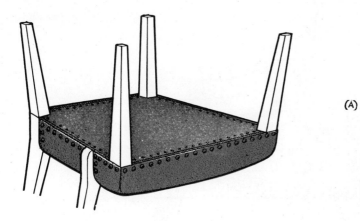

(A)

TACKING CAMBRIC TO BOTTOM

9

(B)

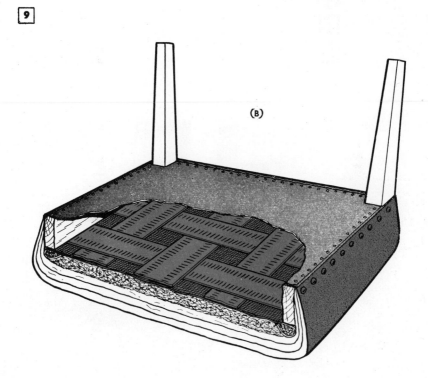

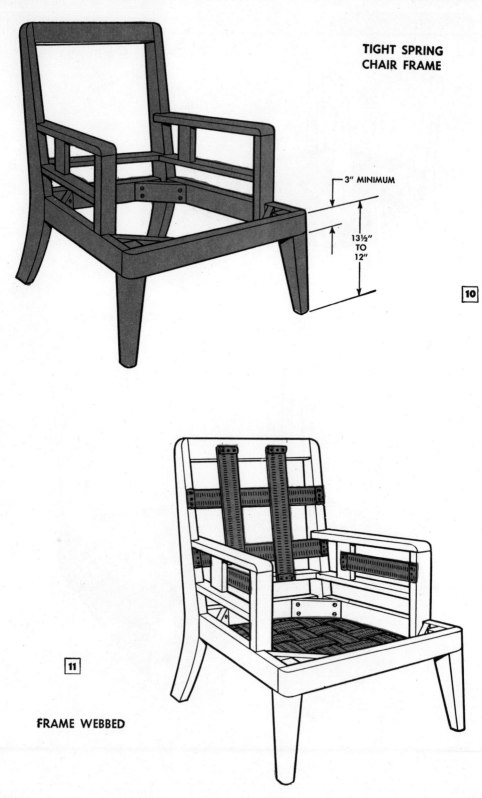

**TIGHT SPRING
CHAIR FRAME**

3" MINIMUM

13½"
TO
12"

10

11

FRAME WEBBED

SPRINGS SEWED AND TIED

12

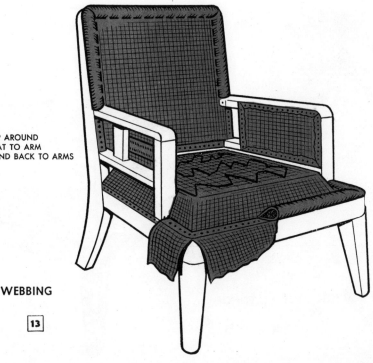

EDGE ROLL BUILT UP AROUND
FRONT EDGE OF SEAT TO ARM
STUMPS AND AROUND BACK TO ARMS

BURLAP OVER WEBBING

13

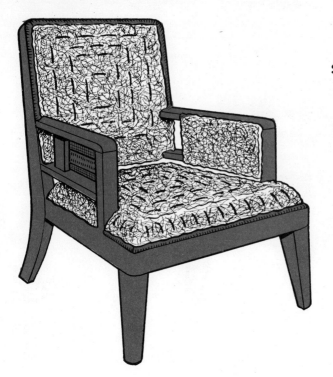

STUFFING STITCHED TO BURLAP

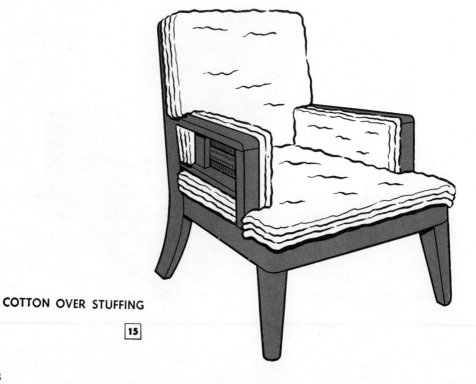

COTTON OVER STUFFING

15

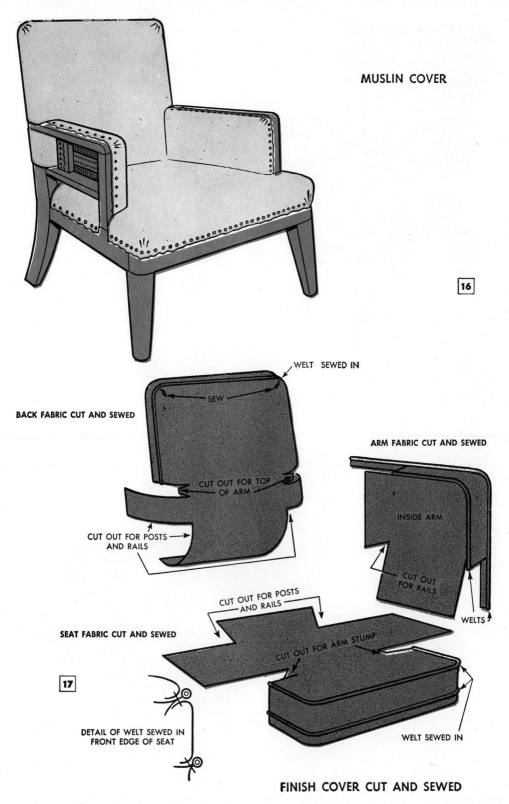

MUSLIN COVER

16

WELT SEWED IN

SEW

BACK FABRIC CUT AND SEWED

ARM FABRIC CUT AND SEWED

CUT OUT FOR TOP
OF ARM

INSIDE ARM

CUT OUT FOR POSTS
AND RAILS

CUT OUT
FOR RAILS

WELTS

CUT OUT FOR POSTS
AND RAILS

SEAT FABRIC CUT AND SEWED

CUT OUT FOR ARM STUMP

17

DETAIL OF WELT SEWED IN
FRONT EDGE OF SEAT

WELT SEWED IN

FINISH COVER CUT AND SEWED

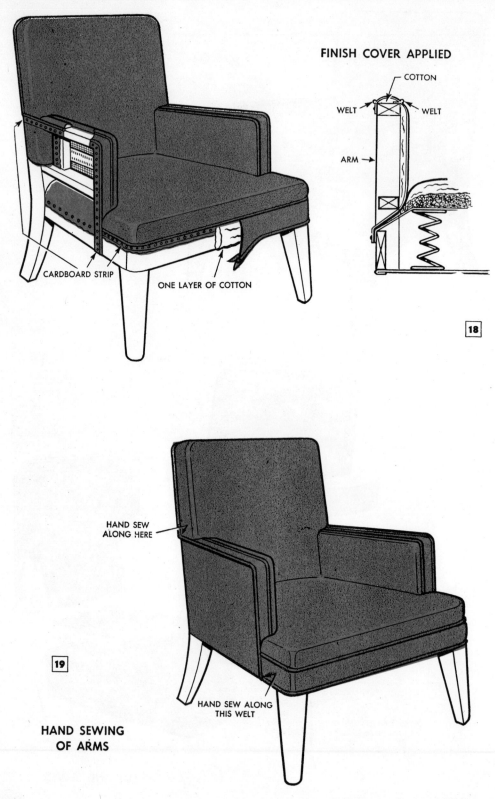

FINISH COVER APPLIED

COTTON

WELT · WELT

ARM →

CARDBOARD STRIP

ONE LAYER OF COTTON

18

HAND SEW ALONG HERE

19

HAND SEW ALONG THIS WELT

HAND SEWING OF ARMS

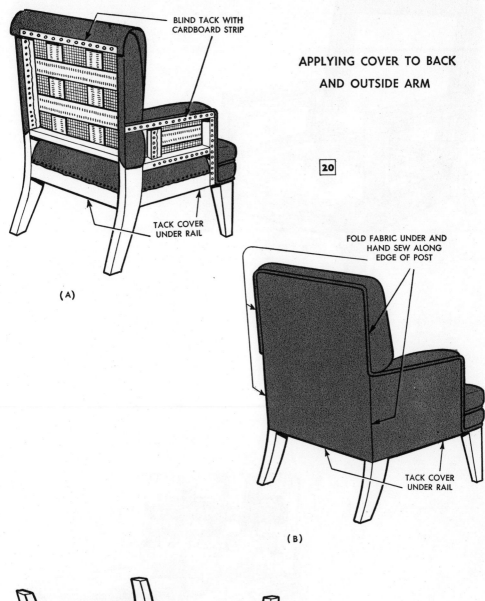

BLIND TACK WITH
CARDBOARD STRIP

TACK COVER
UNDER RAIL

(A)

APPLYING COVER TO BACK
AND OUTSIDE ARM

20

FOLD FABRIC UNDER AND
HAND SEW ALONG
EDGE OF POST

TACK COVER
UNDER RAIL

(B)

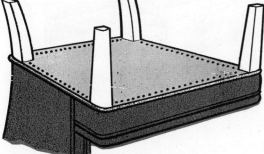

21

TACKING CAMBRIC TO BOTTOM

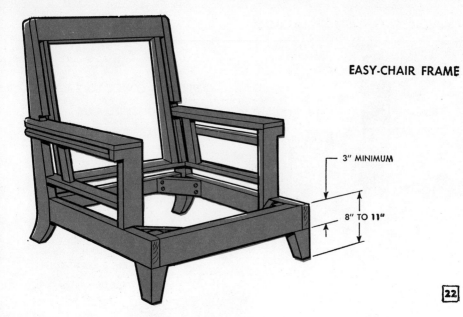

EASY-CHAIR FRAME

3" MINIMUM

8" TO 11"

22

23

FRAME WEBBED

BURLAP OVER WEBBING ON BACK

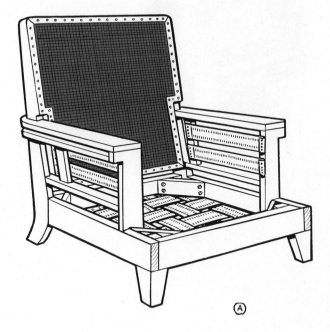

Ⓐ

24

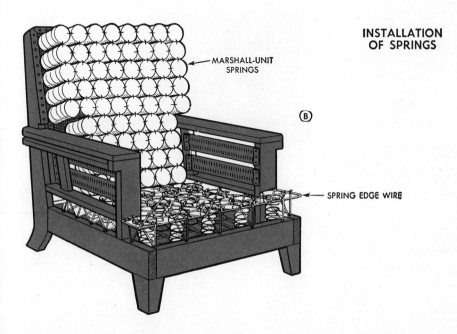

INSTALLATION OF SPRINGS

← MARSHALL-UNIT SPRINGS

Ⓑ

← SPRING EDGE WIRE

BURLAP OVER SPRINGS

 25

EDGE ROLL

SPRING EDGE ROLL

26

EDGE TREATMENT

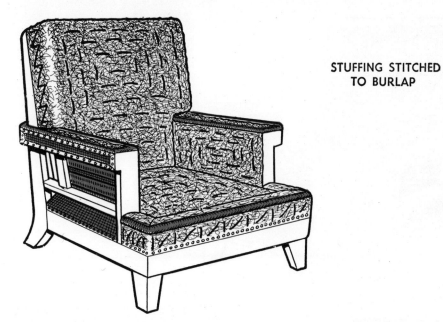

**STUFFING STITCHED
TO BURLAP**

27

FOLD BACK **ALONG**
SIDE OF BACK

28

COTTON

COTTON IN PLACE

MUSLIN COVER
SEWED IN PLACE
IN BACK OF SPRING EDGE ROLL

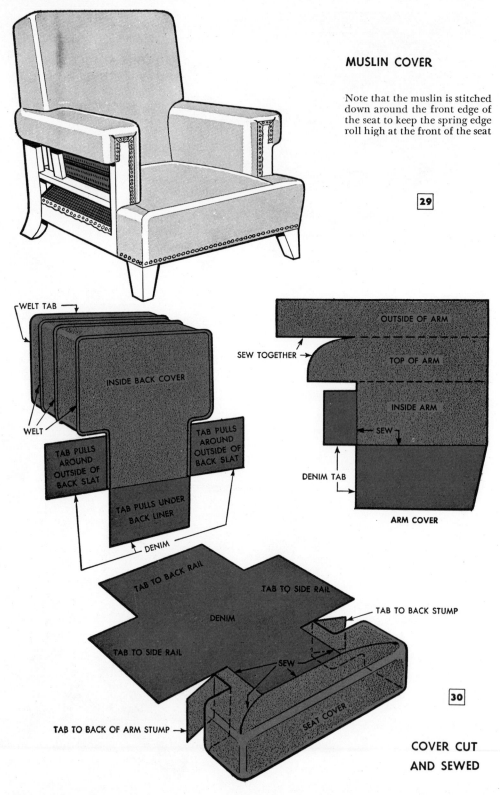

MUSLIN COVER

Note that the muslin is stitched down around the front edge of the seat to keep the spring edge roll high at the front of the seat

29

WELT TAB

INSIDE BACK COVER

WELT

TAB PULLS AROUND OUTSIDE OF BACK SLAT

TAB PULLS AROUND OUTSIDE OF BACK SLAT

TAB PULLS UNDER BACK LINER

DENIM

OUTSIDE OF ARM

SEW TOGETHER

TOP OF ARM

INSIDE ARM

SEW

DENIM TAB

ARM COVER

TAB TO BACK RAIL

TAB TO SIDE RAIL

DENIM

TAB TO SIDE RAIL

TAB TO BACK STUMP

SEW

TAB TO BACK OF ARM STUMP

SEAT COVER

30

COVER CUT AND SEWED

22

CUSHION CONSTRUCTION

**SEWED COVER WITH OPEN FRONT
READY TO BE STUFFED**

INTERSPRING (MARSHALL UNIT)
FOR CUSHION

31

NOTE: The single coils at the front of the marshall unit are left free so that they can be moved to the front of the cushion while being stuffed into the final cover with hand irons or a cushion-filling machine, and are pushed back into the T ends at the front of the cushion later

MARSHALL UNIT COVERED WITH COTTON
READY TO BE STUFFED INTO COVER

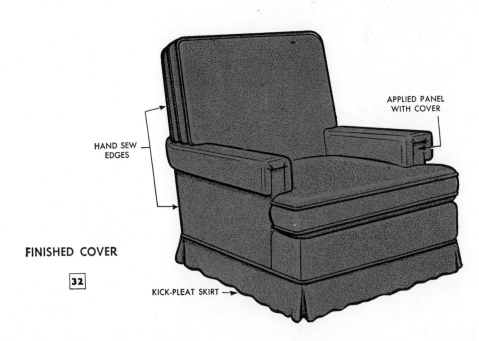

APPLIED PANEL
WITH COVER

HAND SEW
EDGES

FINISHED COVER

32

KICK-PLEAT SKIRT →

holstered as a separate seat and the marshall unit is upholstered as a loose cushion and placed upon the deck.

Figs. 22 to 32 inclusive show the operations in upholstering an easy chair. Fig. 22 shows the frame to be upholstered; notice that the front rail is low, allowing for additional marshall-unit height. Fig. 23 illustrates the webbing of the frame. Burlap has been placed over the webbing on the back of the chair in Fig. 24-A before the marshall-unit springs are sewn to the back. In Fig. 24-B the seat springs have been sewn to the webbing at the bottom and tied eight ways at the top. Notice that the front springs have been pulled forward and a spring-edge wire has been tied to the springs. This wire is fastened to the inside of the arm stump and runs in back of and around the side of the end springs. Fig. 25 shows burlap sewn over the seat and back springs. The inside and upper part of the outside arm also have burlap tacked over the openings. In Fig. 26, the edge roll is being formed around the top edge of the arm and a spring edge roll is being formed around the front and side edges in front of the arm stump on seat. Fig. 27 shows loose stuffing stitched in place. Cotton has been placed over stuffing in Fig. 28. Fig. 29 shows the muslin cover. Fig. 30 illustrates how the cover is cut and sewn. Fig. 31 shows the marshall unit covered with cotton, and the cover case into which the marshall unit and cotton will be placed. Fig. 32 shows the completed chair. The back and arms of the chair are covered the same as were the tight-spring-seat chair in Fig. 20. The cambric bottom is tacked in place before the skirt is put on the chair.

PART TWO

Tools, Materials and Frames

Lesson One – **EQUIPMENT AND TOOLS**

BEFORE YOU CONSIDER taking up upholstering you must first find a space in which to work. You will, of course, need a clear area large enough so that the largest piece of furniture to be upholstered may be moved about without crowding you out. The work space should be well-lighted, preferably by daylight. It should accommodate a worktable on which to cut fabric, make slip seats, fill cushions, etc.

It is not necessary to have all the equipment and tools listed in this chapter. The basic tools needed to upholster are a tack hammer, webbing stretcher, an assortment of straight and curved needles, stuffing regulator, ripping tool, shears and at least two dozen skewer pins. See Fig. 37. With these tools you can do practically any upholstering job. The balance of the equipment and tools listed are merely a convenience and help facilitate the work. They are listed mainly to acquaint you with their availability and uses.

EQUIPMENT

Trestles: You will need a pair of benches to set your work upon. Fig. 33 illustrates how to make the trestles. The shelf may be eliminated if desired. The top should be padded with a piece of rug or several layers of burlap to prevent furniture from being marred. An edge roll is built around the outer edge so furniture will not slip off. See page 58 (Edge Roll).

Worktable: Because cover fabrics are 54 inches wide, the width of the worktable should be at least 54 inches. If you are going to do a great deal of upholstering it is best to have a table 5 feet wide, 8 feet long and 34 inches high. The bottom of the table could be used for storage of upholstery fabrics, materials and tools. See Fig. 34.

Sewing Machine: Machine sewing is an important part of upholstering. For most upholstery sewing, a domestic, home-type machine will do. You will need both a left and right-hand cording-foot attachment. This foot is used in place of the regular presser

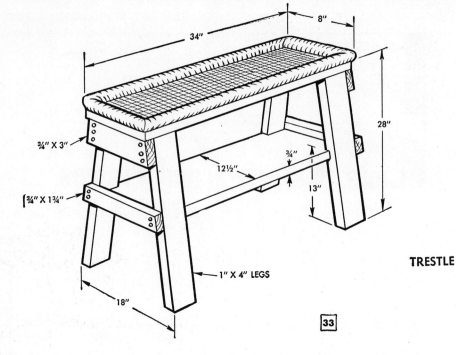

8"

34"

28"

¾" X 3"

12½"

¾"

13"

¾" X 1¾"

TRESTLE

1" X 4" LEGS

18"

33

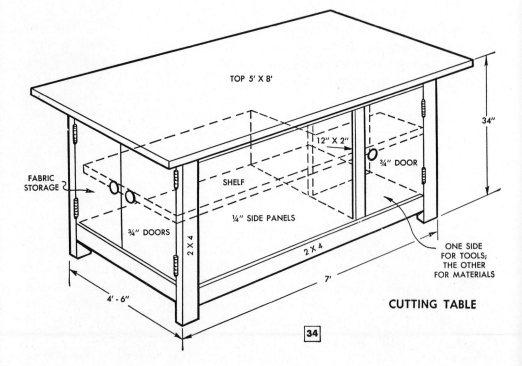

TOP 5' X 8'

34"

12" X 2"

¾" DOOR

FABRIC
STORAGE

SHELF

¼" SIDE PANELS

¾" DOORS

2 X 4

2 X 4

ONE SIDE
FOR TOOLS;
THE OTHER
FOR MATERIALS

7'

4' - 6"

CUTTING TABLE

34

FIG. 35. Industrial sewing machine

those that are hand-operated to the large motor-driven ones. After stuffing has been loosened and fluffed, it should be shaken out to free it of dirt, sticks, stones and other foreign matter. Fig. 36.

Cushion-Filling Machine: See Part 3, Lesson 7, on making loose cushions for operation and illustrations of cushion-filling machine.

FIG. 36. Hand-operated hair picker

foot to sew in welts. Do not attempt to sew heavy fabric or leather on a home machine. For heavy fabric and leather, an industrial-type sewing machine, such as Model #111W155 Singer, should be used. See Fig. 35. Leather can be hand-sewn if volume of work done does not warrant the investment in an industrial sewing machine. Good hand sewing is just as satisfactory as machine sewing and better than poor machine sewing.

Hair Picker: All stuffing comes in bales and must be loosened by pulling apart and fluffing. The same thing should be done on stuffing that is being reused. A hair-picking machine is more efficient and faster in doing this work than working by hand. This machine is a good investment if you are going to do much upholstering. Hair pickers come in sizes varying from

Button Machine: A button machine covers buttons with the same fabric as is being used on the piece you are upholstering. The button molds come in four different types: tuft, loop, tack and clinch. With the addition of attachments, this machine may also be used to secure snap fasteners, eyes, grommets and ventilators. Full

FIG. 37. Basic tools needed to upholster

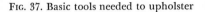

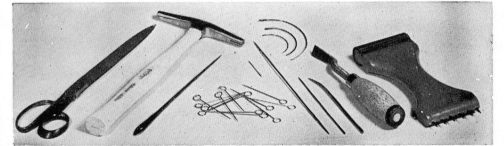

operating instructions come with each machine.

TOOLS

Upholsterer's Tack Hammer: Of all the upholstery tools, the tack hammer is most often in use; therefore, by purchasing the best-quality tool available you will enjoy the lasting satisfaction of a dependable tool. The hammer head is slightly curved and equally balanced, and is 5 to 6 inches long. These double-headed hammers sometimes come equipped with a claw fastened to the heel of the handle. Usually one face is magnetized to hold steel tacks. This hammer is styled for work in deep corners, also for tacking on gimp without marring the wood or cutting the fabric. The side of the head is handy for knocking out tacks that have been slip tacked, also for padding stuffing and smoothing cover into proper shape. Fig. 38.

Webbing Stretchers: There are two types of webbing stretchers—one used with steel-band webbing in repair work, and the other used to tightly stretch jute, canvas and other fabric webbing over the frame in new upholstery. The steel-band webbing stretcher, Fig. 39, is made of cast iron. You can either make or purchase the hardwood webbing stretcher used on fabric webbing. Fig. 40 gives the dimensions for cutting a hardwood block; drive six 2½-inch-long common nails into one end and let them project 1¼ inches. It is best to drill pilot holes into end of block before driving nails, to prevent splitting the block. Cut off heads so they project 1 inch and file them to sharp points. The butt of the stretcher should be padded with leather or rubber to prevent slip-

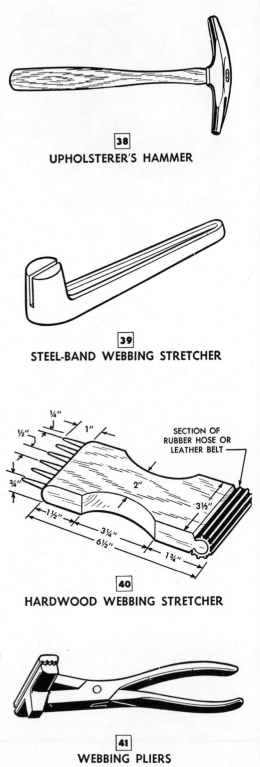

38
UPHOLSTERER'S HAMMER

39
STEEL-BAND WEBBING STRETCHER

SECTION OF RUBBER HOSE OR LEATHER BELT

40
HARDWOOD WEBBING STRETCHER

41
WEBBING PLIERS

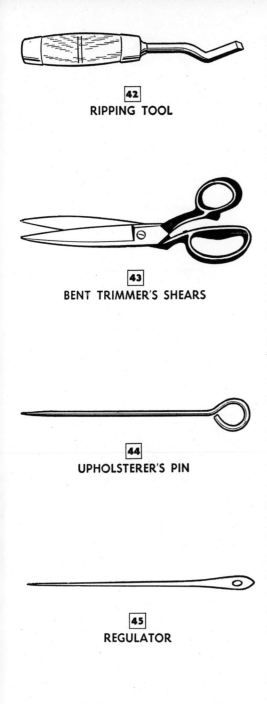

42
RIPPING TOOL

43
BENT TRIMMER'S SHEARS

44
UPHOLSTERER'S PIN

45
REGULATOR

46
STUFFING ROD

page and marring of the wood frame. The webbing stretcher is used to draw webbing tight over the frame.

Webbing Pliers: Webbing pliers are used in place of webbing stretchers and have the added advantage of being able to hold short ends of webbing and draw them tight. They can also be used to stretch fabric, leather and canvas. Fig. 41.

Ripping Tool: The ripping tool is used for driving out tacks and stripping frames that are to be reupholstered. A claw tool does the same work and has a notch in the center of the blade. A good substitute for a ripping tool is a cheap wood chisel. In using a ripping tool, wedge the blade under tack head and tap end of handle sharply with mallet, driving out tack. Always be sure the flat bottom of ripping blade lies flat on the frame to prevent gouging into the wood frame. Fig. 42.

Upholsterer's Shears: Shears should be of the heavy-duty type with sharp-pointed tips. The shears can be either straight or bent-handle patterns. The blades should be from 4 to 6 inches long. Shears are used to cut webbing, twine, burlap, fabric and leather. Figs. 37 and 43.

Upholsterer's Pin or Skewer: The skewer is used to baste and temporarily pin cover fabric in place, helping to get it straight and fitted for final tacking and sewing. The pin has a loop head and comes in 3, 3½ and 4-inch lengths. You should have about two or three dozen of these pins on hand. Fig. 44.

Stuffing Regulator: Regulators come in light and heavy gauges and are made in sizes from 6 to 12 inches long. The best size is a 10-inch light gauge. The regulator is used to even out irregularities in stuffing under temporary cover. It is also used to assist in shaping edges. The point of the regulator is pushed through temporary cover where irregularity of stuffing occurs. It is held between the thumb and fingers of one hand close to the cover and is manipulated back and forth and to the sides with the other hand held at top of regulator until stuffing has been worked even. The blunt end of the regulator is used for pleating and placing wads of cotton. Never use regulator through the finished cover, for it is likely to leave a hole in cover. Fig. 45.

An ice pick may be used in place of stuffing regulator. Be sure the point of the ice pick is smooth and straight or it will snag and pull stuffing out of place and leave a hole in padding.

Padding Stick: A padding stick is also called a stuffing iron or stuffing rod and is made of forged steel. An ideal size is 18 inches long. This tool is used to push stuffing into corners and places that cannot be reached by hand. Fig. 46.

Needles: Fig. 47. A large variety of needles is required in hand sewing. For fabric, use round-body needles. For sewing leather and heavy leather substitutes, use triangle-point needles. Triangle-point needles are also better on cotton and kapok. Today all needles sold are of fine quality. Straight needles come in light and heavy-gauge bodies, their sizes being 4 to 20 inches long. Straight needles also come double-pointed so you can sew through and back without turning the needle.

Curved needles also come in light and heavy weights and are from 2 to 10 inches over-all length.

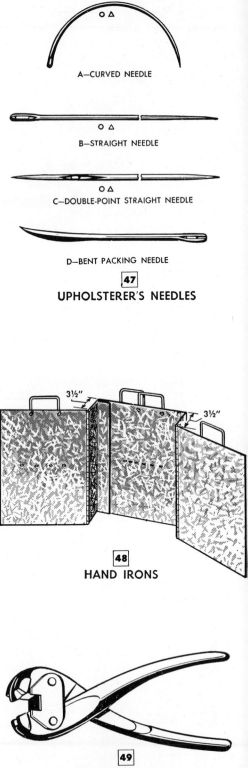

A—CURVED NEEDLE

B—STRAIGHT NEEDLE

C—DOUBLE-POINT STRAIGHT NEEDLE

D—BENT PACKING NEEDLE

47

UPHOLSTERER'S NEEDLES

3½″   3½″

48

HAND IRONS

49

SPRING-CLIP PLIERS

A packing needle is desirable to have for heavy rough sewing. This is a heavy-gauge needle with a straight body and a slightly curved spear point. These needles come in 3 to 10-inch lengths.

Both straight and curved needles come with round and triangle points. Use light-weight needles for sewing finished cover. Use heavy-weight needles for sewing through stuffing with light twine or heavy thread.

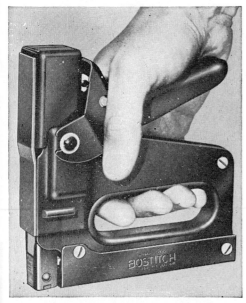

FIG. 50. Spring-driven tacker

A good assortment of needles to have is one or more of the following: 4 and 6-inch, light, straight, single-point, round-body needles; 4 and 6-inch, curved, light-weight needles, both in round and triangle points; 8 and 10-inch, heavy, triangle-point, straight, double-pointed needles; 6-inch-long packing needle.

Hand Irons: If volume of work does not warrant the investment in a cushion-filling machine, hand irons will do the same operation; however, it will require more labor and time

to fill cushions. Hand irons are made of sheet metal. The top and bottom plates can be adjusted to the width of the cushion to be filled, anywhere from a 15⅜-inch to 23⅜-inch-wide cushion. The sides hook on to the top and bottom panels. See Fig. 48 for over-all size and construction of irons. For use of irons see Part 3, Lesson 7, on making loose cushions.

Spring-Clip Pliers: Spring-clip pliers are used for setting metal clips to fasten springs to edge wire of seats and backs. These pliers are made for setting clips with three or five prongs. A common pliers will do the same job but is much slower. Fig. 49.

The following tools are not essential except for those of you who are going to do a volume of work. These tools will enable you to do a better job, more easily and quickly.

Spring-Driven Tacker: This machine is ideal for tacking on burlap, muslin, cambric and the finished cov-

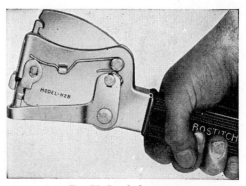

FIG. 51. Staple hammer

er where staples will not be seen. This machine will drive staples faster than one could tack; also the holding power of a staple is greater than that of a tack. Fig. 50.

Staple Hammer: The staple hammer is ideal for tacking down webbing. A hammer that drives ½-inch-

Fig. 52. Klinch-It tool in use

Fig. 53. Hog-ring pliers

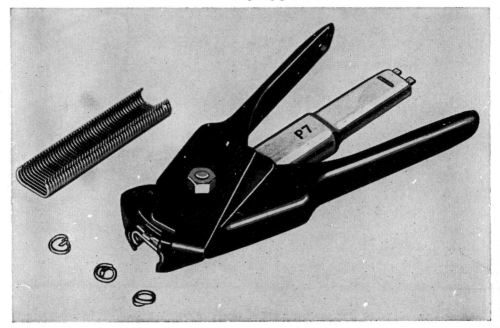

long staples is recommended. This stapler will drive staples as rapidly as you can swing your arm. Fig. 51.

Klinch-It Tool: This is another time and labor-saving tool that does a better job than hand sewing. It is used to fasten coil springs to webbing or burlap base, eliminating hand sewing of springs to webbing or burlap base. With the Klinch-It tool all the work of fastening the springs is done from the top side with no chance of the spring slipping out of place while being fastened. The Klinch-It tool utilizes a staple with great holding power. With this tool there is less risk of springs coming loose from the webbing. This is generally the first failure of upholstered work, because in hand sewing several springs are sewed in place with the same length of twine, and when one spring breaks loose the others will also become loose.

With the Klinch-It tool each spring is held in place by itself. Full operating instructions come with the tool when purchased. See Fig. 52.

Measuring Tools: For measuring you should have a 6-foot steel tape, a wood yardstick and framing square. Chalk is used for marking fabrics.

Hog-Ring Pliers: A pair of hog-ring pliers is convenient to have. Their use will eliminate a great deal of hand sewing in fastening burlap to springs, making up marshall units and fastening ready-made edge rolls to burlap. Fig. 53.

Miscellaneous Tools: Here is a list of tools that will help you in remodeling, repairing and preparing frames for upholstery: rubber mallet, claw hammer, crosscut saw, rip saw, coping saw, knife, brace, bits and countersink bit, rasp, file, screw driver, wood chisel, plane and pliers.

Lesson Two — MATERIALS

THERE IS no product that is as dependent upon a supply of material from all parts of the world as is upholstered furniture. Lumber from the northern part of the United States, cotton and moss from the southern states, animal hair from South America and Europe, sisal, palm, coco fiber from the tropics, twine and webbing made in Italy, burlap from India, and steel from mills in the United States all are needed. With material coming from so many parts of the world, price and supply on hand fluctuate greatly and at times substitutions are needed.

Listed here are most of the various materials from which you may choose.

Upholstery Tacks: This tack has a smooth flat head and is used for almost all of the upholstery tacking. Sizes under 6 oz. are used for tacking fabric. Sizes over 6 oz. are used for tacking springs, twine and webbing. A supply of 2, 4, 6, 10 and 12-oz. sizes will be needed. See tack chart, Fig. 55.

Webbing Tacks: This tack is similar to an upholstery tack except that it has barbs which project from the shank to give the tack more holding power. Sizes 12 and 14-oz. are most commonly used.

Gimp Tacks: This tack has a small round head and is used where the head of the tack must show—such as

Fig. 54. Upholsterers' materials

around the arms and down the back. It is used primarily to tack cloth gimp in place. A supply of 3 and 6-oz. tacks will do for most jobs. Tacks can be purchased in 4-oz. and 1-lb. paper boxes, or in 5 and 25-lb. cartons.

Glides: Metal glides should be installed under all upholstered furniture to prevent marring of floors and chipping of legs and to assist in sliding furniture over floor and carpets easily. Three-prong glides are most commonly used, ranging from ⅜ inch and increasing in size by ⅛ inch to 1⅛ inches in diameter. A better quality glide, having a nail prong and mounted in rubber, is available in sizes ⅝ inch to 2 inches in diameter.

Webbing (Jute): Always purchase the best grade of webbing, for this is the foundation on which upholstery is built. Jute yarn is used in making webbing because it is exceptionally strong and has very little stretch. Jute webbing is a coarsely woven band and comes in 3, 3½ and 4-inch widths. The 3½-inch width is most commonly used.

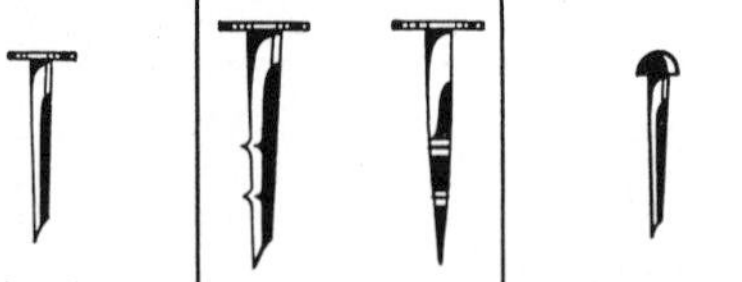

UPHOLSTERY TACK	WEBBING TACK	GIMP TACK
Size — Length	Size — Length	Size — Length
1 oz. ³⁄₁₆ in.	12 oz. ¹¹⁄₁₆ in.	2 oz. ⁵⁄₁₆ in.
1½ oz. ⁷⁄₃₂ in.	14 oz. ¾ in.	2½ oz. ⅜ in.
2 oz. ¼ in.		3 oz. ⁷⁄₁₆ in.
2½ oz. ⁵⁄₁₆ in.		4 oz. ½ in.
3 oz. ⅜ in.		6 oz. ⁹⁄₁₆ in.
4 oz. ⁷⁄₁₆ in.		8 oz. ⅝ in.
6 oz. ½ in.		
8 oz. ⁹⁄₁₆ in.		
10 oz. ⅝ in.		
12 oz. ¹¹⁄₁₆ in.		
14 oz. ¾ in.		
16 oz. ¹³⁄₁₆ in.		
18 oz. ⅞ in.		
20 oz. ¹⁵⁄₁₆ in.		

Use of Gimp Tack Sizes:

2 to 2½ oz. for gimp and fringe.
3 to 4 oz. for back panel along post.
6 oz. for cover around arms.
8 oz. on overlay panels.

Use of Upholstery Tack Sizes:

1 and 1½ oz. on post panel covering fabric.
2 oz. on post-panel welts.
2 to 4 oz. for muslin, light and medium weight fabric.
4 to 6 oz. for burlap, heavyweight fabric and leather.
4 to 8 oz. for cardboard and blind tacking.
8 to 14 oz. for webbing, blind tacking through welt and tacking down back-spring twine.
14 to 18 oz. for seat-spring twine and large readymade edging.

Note: If the frame is made of soft wood or severely pitted with nail holes, use a tack the next size or two larger to tack down webbing and spring anchoring twine.

Fig. 55. Tack chart

Webbing can be bought by the yard or in 72, 100 or 144-yard rolls.

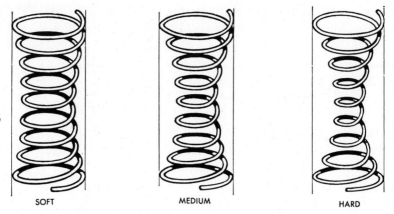

SEAT SPRINGS

SOFT   MEDIUM   HARD

FIG. 56. Spring softness is governed by the width of the center coil

Webbing (Steel): Steel webbing should be used only for repair work. It is used to reinforce weakened jute webbing. Steel webbing comes in ⅝ and ¾-inch widths, and is perforated for nails. Strong-hold nails, 1 inch long, are used in tacking down this webbing. Steel webbing is purchased in 75, 250 and 500-foot rolls.

Webbing (Decorative): Decorative webbing is used on modern and garden furniture as a base to sit upon or as a base for loose cushions. Jute webbing, when exposed to view, is too coarse in appearance. Decorative webbing is made of many materials such as cotton, linen and plastics, and comes in widths ranging from ¾ to 5 inches and is available in many colors and patterns.

Springs: The function of springs in upholstered furniture is to absorb shock and give added resilience to the seat. Springs used in upholstery are classified according to their usage, firmness, shape and end of coil. They are selected to suit the use, the load they are to carry, and the depth of the frame in which they will be placed.

Seat Springs: Seat springs are made in three firmnesses and several sizes.

These springs are made of heavy 9 to 11-gauge wire and range in height from #00-4 inches to #6-14 inches. Seat springs are open at both ends— that is, the wire is not knotted to close the last coil. Each size can be obtained in soft, medium and hard. Springs of the same size have the same number of coils, but the width of the center of the spring varies. See Fig. 56. You will notice that the soft spring has a wider center than the medium spring and that the medium spring has a

FIG. 57. Spring chart

SEAT SPRINGS	BACK SPRINGS	CUSHION SPRINGS
SIZE	SIZE	SIZE
00 - 5 in. high	4 in.	4 in.
0 - 6 in. high	6 in.	6 in.
1 - 7 in. high	8 in.	
2 - 8 in. high	10 in.	
3 - 9½ in. high		
4 - 10½ in. high		
5 - 12 in. high		
6 - 14 in. high		

Note: Soft seat springs can be tied 2 in. lower than normal height. Medium seat springs can be tied 1 in. lower than normal height. Hard seat springs should never be tied below normal height but can be tied 1 in. above normal height. Seat springs, before tying, are from 1 to 1½ in. over normal height.

wider center than the hard spring. Some spring manufacturers vary the gauge of spring wire used to obtain soft, medium and hard springs instead of changing the width of the centers. The medium spring is preferred in most work. If the desired spring size cannot be obtained, use the next size larger and softer, or the size smaller and firmer. See chart, Fig. 57, for spring size. Try not to use springs over size No. 4. Larger springs, because of their height, have a tendency to wobble and fall over. Seat springs are sold by the pound and in 25-lb. bundles.

Back or Pillow Springs: These springs are made from 12 to 15-gauge wire and are used on backs and arms. They can be obtained in 4, 6 and 8-inch heights and are knotted at both ends.

Cushion Spring: This spring is similar to a seat spring except that it is knotted at both ends. Cushion springs are used in automobile seats and come in 4 to 6-inch heights.

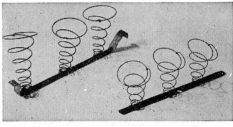

FIG. 58. Spring bars for seats (left) or arms and backs (right)

Spring Bars: Seats of popular-priced factory-built furniture use spring bars on which to mount conical springs. These bars are used to replace webbing and thus eliminate sewing the springs to the webbing. Seat bars range from 16 to 26 inches long and have about a 1½-inch drop. They are nailed or screwed to the top side of

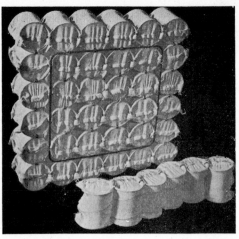

FIG. 59. Innersprings, or marshall unit

the front and back rails. Springs mounted on bars vary from 4 to 7 inches high. The tops of the springs are tied in the same manner as springs mounted on webbing. Straight bars are suitable for backs and arms. See Fig. 58.

Innerspring or Marshall Unit: Fig. 59. Innerspring units are used in filling loose cushions. These springs are 3½ inches high and 3 inches in diameter and are sewn in separate pockets of burlap or muslin. Marshall units are also made for backs. These springs are 6 inches high and 3 inches in diameter. Marshall springs are sold as ready-made units or in strips. Thus you can build a cushion to any size or shape needed.

Spring-Edge Wire: Edge wire for seats should be 9 or 10-gauge; for backs, 12 to 14-gauge. Spring-edge wire is highly tempered steel wire, used to unite springs, and shape and strengthen exposed edges. The wire is sold by the pound and comes in 5 to 12-foot lengths.

Stitching Twine: Flax twine is used to sew springs to webbing and burlap. It is also used to stitch stuffing to burlap and in sewing edge rolls and spring edges. Flax twine is sold in ½-lb. balls.

Spring Twine: Spring twine is used to tie down heavy seat springs. Spring twine is made of 6-ply hemp, and often has a wax finish. It pays to buy the best twine available because it is under constant strain. A poor grade of twine would not hold. Twine, if properly used and tied, will last as long as the upholstery. Spring twine comes in 1-lb. balls.

Back-Spring Twine or Packing Twine: This is a softer twine made of 5-ply jute. It is used for tying back and arm springs. This twine is sold in 1-lb. balls.

Burlap: Burlap is woven from jute. It is primarily used to cover springs and as a base on which to upholster. It is also used in making edge and spring-edge rolls. Burlap comes in 36, 40 and 45-inch widths, but the 40-inch width is most commonly used. It also comes in several weights: 8, 10 and 12 oz. The 8-oz. weight is used for light work such as edge rolls; 10-oz. weight for medium-heavy work over the back, arms and marshall units, and the 12-oz. weight is used for heavy duty as over seat springs or as a base or foundation for upholstery.

Stuffing: The word *stuffing* is a loose term describing the various fibers used in the filling of upholstered furniture. Stuffing is used to accomplish several ends: first, it must eliminate the feel of springs if they are used; second, it must give a softness to the seat and arms, and third, it must help the seat resume its original appearance when the load is removed. Stuffing should be clean and easy to work with. Fibers that are to

be used as stuffing should be long and curly, elastic, and tough enough so that they will not tend to break. All stuffing will pack down to some extent, but if you are careful in your selection and preparation of the stuffing you use, it will not lump or pack hard. All types of loose-hair or fiber stuffing should be run through a picking machine or picked by hand to break up the hard lumps and balls, and to remove small sticks, stones and caked dirt before it is used. If you choose to hand-pick the stuffing you use, take care to shred and shake out only a small handful of fibers at a time.

Hair: Curled hair is the finest stuffing that can be used in upholstering. It is processed hair from the tails and manes of horses, the tails of cattle, and hog hair. It is graded for type, length and color. Hair from the tails and manes of horses is the best kind available. The addition of hog hair to the stuffing mixture reduces the quality of the mixture. Hog hair should never be used alone—due to its shortness and lack of curl, it does not hold together. Tampico or sisal are sometimes added to hog hair to strengthen and hold the hair mixture together; this, however, is the poorest type of hair-stuffing available. Hair should be treated with a moth repellent before it is used. Curled hair is sold by the pound and in 25 to 50-lb. bags.

Moss: Known as *southern moss*, *Louisiana* and *Spanish moss* are the fibers of a plant growing on the live oak and other trees in the southern states. Moss is considered to be the second best type of stuffing, because the fibers are resilient, strong and easy to work with. Moss is not a clean stuffing and must be pulled apart and shaken free of foreign matter and dirt. The resilience and grade of moss depends upon how many times it has been processed. XXXX moss is the best grade, XX moss the poorest grade. The X indicates the number of times the moss has been cured and ginned. In processing XXXX moss, the fibers turn black or dark brown. The poorest grade, XX moss, has a greenish color.

The best grade of moss is much better than the cheaper grades of hair. Moss is sold by the pound and in bales of 100 to 150 lb.

Tow: The stalks of the flax plant are used in making tow. The fibers of tow are strong and clean; however, it mats and packs into hard layers. It is best to use tow as an insulator over springs and then top it with curled hair or moss for resilience. Tow is also excellent for building edge rolls. It is sold by the pound and in 125 to 150-lb. bales.

Sisal: Sisal grows in tropical countries, and the fibers used for upholstery are processed from the plant's leaves. Sisal fibers are long, strong and clean. The grade of sisal is determined by the length and thickness of the fiber. Sisal is not only sold as a loose filler, but also in felted pads. Sisal is white in color. In good-quality upholstery, sisal is used as an insulator over the springs only, and should be covered with hair or moss for greater resiliency.

Palm Fiber: The fibers from the leaves of palm trees are coarse and have little resilience, but are strong, durable and clean. The fiber is light green when new. In cheaper upholstery, palm fiber is often the only stuffing used, but, like sisal and tow, it is best to use palm fiber as an insulator over the springs, with the addition of moss or hair stuffing.

Coco Fiber: This fiber comes from the outer husk of the coconut and is strong, clean and durable, but tends to mat down and pack. Because it is short, flat and coarse, it is quite difficult to handle. Coco fiber is light brown. Like tow, coco fiber should be used only as an insulator.

Tampico: This fiber is similar to sisal and, while it is shorter, it holds a better curl. Tampico is often used alone in popular-priced upholstered furniture, but in the better-quality upholstery it is used only as an insulator over the springs.

Excelsior: This product is made by shredding wood with knives. The best grade is called *wood wool* and is made of basswood. While excelsior is a good insulator, it soon mats down and breaks up into fine particles, and should never be used in fine quality upholstery.

Kapok: This is a silky fiber that comes from seed pods of a tree known as the *Ceiba pentandra*. It is used in filling cushions, but tends to separate and lump.

Cotton Felt: For upholstery cotton, only cotton linters are used. The linters are placed in a garnetting machine, where the fibers are combed out and woven into sheets, layer upon layer, until it is built up in a pad suitable for upholstering. Cotton felt is 1 inch thick and 27 inches wide, and weighs about 20 oz. per yard. It should never be used as a filler except on pad seats, as kitchen chairs or dining-room chairs, or for padding arms, making channels, or as a corner filler, for **it**

packs down into very hard layers. It should be used over all stuffing before the final cover is applied, for it acts as a barrier to prevent a scratching sound between the fibers and the cover, and keeps the fibers from working through the finished cover.

The following tips should be observed when working with cotton: always *tear* or *pull* cotton apart—when cut with shears a hard edge results; never fold cotton in upholstery work, as this will show as a ridge or lump; don't wad or roll cotton into balls; don't compress cotton felt when installing it—press it into place but let the final cover do the compressing; and finally, if you have a correction to make in the stuffing, do it *under* the cotton felt—never on the top surface.

FIG. 60. Tufflex—a cotton substitute

Cotton Substitute: Tufflex (trade name), Fig. 60, is made from clean, new wood, felted and bonded into a fleecy, homogeneous mat. It is processed to resist mold and vermin. Tufflex is made in three densities; light, medium and heavy, and in ¼, ½, ¾, 1 and 1½-inch thicknesses. It comes in rolls 6, 11, 22, 33 and 66 inches wide, and in lengths of 35 feet for the 1½-inch material, 50 feet for the 1-inch, 75 feet for the ¾-inch and 100

FIG. 61. Down (left) and goose feather

feet for the ½ and ¼-inch-thick material. Tufflex is used for the same purpose as felted cotton. Its resilience is greater, however, and it does not mat down as much as cotton. Do not tear Tufflex—cut it either with shears, a sharp knife or a bandsaw.

Down and Feathers: Fig. 61. It is best to use a mixture of down and feathers in filling cushions, because feathers added to down give a cushion more body. The best mixture is 60 percent down and 40 percent feathers, although half and half is considered adequate. Both are sold by the pound, and while pure down is more expensive than feathers, a pound of down will go farther in filling a cushion than will a pound of feathers. Because of their cupped and curved shape and their springy lightness, only goose and duck feathers should be used in upholstery work. Of the two, goose feathers are the best, for they are stronger and have a greater number of soft fibers on the quill. Goose feathers are the nearest thing to down for comfort, for their many fine fibers radiating from the center most nearly approximate the pointless quill found in down.

Never mix cotton with down and feathers, as this will form lumps.

Ready-Made and Spring Edge Rolls: Ready-made edge rolls save a

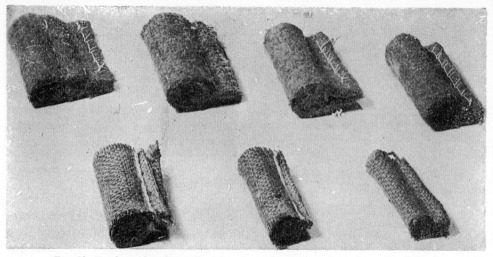

FIG. 62. Ready-made edge rolls (above); ready-made spring edge rolls (below)

lot of time and labor when used around arms and rails where soft edges are required. Edge rolls come in ½, ⅝, ¾ and 1-inch diameters. Ready-made edge rolls need only be tacked or sewn in place.

Spring edge rolls also come ready-made and need only be sewn in place. They are available in several sizes and shapes and with various fillers. Edge and spring edge rolls are sold by the foot or in rolls of 250 to 1000 feet. See Fig. 62.

Muslin: Muslin is used as a temporary cover in upholstering. It is sold bleached or unbleached in bolts 36 to 54 inches wide. Unbleached muslin of a cheaper grade is satisfactory for use as a temporary cover.

Denim: Denim is used to cover platforms under loose cushions, and as tabs on expensive cover fabrics as an economy measure. Denim is a strong, twilled, cotton fabric of good wearing quality. It is made in plain dark colors and in a speckled surface that has a dark-colored background with white flecks. Denim comes in 28 and 36-inch widths.

Cambric: Cambric is used to cover the bottom side of a seat to prevent dust and loose stuffing from falling to the floor. The cambric used in upholstery is a stiff cotton fabric with a calendered glazed surface. It comes either in black or white, 30 or 36 inches wide, and in light or heavy weights. Black cambric is used for tacking under seats, while the white is used for cushion and pillow casings.

Ticking: Ticking is used in making casings for loose cushions and pillows that are to be stuffed with down and feathers. It is made of extra-closely woven cottons, and has a smooth, linen-like finish. Ticking is down, feather and dust-proof. It comes in 28½, 32 and 36-inch widths.

Tacking Strip: The tacking strip is used in blind-tacking on finished covers and to assist in holding a straight line in blind-tacking welt seams in place. It also helps to hold blind-tacked edges of cover fabrics and welts close to the surface of the surrounding cover. The tacking strip is made of stiff cardboard and comes in ⅜ and ½-inch-wide rolls.

Lesson Three — FRAMES

THE FRAME is the form on which upholstery is placed. The outside lines of the frame indicate the shape and nature of the finished upholstered piece. The frame also dictates the type of upholstery to be used in order to give a proper seating height. Fig. 63 illustrates several types of frames.

Fig. 64 shows a wing-chair frame. Here the names of the chair parts are given. It is necessary to learn the names and functions of these parts because there will be constant references to them. Fig. 65 illustrates a sofa frame. Notice that the seat and back slats have been added to the frame. The back requires two slats to permit pulling fabric between them if a divided back is desired. Seat and back slats are required in all frames that are to seat more than one person. The maximum distance between the center lines of the slats should be no more than 22 inches. The color lines shown in Fig. 65 indicate how cover fabrics are pulled around a frame.

Seat rails, back posts, arm posts, boards, legs, wing posts, top wing rails and the top rail are the structural parts of the frame which support the weight of a seated person. Slats and liners of tacking strip are the pieces that shape and hold the upholstery and fabrics. Many upholsterers prefer to buy frames without liners and slats in place so that they can install these pieces themselves to suit their upholstery requirements. Wood that shows after the frame has been upholstered is called *show wood*.

Lumber: The lumber used in making frames should be straight, close-grained hardwood. Woods that split easily, or woods too hard to drive tacks into, are not suitable for making frames. The following hardwoods should be used: walnut, mahogany, soft maple, birch, gum, chestnut, poplar and sycamore. Walnut and mahogany, because of their high cost, are seldom used for whole frames, but are used for legs and other exposed show wood. White oak, primavera and other fine cabinet woods are also used where show wood is to match the woods, color or finish of other pieces of furniture. All lumber should be kiln-dried to avoid warping, shrinking and glue-line failure.

The minimum thickness of straight rails in better frames should be 1¹⁄₁₆ inch thick. The liner on the slats can be ¾ inch thick unless they are curved, in which case they should not be under 1¹⁄₁₆ inch thick. All lumber used in building frames should be surfaced smooth on all four sides to prevent upholstery materials and cover from being snagged on rough surfaces.

Frame Joinery and Construction: The preferred method of assembling frames includes the use of glue and dowels. Arms, liners and slats can be set in place with glue and wood screws. To obtain a satisfactory glued joint, be sure that the pieces being glued are kept under pressure. This is best accomplished by using clamps that are long enough and sufficiently strong to apply about 35 pounds of pressure per square inch. Be sure that you have enough of these clamps to maintain equal pressure on all parts being assembled. The home craftsman

41

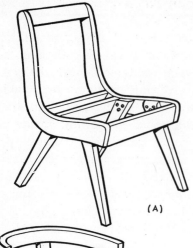

(A)

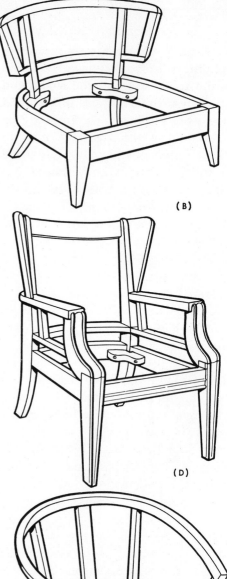

(B)

63

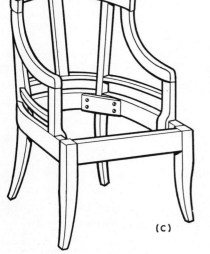

(C)

(D)

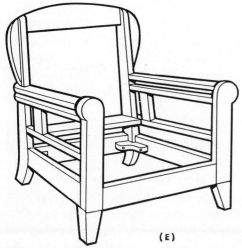

(E)

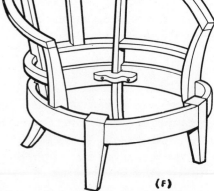

(F)

FRAMES

will find it best to use prepared glues or resin glues that have to be mixed with water or a catalyst before use. For larger-scale operations, such as in upholstery shops, hot glue may be used. A 70° F. temperature should be maintained in the room in which glue work is done, and the wood itself should be warm enough to avoid chilling the glue. Do not use nails to assemble frames, because the lumber splits when nailed and thus weakens the frame.

Side rails, back posts and arms are subassembled. After the side rails and posts are assembled, front, back and top rails are assembled to the sides. Next the arms are placed. The liners are then assembled and fastened in place and the slats are added. The front legs can be fastened to the side rail when the back post is assembled,

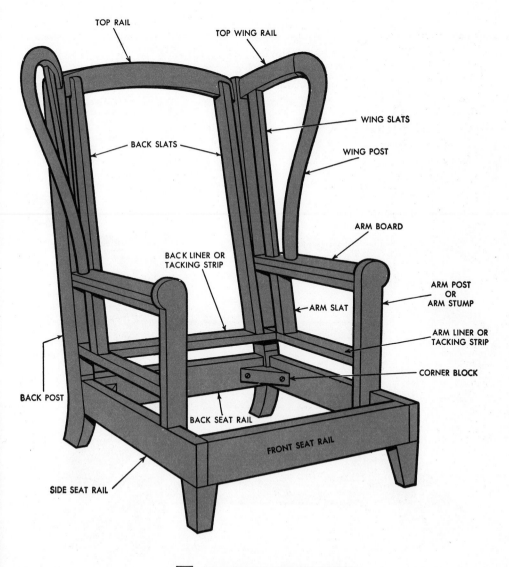

TOP RAIL

TOP WING RAIL

WING SLATS

BACK SLATS

WING POST

ARM BOARD

BACK LINER OR TACKING STRIP

ARM POST OR ARM STUMP

ARM SLAT

ARM LINER OR TACKING STRIP

CORNER BLOCK

BACK POST

BACK SEAT RAIL

FRONT SEAT RAIL

SIDE SEAT RAIL

64 NAMES OF FRAME PARTS

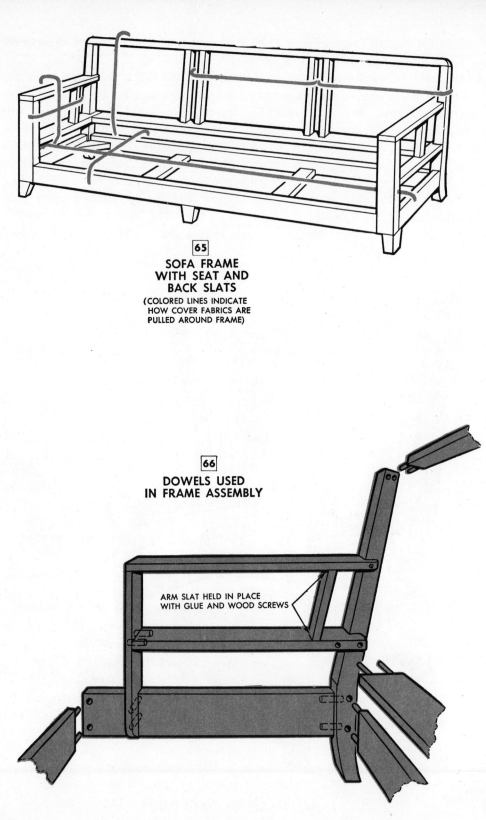

65

SOFA FRAME
WITH SEAT AND
BACK SLATS
(COLORED LINES INDICATE
HOW COVER FABRICS ARE
PULLED AROUND FRAME)

66

DOWELS USED
IN FRAME ASSEMBLY

ARM SLAT HELD IN PLACE
WITH GLUE AND WOOD SCREWS

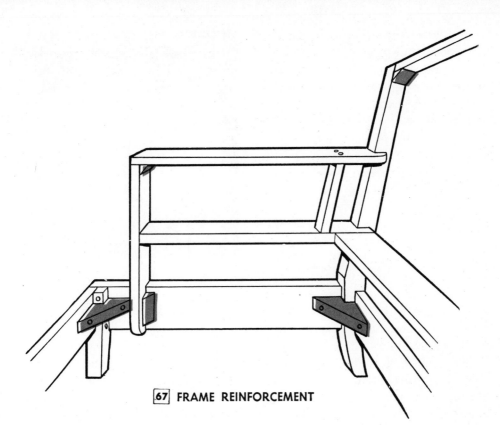

67 FRAME REINFORCEMENT

or notch the leg on two sides and then glue and screw it in place after the frame is built. See Fig. 66 for typical frame assembly. The corner and glue blocks are added last to reinforce the frame and prevent the joints from racking loose. Fig. 67.

It is important to cut the joints square, or at the exact angle needed, so that they fit together tightly when the frame is assembled. The dowel holes should be exactly aligned, and dowels of the correct diameter should be cut so that there will be no binding or looseness when the joints are set together.

Preparation of Frame for Upholstery: The first step in preparing the frame for upholstery is to make sure that the glides on the feet and back posts are secure. If these glides are missing, they should be driven in

place with a rubber-headed mallet (this will avoid marring the face of the glide).

Fig. 68 shows procedure to be followed on frames that are to have spring seats. The inside top edges of the front rail should be rounded off or beveled as shown to prevent springs and ties from being damaged by rubbing against sharp frame edges. This beveling may be done with a rasp or spokeshave. It is good practice to round off the bottom inside edges of the slats where the upholstery will be pulled around, and all sharp edges on the arm posts and boards should be smoothed off when edge rolls will not be used. This will reduce wear on the final cover.

Finishing Frame: All the show-wood parts of the frame should be sanded smooth with 1/0 or 2/0 sandpaper. Always sand *with* the grain of the wood. Sanding across the grain will leave scratches that are difficult to remove. This light sanding will be sufficient if the exposed parts are to be painted. If they are to be stained and top-coated with shellac, varnish or lacquer, it is best to sand the wood to a satin smoothness with 4/0 sandpaper. Be sure that there are no glue or grease spots left on the wood.

If there are carvings or deep grooves on the show wood, or the wood is fuzzy, size the wood with a thin, watery glue size. The sizing will raise the grain, and the surface will have to sanded again with 4/0 sandpaper when the wood is dry. Do not use a heavy glue size, as this will build up and be extremely difficult to remove. This sizing process will help control the amount of grain raising that will occur when you stain the wood and, particularly on the carved show wood, you will find that the more grain raising you can avoid, the easier will be the finishing down of the wood.

Water, acid or oil stain can be used to give the exposed wood the desired color. When using a water stain, the grain will raise once again and need more sanding. It is best to use oil stain on show wood that is carved, because these stains have a little slower action on the wood, and you can work them in, or remove excess at will. The water or acid stains effect an almost immediate reaction on the wood, and the inexperienced upholsterer might find that he had applied an over-abundance of the stain and upset the carved-wood effect almost irreparably.

A paste wood filler should be used on show wood with open pores after it has been stained. This filler should

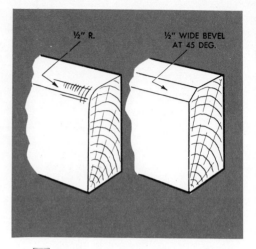

68 EDGES ROUNDED OR BEVELED

be wiped across the grain with burlap. When the wood begins to get light spots, or the appearance becomes dull, remove the surplus filler. Allow the filler to dry for at least 24 hours. Then sand again with 4/0 sandpaper.

At this point the show wood is ready to be sealed. If an oil stain has been used, it should be sealed with shellac. Water or acid stains can be sealed with either shellac or lacquer sealer. When the sealer coat is dry, sand the surface lightly with No. 300 finishing paper. Now apply one or two coats of varnish or lacquer.

To give the wood a dull finish, rub it with pumice stone first, and then with rubbing oil applied with a felt pad. Wipe the surface clean and give it a final rubbing with rottenstone and rubbing oil applied with a felt pad.

If a high-gloss finish is desired, follow the same rubbing procedures outlined above, but use water instead of rubbing oil. Then wipe the surface clean and apply a coat of wax. Let the wax dry and later polish it to the desired luster.

PART THREE

Upholstery Procedure

Lesson One — **WEBBING**

ALL OPEN FRAMES need to be webbed before upholstery can be built over them. Because the webbing is the foundation for all upholstering which follows, only the best grade of jute webbing should be used. When the webbing fails, the upholstery fails. If a good grade of webbing is properly installed and tacked on a well-built frame, the upholstery should wear well under all normal use. Webbing is *not* needed when upholstery is to be built over a solid base.

Application of Webbing: The tools required during the application of webbing are a tack hammer, a webbing stretcher and a pair of shears. The size of the tacks to be used will depend upon the width, lumber and condition of the frame rails. No. 8 to No. 14 tacks are customarily used. The webbing should first be tacked to the front rail, then stretched across the frame and finally tacked to the back rail. This procedure will avoid any possible damaging of the front rail by slippage of the webbing stretcher.

The first end of the webbing to be tacked should be folded under 1½ inches and tacked ½ inch in from the outside edge of the rail as shown in Fig. 69-A. Notice that the tacks are staggered to prevent the wood from splitting. The webbing is then drawn across the frame and pulled tightly over the frame by hand as illustrated in Fig. 69-B. The padded end of the webbing stretcher is placed against the outside of the frame with the pointed end up. The points of the webbing stretcher are then pierced through the webbing and the stretcher is pulled down, thus drawing the webbing taut. With the webbing stretched, it is next tacked down with four tacks equally spaced. Fig. 69-C. The webbing is then cut off 1½ inches from the tack heads and the ends folded ½ inch *in* from the outside edge of the back rail toward the inside of the frame. The folded webbing end is tacked down with three tacks between the first four. Fig. 69-D. The reason for tacking the folded webbing ½ inch

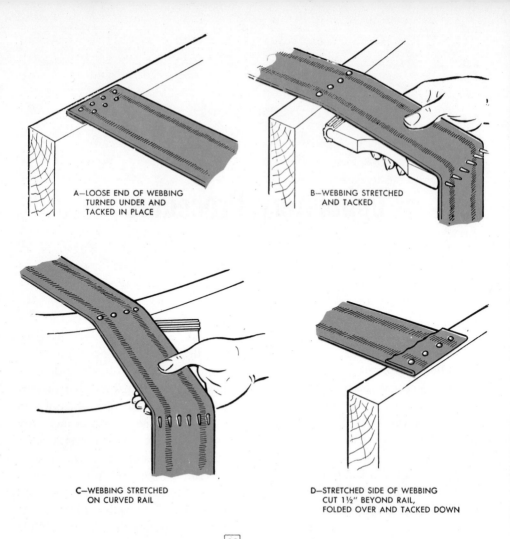

A—LOOSE END OF WEBBING
TURNED UNDER AND
TACKED IN PLACE

B—WEBBING STRETCHED
AND TACKED

C—WEBBING STRETCHED
ON CURVED RAIL

D—STRETCHED SIDE OF WEBBING
CUT 1½" BEYOND RAIL,
FOLDED OVER AND TACKED DOWN

69

TACKING AND STRETCHING OF WEBBING

in from the outside edge of the back rail is that by so doing, the webbing will not show through or interfere with applying the finished cover.

The amount of stretch to put on the webbing will depend on the condition of the frame and the amount of elasticity in the webbing. Webbing should never be stretched to its breaking point, or to the point when the nail heads are being pulled. Care should be exercised to put the same amount of stretch on each subsequent band of webbing as was put on the first bands. When the bands of webbing are stretched, they should yield slightly under pressure, but must still be taut enough to prevent the springs from bulging down when they are tied. It is best to stretch the webbing bands in straight lines so that they can be used as guides when the springs are sewn in place. All cross-webbing bands should be interlaced between the front and back webbing bands, so that a sturdy foundation will result. This will prevent any possible sagging due to some bands being stretched more tightly than others.

The number of bands of webbing to be used will be determined by the size of the frame opening, the width of the webbing and the weight to be carried by the seat. The closer the webbing is placed together, the stronger will be the foundation. Webbing bands should never be overlapped, however. It is usually spaced ¾ to 1 inch apart.

When the desired position of the webbing bands has been determined and marked on the frame, it is best to begin with the center band, placing and tacking it down, and then working toward the ends. *Never cut strips of webbing to length.* This will not permit stretching them with a webbing stretcher.

A time-saving method for placing webbing is as follows: first, tack down both the inside and outside ends of a roll of webbing to one side of the frame; then, stretch the webbing across the frame, tack it and trim it on the opposite side. When more than one roll of webbing is available, it is best to use two or three rolls at the same time so that more work can be done on the first side of the frame before the webbing is stretched across it and tacked on the opposite side. See Fig. 70.

Webbing of Pad Seat: When webbing a pad seat, the webbing is always stretched across the top side of the open seat frame. If the webbing were tacked to the bottom side of the frame, it would require more stuffing and it would be much more difficult to eliminate the feel of the hard edges of the seat rails.

Webbing of Spring Seats: Spring seats are webbed on the bottom side of the seat rails so that the springs may be tied closer to the top of the seat rails. This practice holds the springs upright and prevents them from tipping over.

When webbing a spring-edge seat, it is best to have the front crossband of webbing as close as possible to the front rail of the frame because the front row of springs in this type of seat is always placed just against the front seat rail. The rear band of webbing does not have to go all the way to the back seat rail because the springs in this type of upholstery are not usually placed close to the back side of the frame. Fig. 71.

When webbing love seats or sofas, a band of webbing is folded double and tacked across the seat slats to give additional support to the crossbands of webbing. Notice how the tacks have been staggered. Fig. 72.

Webbing of Saddle and Sag Seats: The front rail and back seat rails of saddle-seat frames are usually curved down at the center. The webbing should be stretched taut from the front to the back rail with a webbing stretcher. The crossband webbing is interwoven and pulled up just tight enough to bring bands of webbing up to those running from front to back, and is tacked to the side rails. This tightening may be done by hand. Fig. 73.

The front rail of the frame to be upholstered with a scoop or sag seat is always curved down at the center. These seats should be webbed without the use of a webbing stretcher. The center band of front-to-back webbing is fastened in place first, allow-

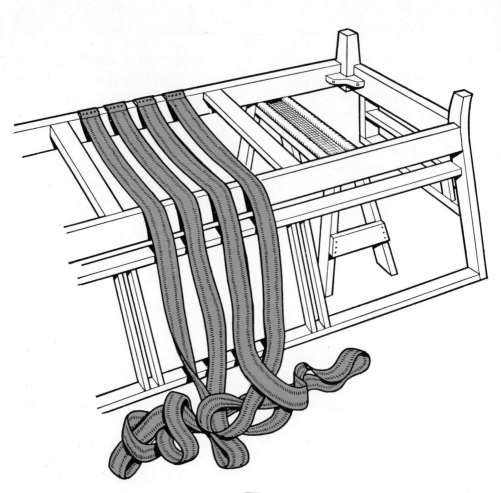

70
USING TWO ROLLS OF WEBBING

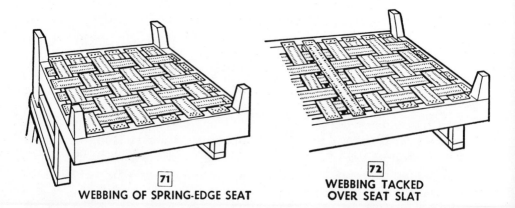

71
WEBBING OF SPRING-EDGE SEAT

72
WEBBING TACKED
OVER SEAT SLAT

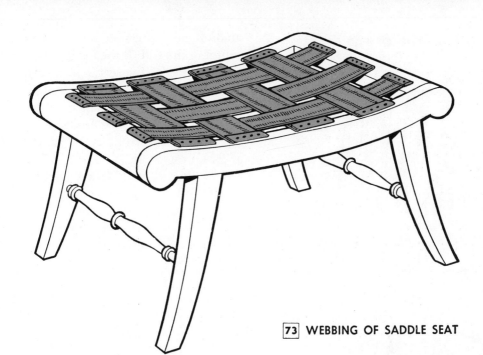

73 WEBBING OF SADDLE SEAT

ing the center of the webbing to sag slightly. The center crossband of side-to-side webbing is tacked in place next, with its center touching the front-to-back band. Place the rest of the front-to-back webbing by weaving it over and under the side-to-side center band of webbing, allowing enough slack in the webbing so that it will touch the side-to-side band. Repeat this process on the side-to-side webbing, weaving the webbing as you go. Be sure that each band of webbing is left as slack as the preceding one. Fig. 74. The comfort of a scoop or sag seat will greatly depend on the

74 WEBBING SCOOP OR SAG SEAT

(A)

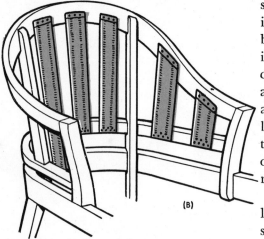

(B)

(C)

amount of depression built into the center of the seat. If the sag is *too* deep at the center of the seat, it will be difficult to get in and out of the seat. The center of the front-to-back center band of webbing should be from ¼ to ⅜ inch below the front and back rails at its lowest point.

Webbing of Pad Backs: Backs can be webbed with a lighter-weight webbing than that used in seats. The webbing is tacked to the inside face of the top back rail and to the inside edge of the back liner. It needs to be only hand tightened over the opening and tacked in place. Narrow pad-back chairs need only two or three upright strips of webbing. If the back is high, it is best to place a crossband of webbing over the tops of the arms and tack it to the front of the back posts. On curved backs, care should be taken to avoid drawing this crossband so tightly as to pull the upright bands out of line. It is good practice to tack-sew the crossover bands together at their centers. Barrel-type chairs need upright webbing only. See Fig. 75.

Webbing of Spring Backs: The lighter-weight webbing is used also in spring backs. The placement of the webbing will be determined by the number of rows of springs you plan to use. The springs should be centered over the upright bands of webbing. Usually two or three rows of cross webbing are needed to give added support. On curved backs, upright bands of heavy-weight webbing should be used. This webbing will be spaced farther apart than the webbing on a straight back, because the face of the springs will be closer together at the front. No crossbands are used on deeply curved backs.

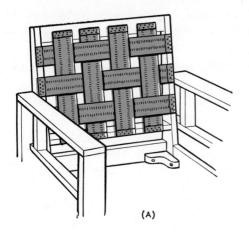

(A)

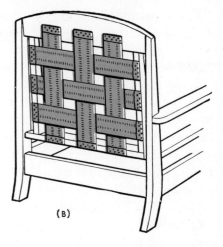

(B)

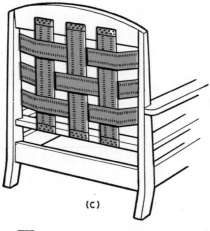

(C)

76 WEBBING OF SPRING BACKS

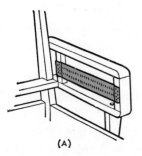

(A)

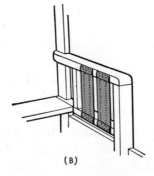

(B)

(C)

77 WEBBING OF ARMS

The depth of the frame liner and the height of the springs being used will determine whether the webbing should be tacked to the inside of the back top rail, the back liner and posts, or to the outside back top rail, back liner and posts. Fig. 76 illustrates three frames webbed for springs. If the front of the back liner is 4 or more inches from the back side of the back post, it is usually tacked to the back side of the back. The chart on springs in Part 2, Lesson 2 will help you to determine whether the webbing should be placed on the face or back side of the back.

In sofa or love-seat frames that are to have divided backs, the crossband webbing should not cross the dividing back slats.

Webbing of Arms: Arms that are to be enclosed in upholstery should be webbed on the inside to give added support to subsequent upholstery. On high arms it is best to use two bands of light-weight webbing tacked upright from the inside of the arm liner to the inside of the arm board. Low arms need only one band of webbing drawn from the inside of the arm stump to the inside of the arm slat. As on the back, the webbing may be tightened satisfactorily by hand. See Fig. 77.

Estimating Amount of Webbing Needed: Count the number of bands of webbing needed and multiply this number by the number of inches between the front and back of the seat—outside edges in both instances. Add an extra 3 inches per band to allow for tacking. Use the same process to determine the amount of cross webbing needed, and the amount needed to web the back and arms.

Lesson Two — **SLIP SEATS**

SLIP SEATS are the easiest type of seat for the home craftsman to upholster. They are the seats that can be removed from the main frame of a chair by removing screws or fasteners, and are usually found in kitchen chairs, dining-room chairs, benches and some occasional chairs.

The slip-seat base can be a plywood panel, a piece of solid wood or an open frame. See Fig. 78. The open-frame base will produce a more comfortable slip seat than will the solid panel. This frame should be webbed as illustrated in Fig. 79A, unless sagless construction is planned. If you plan to use the sagless construction, Fig. 79B, the frame members should

be made of hardwood stock at least $1\frac{3}{16}$ inch thick and $1\frac{3}{4}$ inches wide.

Sagless construction requires a piece of 12 or 14-gauge spring-edge wire bent to the shape of the frame, with hooks bent on the ends of the wire so that they can be hooked into screw eyes. This wire frame should be 4 inches narrower than the inside width of the open frame and 2 inches shorter than its inside front-to-back opening. After the wire has been bent to shape, it is sewn into a piece of heavy-weight burlap or canvas duck, leaving about $1\frac{1}{2}$ inches of the burlap or canvas overhanging the open end of the edge-wire frame. The seam sewn around the edge wire should be about $\frac{3}{4}$ inch

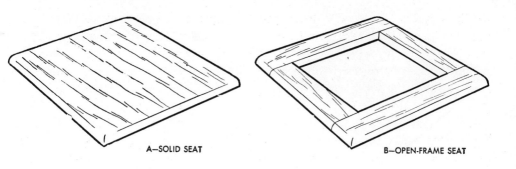

A—SOLID SEAT

B—OPEN-FRAME SEAT

78
SLIP SEAT
BASE AND FRAME

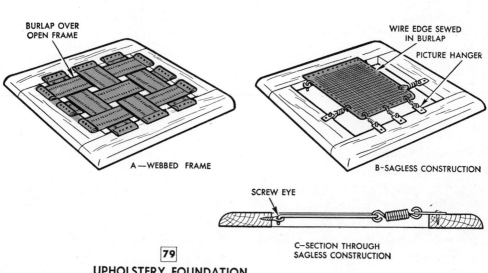

BURLAP OVER
OPEN FRAME

WIRE EDGE SEWED
IN BURLAP

PICTURE HANGER

A—WEBBED FRAME

B—SAGLESS CONSTRUCTION

SCREW EYE

C—SECTION THROUGH
SAGLESS CONSTRUCTION

79
UPHOLSTERY FOUNDATION
FOR OPEN-FRAME
SLIP SEAT

wide and double stitched. Five picture-hanger straps are nailed or screwed to the inside edge of the open frame, and two screw eyes are fastened 2 inches in from the sides on the inside of the back rail of the frame. The spring-edge-wire hooks are then hooked into screw eyes and the 1½-inch tab at the open end of the wire frame is tacked securely to the top side of the back frame rail. One-inch helical springs are then hooked through the burlap over the spring-edge wire. Then the helical springs are pulled tight and hooked into the eyes of the picture-hanger straps.

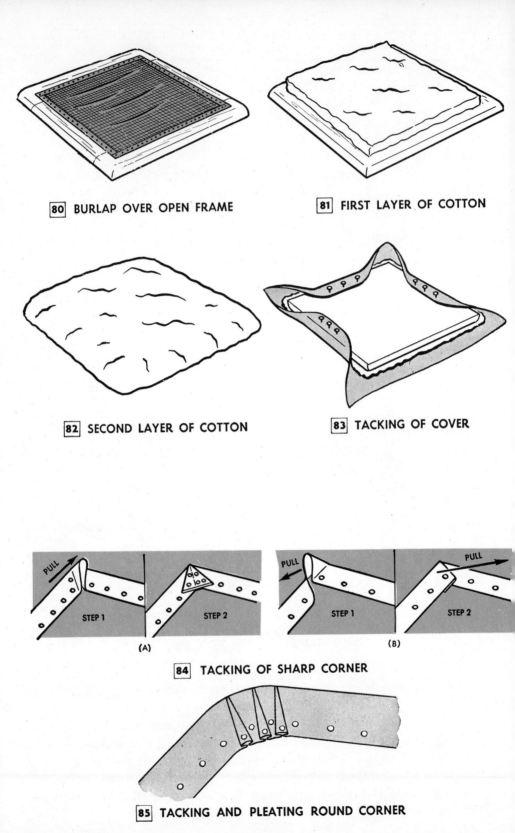

80 BURLAP OVER OPEN FRAME

81 FIRST LAYER OF COTTON

82 SECOND LAYER OF COTTON

83 TACKING OF COVER

PULL

STEP 1

STEP 2

(A)

PULL

STEP 1

STEP 2

PULL

(B)

84 TACKING OF SHARP CORNER

85 TACKING AND PLEATING ROUND CORNER

When the open slip-seat frame has been webbed, or the sagless construction has been built, burlap is tacked over the opening to cover all the openings between the webbing or the open areas around the sagless construction. Fig. 80. The burlap must not be too tightly drawn over the webbing or sagless construction, for the weight of the seated person should be upon the webbing or sagless construction and not on the burlap.

Padding of Slip Seats: Most commercially upholstered slip seats are padded with cotton or Tufflex (trade name). Because slip seats are usually thin, loose stuffing would give little added resilience and is, therefore, rarely used. Two layers of upholsterer's cotton will be sufficient padding in most cases. The first layer of cotton should be torn to the shape of the slip seat and should be 2 inches shorter in width and depth than the seat. Place this piece of cotton at the center of the slip seat, leaving a 1-inch margin of slip seat exposed on each side. Fig. 81. The second layer of cotton should be torn to the shape of the slip seat, only this time large enough to permit an overhang to cover the edges. Fig. 82. To pad sagless construction, tear a piece of cotton to fit the cavity inside the frame before the two padding layers are placed.

When Tufflex is used, only one 1-inch-thick layer is needed. Cut this layer to the size and shape of the frame. A ½-inch-thick layer of Tufflex should be used to fill the cavity in sagless construction before the 1-inch layer is applied.

Covering Slip Seats: The cover should be cut large enough to allow for a 2-inch overhang on each side of the seat when folded under. Lay the seat top face down and start tacking the cover at the center of each side, working toward all four corners at the same time. Fig. 83. If the cover has a large figure or pattern that needs to be centered, it is best to slip tack (drive tacks only part way in) before proceeding further. In this way the cover can be checked for alignment as well as tightness and smoothness. For that matter, it is good practice to slip tack all tacks so that when a correction in the cover needs to be made the tacks can be easily removed by striking them with the side of an upholsterer's hammer. Tacks should be driven in place permanently only when the cover is exactly positioned and free from wrinkles.

There are two ways to corner tack the cover of a slip seat with sharp corners. Fig. 84A shows the following method: tack the sides to the point where the two sides meet; fold the tab of the cover at the corner, pull it tight and tack it down at each corner of the fold; finally, cut away any surplus material which would cause a lump. Fig. 84B illustrates a second method: tack the sides down to within 3 inches of the corner; at the corner draw one side of the cover tight as indicated by the arrow in step 1, and tack it down; then fold the corner under, draw it back as indicated in step 2, and finally tack it at the fold.

When the slip seat has rounded corners, several small pleats should be made as illustrated in Fig. 85.

If unsupported plastic (vinyl) sheeting is to be used as the cover, a few precautions must be taken to obtain good results. Room temperatures of 70° to 75° F. should be maintained when working on this plastic sheeting. The sheeting itself should be warmed to 90° F. to assure pliability and elasticity. Place the tacks at least ¾ inch from the edge of the sheeting, and drive the tack heads flat and tight to the sheeting. (See Part 4, Lesson 2, *Plastic Sheeting*.)

Lesson Three — PAD SEATS AND BACKS

THE SOFTNESS and resilience of a pad seat depend upon the amount of loose stuffing used and the thickness of the pad. An edge roll or stitched edge should be built along all the exposed edges of seats and backs that are to be padded. This edge roll or stitched edge forms the shape of the edge. Its purpose is to keep the stuffing from working over the edges and to prevent bare wood from wearing out the cover.

MAKING A PAD SEAT ON A BOARD BASE

Footstools, benches, toy chests, storage boxes and stools are usually upholstered on a board base. The top edges of the board should be chamfered at a 45-degree angle about ¼ inch. Fig. 86.

Edge Roll: The required diameter of the edge roll must first be determined. For example, if the top of the board to be padded is 17 inches above the floor, and the desired seating height is 17½ inches above the floor, the edge roll should be made ½ inch thick. In all cases, the difference between the height from the floor to the top of the board to be padded and the desired seating height will be the required diameter of the edge roll. Do not plan to make an edge roll more than 1½ inches in diameter because larger ones are hard to build and become weak under use.

Cut a piece of lightweight burlap 4 to 6 inches wide, depending on the size of the edge roll required, and long enough to go around the board to be upholstered. Allow about 1 or 2 inches at each corner for pleats, and 2 inches for overlapping ends. Cut the burlap along the thread to keep the edge straight and unraveled. Tack this strip of burlap along the chamfered edge as shown in Fig. 87. The burlap is pleated on each corner to allow for fullness in the edge roll. No. 4 or 6 tacks are used. Space the tacks about 1¼ inches apart, and keep the weave of the burlap straight with the edge of the board.

The burlap is now ready to be stuffed. If a firm edge is desired, stuff the edge roll with tow. Hair or moss stuffing will produce a soft edge roll. A firm edge roll will wear better, and will improve the wearing quality of the cover.

The amount of stuffing needed can be discovered only by drawing the burlap over the stuffing and shaping the roll. Be sure to pick the loose stuffing free of lumps and foreign matter before starting to build the roll. Start stuffing and forming the roll near one corner. Work the stuffing firmly into place with a kneading motion. Work the loose end of the burlap under the roll and tack it down at the back close to the bevel. Catch

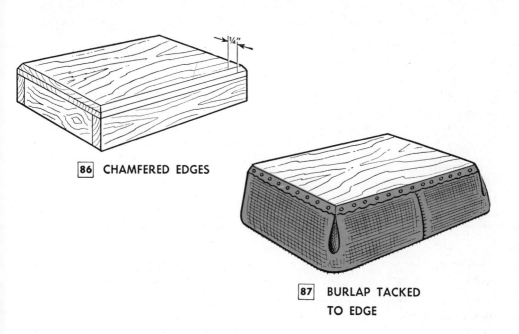

86 CHAMFERED EDGES

87 BURLAP TACKED
TO EDGE

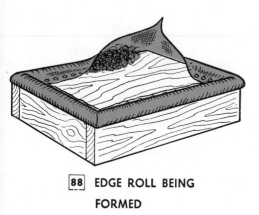

88 EDGE ROLL BEING
FORMED

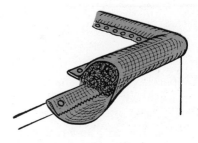

A—EDGE ROLL OVERHANGING EDGE

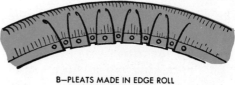

B—PLEATS MADE IN EDGE ROLL
AT ROUND CORNERS

some of the stuffing with each tack to keep it from shifting. Fig. 88. To give fullness, the edge roll should slightly overhang the edge of the board. Fig. 88A. To form a roll of uniform diameter, tack straight with the weave of the burlap along the back edge. The stuffing should be distributed as evenly as possible. The roll should be kept free of lumps and hollows, for the desired result is a smooth, firm roll of even diameter. If slight irregularities in the roll occur, these can be worked out by probing the roll with the point of a regulator, breaking up the lumps, and redistributing the stuffing.

The corners are usually formed last. Fill and form each side of the corner. Then form a mitered edge by folding the burlap under and tacking the end down at the back side of the corner. Corners should be firm and square, and have the same overhang as the sides. When both sides of the corner are formed, stitch it closed with a small curved needle. Rounded corners are stuffed in the same way as is the straight edge, except that small, evenly spaced pleats are made in the burlap as shown in Fig. 88B.

Ready-Made Edge Roll: Beginning upholsterers will find ready-made edge rolls a great convenience. They are just as effective as a built-up edge roll, and are better than a poorly formed roll. Ready-made edge rolls need only be tacked in place so that the front of the roll overhangs the edge slightly. Fig. 89. At sharp corners, it is necessary to cut a notch on the inside of the roll so that the corner may be formed. Pleat the tacking tab to form round corners. After the edge roll is tacked in place you are ready to start stuffing the board.

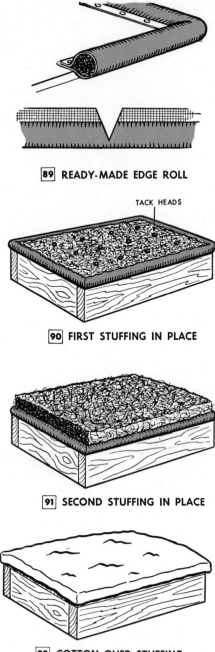

89 READY-MADE EDGE ROLL

TACK HEADS

90 FIRST STUFFING IN PLACE

91 SECOND STUFFING IN PLACE

92 COTTON OVER STUFFING

First Stuffing: Hair, moss or sisal may be used for the first stuffing. It should be picked free of lumps and foreign matter, fluffed out and loosened thoroughly, so that its full resiliency may be realized.

Lay handfuls of the fluffed stuffing on the base, distributing and weaving it together with the fingers of one hand while placing more stuffing with the other hand. The board should be covered to the height of the edge roll. Fig. 90.

When the stuffing has been built up to the desired height and is free of lumps and hollows, it is tacked down with No. 4 or 6 tacks 3 to 4 inches apart. Drive the tack heads flush to the board to keep the stuffing from shifting out of place. Place the tacks about 2 inches in from the edge roll.

Top Stuffing: The top stuffing should consist of hair or moss. The muslin cover will compress this layer, so it should be built up two or three times as high as the desired thickness of the finished pad. Ample stuffing must be used to avoid any possible discomfort along the rolled edges. Fig. 91. Spread and weave the fluffed stuffing as before, building the center higher than the edges to make the cover fit tighter and avoid producing a seat with a dished appearance.

Muslin Cover: A layer of upholsterer's cotton may be placed over the stuffing under the muslin cover, or the cover may be placed first with the cotton laid between the muslin cover and the final cover.

The purpose of a muslin cover is largely that of holding the stuffing in place. By using a muslin cover, you can readily see whether the stuffing is evenly distributed or needs redistributing through use of a stuffing regulator poked through the muslin. Redistributing cannot be done after the final cover is placed.

To estimate the size of the muslin cover, place a tape measure over the stuffing, pulling the stuffing down to the desired seat height, and measure the distance from front to back and side to side of the seat. Add several inches each way for handling, then cut the muslin to size. If the pad is for a slip seat, or a loose cover for a storage box or bench, tack the muslin to the underside of the seat. If the front, side and back rails are to be covered, the muslin can be tacked either under the edge roll or on the underside of the rails. If the rails have exposed wood, the muslin should be tacked above the exposed wood so that the final cover will conceal the muslin.

Just as much care should be taken when applying the muslin cover as is required when working on the final cover. Start slip tacking the muslin cover in place by tacking it at the four centers first and working toward all the corners simultaneously. Fig. 93A. The muslin cover will compress the stuffing to the desired height and crown when correctly applied, so the primary process of slip tacking will be well followed in case any corrections have to be made. By tacking the muslin halfway between the existing tack and the section of muslin being drawn taut by the hand, pull marks in the muslin can be avoided. Fig. 93B. If pull marks do show, knock out the tack causing the pull mark or make a slight cut in the muslin over the tack head to release the tension. Form the corner muslin into neat flat folds on square corners, as shown in Fig. 94. Several evenly spaced small pleats should be made at round corners.

After the muslin cover has been applied, providing that the cotton pad

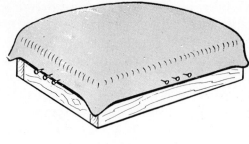

(A)

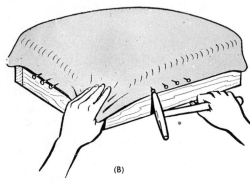

(B)

93 MUSLIN COVER

was placed directly over the stuffing, the seat is ready for the application of the final cover and trim. When the muslin cover is placed over the stuffing, only the cotton pad needs to be added before applying the final cover. See Part 4, Lesson 1.

PAD SEATS AND BACKS ON OPEN FRAMES

All conventional open-frame chairs may be classified as shown in Fig. 95. All open chair frames must first be webbed in order to form a foundation upon which upholstery can be built. The webbing is always tacked to the top side of the frame in making pad seats. See Part 3, Lesson 1.

Burlap: Either heavy or light-weight burlap may be used to cover the webbing on pad seats and backs. Burlap is placed over the webbing to prevent the loose stuffing from falling out between the bands of webbing.

Plan the size of the burlap piece needed before cutting it. The piece should be large enough to cover the frame, allowing 1 inch to overlap the rails not having an edge roll. When the rails are to have an edge roll, make the burlap large enough to cover the frame, allowing 5 to 8 inches for the overlap. The amount of overlap required will, of course, depend upon the size of the edge roll used. A 5-inch overhang is sufficient for a 1-inch roll, while a 1½-inch-diameter roll will require an 8-inch overhang. In some cases an extra strip of burlap cut and tacked to form an edge roll, after the burlap has been tacked over the webbing, is easier to use. If this method is to be used, cut the burlap edge-roll strip along the thread of the weave. In this way, the weave will also serve as a guide to keep the edge roll a uniform diameter. An extra 2 inches of width in the burlap strip will be needed for edge rolls that are to be made on curved rails, to allow for pleating.

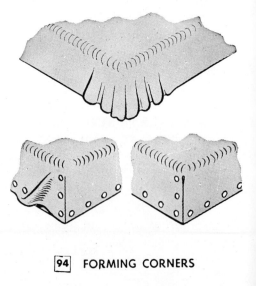

94 FORMING CORNERS

62

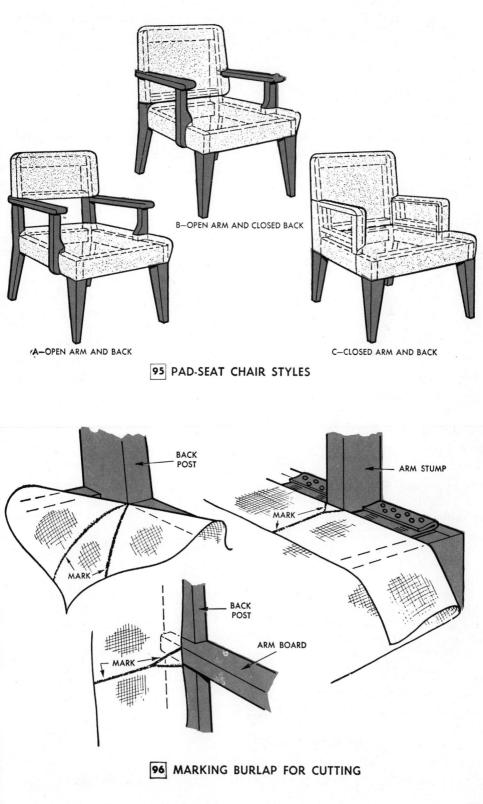

B—OPEN ARM AND CLOSED BACK

A—OPEN ARM AND BACK

C—CLOSED ARM AND BACK

95 PAD-SEAT CHAIR STYLES

BACK POST

ARM STUMP

MARK

MARK

BACK POST

ARM BOARD

MARK

96 MARKING BURLAP FOR CUTTING

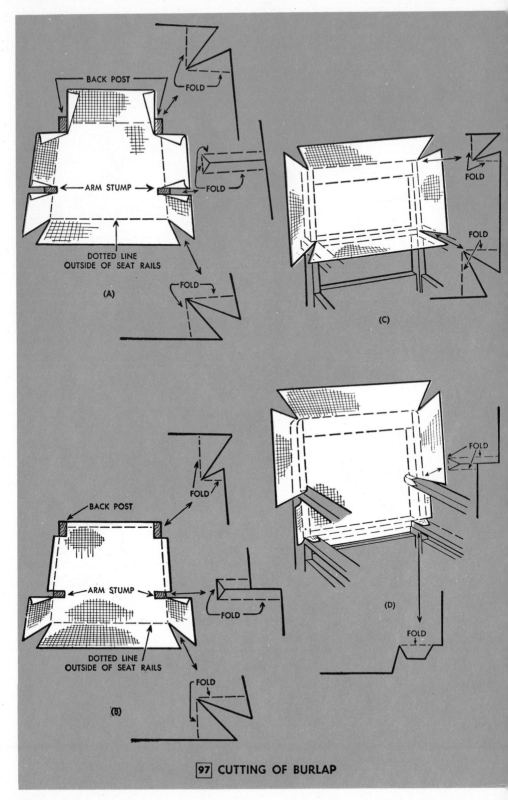

97 CUTTING OF BURLAP

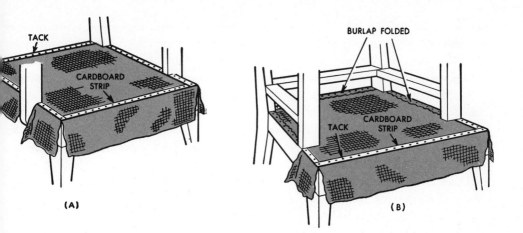

(A)

BURLAP FOLDED

CARDBOARD
STRIP

TACK

(B)

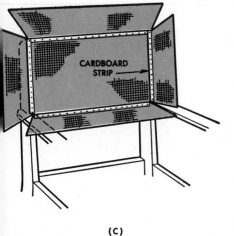

CARDBOARD
STRIP

(C)

CARDBOARD
STRIP

BURLAP FOLDED
AND TACKED

(D)

Now lay the burlap over the webbing, center it in place and slip tack it at the center of each side. Chalk marks to indicate cutting of notches for post, arm stumps, arm board and corners should be made on the back side of the smoothed burlap. Fig. 96. Cut the burlap and fit it around the posts, arm stumps, arm boards and corners as shown in Fig. 97A, B, C and D. The slip tacks are driven in place and edges not having edge rolls are turned over to the inside of the seat and tacked down. Edges that are to have an edge roll are tacked in place with cardboard tack strips. Starting at the center of each side and working toward the corners, the burlap is tacked in place. By working alternately on all four sides, the burlap can be kept tight and smooth. No. 4 or 6 tacks should be placed about 1¼ inch apart when tacking the burlap. Fig. 98 shows the tacking procedure.

When tacking burlap on chairs with curved backs, start tacking at the center and work toward the outside edges, stretching the burlap from *top to bottom only*. Finally tack the sides in place.

Height and Depth for Pad Seats and Backs: The height and depth of a seat affect the seating comfort as much as does the resilience of the pad. A board seat that is of proper seat height and depth, even without padding, is more comfortable than a well-padded seat of improper height and depth. A short person will be seated more comfortably in a seat that is lower to the floor and shallower in depth, than in a seat that is high and deep enough to comfortably seat a tall person. One of the great advantages of custom upholstering is that the seat can be built to fit the seating requirements of the individual. For a short person, the total height and depth of a seat should be 34 inches, for a tall person, 36 inches. The seating chart, Fig. 99, gives various heights of seats compared to depths of seats. Fig. 99A shows the measuring point for determining the seat depth of open-back chairs. Seats built low to the floor are for lounging; those built high from the floor are for dining or other short-period-seating use. Slight alterations in the height of frames can be achieved by cutting down the legs at the bottom. The pitch-back of the seat also affects seating comfort. For a short person the seat should pitch back ¾ of an inch, while it may pitch as much as 1½ inches for a tall person. A pitched seat may be achieved by cutting down the back legs. The most practical procedure is to completely upholster the chair, try it for comfort and then cut the back legs down until the most comfort is enjoyed.

The backs of pad chairs are usually padded with 2 inches of stuffing or less. The back must never be thicker than the seat or the chair will appear awkward.

Edge Roll: The edge roll should be built after burlap is tacked over the webbing. When a 1½-inch edge roll is to be used, a strip of burlap tacked as shown in Fig. 98 will do; however, when the edge roll is to be larger than 1½ inches in diameter, the burlap strip should be sewn to the burlap over the webbing. Fig. 101.

Small Edge Roll: Edge rolls 1½ inches in diameter or smaller may be filled with hair or moss. Prepare a quantity of stuffing by picking and fluffing it, making sure that the stuffing is free of lumps and foreign matter. Place a handful of stuffing over the burlap strip, knead and twist the burlap upwards, and tack it down on the top side of the rail, catching some of the stuffing with each tack. Keep repeating this operation, tacking the burlap straight with the weave to produce a roll of even diameter. Pull the burlap taut with each tacking so that it will be free of wrinkles. It will take a little experimenting to determine

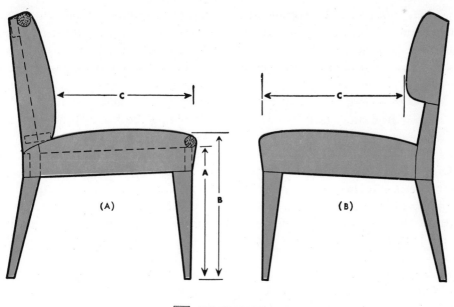

(A)   (B)

99 SEATING CHART

HEIGHT AND DEPTH OF SEAT							
34 IN.				36 IN.			
A	B	C	Height of Seat Pad	A	B	C	Height of Seat Pad
14 in.	16 in.	18 in.	2 in.	14 in.	16 in.	20 in.	2 in.
14 in.	16½ in.	17½ in.	2½ in.	14 in.	16½ in.	19½ in.	2½ in.
14½ in.	16 in.	18 in.	1½ in.	14½ in.	16 in.	20 in.	1½ in.
14½ in.	16½ in.	17½ in.	2 in.	14½ in.	16½ in.	19½ in.	2 in.
15 in.	16½ in.	17½ in.	1½ in.	15 in.	16½ in.	19½ in.	1½ in.
15 in.	17 in.	17 in.	2 in.	15 in.	17 in.	19 in.	2 in.
15 in.	17½ in.	16½ in.	2½ in.	15 in.	17½ in.	18½ in.	2½ in.
15½ in.	16½ in.	17½ in.	1 in.	15½ in.	16½ in.	19½ in.	1 in.
15½ in.	17 in.	17 in.	1½ in.	15½ in.	17 in.	19 in.	1½ in.
15½ in.	17½ in.	16½ in.	2 in.	15½ in.	17½ in.	18½ in.	2 in.
15½ in.	18 in.	16 in.	2½ in.	15½ in.	18 in.	18 in.	2½ in.
16 in.	17½ in.	16½ in.	1½ in.	16 in.	17½ in.	18½ in.	1½ in.
16 in.	18 in.	16 in.	2 in.	16 in.	18 in.	18 in.	2 in.
16 in.	18½ in.	15½ in.	2½ in.	16 in.	18½ in.	17½ in.	2½ in.
16½ in.	17½ in.	16½ in.	1 in.	16½ in.	17½ in.	18½ in.	1 in.
16½ in.	18 in.	16 in.	1½ in.	16½ in.	18 in.	18 in.	1½ in.
16½ in.	18½ in.	15½ in.	2 in.	16½ in.	18½ in.	17½ in.	2 in.
16½ in.	19 in.	15 in.	2½ in.	16½ in.	19 in.	17 in.	2½ in.

This chart is given in ½-in. dimensions. If the frame-height measurement is an odd fraction, use a seat height either lower or higher, and make up the variation in the height of pad. The diameter of the edge roll will be the same as the height of the seat pad. Edge rolls that are over 1½ in. in diameter should be stitched to give the roll firmness and shape. The depth of open-back chair (B) is measured from the bottom where back ends.

exactly how much stuffing will be required to form a roll of the desired diameter.

Keep the stuffing evenly distributed and free of lumps and hollows as the stuffing progresses. If irregularities do occur, use the point of a regulator as a probe to break up the lumps and redistribute the stuffing. If you are not successful in this attempt, open the roll and change the amount or placement of the stuffing. The edge roll should be quite firm throughout.

Make the corners firm and square. Pleat and tack down the surplus burlap inside the corner of the roll. Stitch the corners closed with a small curved needle. When the edge-roll end butts up against the frame, tack its edge to the frame to prevent the stuffing from working out. Fig. 100.

Large Edge Roll: Edge rolls that are to be 1½ inches in diameter or larger, are made by sewing a burlap strip to the burlap in back of the rails. Fig. 101. The line of stitching should be the same distance in back of the rail as the desired height of the roll. Chalk mark a guideline before stitching the burlap in place. Follow the weave of the burlap strip to assist the formation of a roll uniform in diameter. Use a double-pointed straight needle for this sewing.

Pick and shred tow for filling these larger edge rolls, making sure that the tow is free of lumps and foreign matter. Lay the burlap strip back and place a few handfuls of tow in the front of the strip. Draw the strip over the tow and tack it to the front of the top edge of the rail. Fig. 102. Repeat this operation, following the weave of the burlap to keep the roll uniform in size and placing tacks about 1 inch apart. The burlap should be pulled taut as the work progresses to keep the roll smooth. Some experimenting will be required to find the proper amount of tow required to form a roll of the desired size.

The corners and finishing processes for large edge rolls are exactly the same as those described above for smaller rolls, except for the final stitching, as described below.

Fig. 103 shows tapered edge rolls.

These are applied to the side rails of a seat to give additional pitch if needed, or along the face of the back posts to fill out the lower side of the back to make up the difference in pitch between the post and back webbing.

Stitching the Edge Roll: Edge rolls 1½ inches in diameter or larger, or those that need to be especially firm, are stitched. This stitching will form the roll into a triangular shape.

When the roll has been correctly stuffed and uniformly shaped, it is ready to be stitched. A straight, double-pointed needle will be the easiest to use.

Thread the needle with a length of sewing twine. Start sewing the roll at the left-hand corner. Pierce the needle back through the roll and tie the first stitch. Fig. 104A. When tying the knot, begin shaping the roll into a triangular shape by pressing the back of the roll *forward*, and the lower part of the front of the roll *back*, so that the top outside edge of the roll comes to a firm point which projects slightly over the rail. (Note the difference in the shape of the roll shown in Fig. 104A, where it is a soft half-round, compared to the triangular shape it has assumed in Fig. 104B.) Proceed with the stitching as illustrated in Fig. 104B. Pierce the needle through the roll at point 1; bring the needle out at point 2; enter it again at point 3; bring it out again at point 4, pulling the stitch tight and shaping the roll as you did when tying the knot. Continue this procedure, working to the right, making each stitch 1 to 1½ inches long. Use the regulator whenever necessary to keep the roll even and smooth. Knot the end of the twine to the last stitch when the stitching is

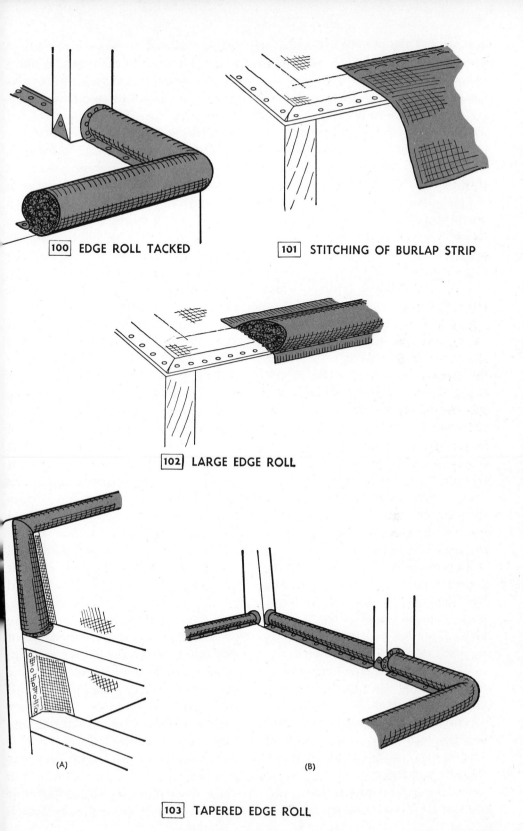

100 EDGE ROLL TACKED

101 STITCHING OF BURLAP STRIP

102 LARGE EDGE ROLL

(A)

(B)

103 TAPERED EDGE ROLL

complete. Take care to avoid pulling the corner out of shape as you stitch.

Second Stitching: The edge roll can be built higher and firmer by making a second row of stitches just above the first row.

The second stitching should be done with a large curved needle threaded with twine. Fig. 105 shows the stitching procedure: starting at the left corner, pierce the needle through the roll at point 1; bring the needle out at 2; enter it again at 3; bring it out at point 4, pulling the roll forward and shaping it between thumb and finger as you tighten the stitch. Continue this operation through point 8, at which point loop a turn of the twine hanging from point 5 around the needle, pull the needle through the loop and tighten the stitch by pulling the thread to the right. Repeat this process, making the stitches from ¾ to 1¼ inches long, connecting each stitch at the front, and pulling the thread to the right to tighten the stitches. The needle should be pierced through the roll at right angles. The stitches should not be connected at the back side of the roll.

First Stuffing: When the edge roll is completed the pad is ready for stuffing. Hair, moss or sisal is suitable for the first stuffing. The seat is usually padded and covered in muslin before the back of the chair is padded.

When the stuffing has been properly picked, fluffed and freed of foreign matter, place a handful of the stuffing over the burlap in a thin layer. Overlap each handful and work the stuffing together. When the first layer of stuffing covers the burlap, start the second layer, and so continue, weaving and felting the stuffing together as

you go, taking care to eliminate lumps and hollows as you spread the stuffing, until it is built up high enough to project slightly over the top of the edge roll.

Stitching Stuffing: After building up the stuffing, it should be stitched to the burlap and webbing to avoid having it shift out of place. Use a double-pointed straight needle threaded with stitching twine. Fig. 106A shows how to stitch the stuffing of the seat. Start at the center of the pad, point A, and work toward the outside of the pad, ending at point B. Fig. 106B shows the corresponding back stitching. Make the first stitch as short as possible. Tie it with a slip knot as shown in Fig. 107. Enclose as little stuffing as possible in the knot, as this may cause a lump. Use running stitches 2 or 3 inches long over the stuffing and ½-inch stitches under the burlap. Set the stitch rows 2 or 3 inches apart, and pull each stitch tight before tying the twine at the last stitch. Use a simple overhand knot to tie the final stitch.

Top Stuffing: When the primary stuffing is stitched in place, the pad is ready for the top stuffing. Hair or moss, prepared as described earlier, should be used.

Because the final cover will compress the padding more at the edges of the seat than at the center, all upholstery should have a certain amount of crown at the center of the pad. This will equalize the pressure of the cover and fill the slack which naturally appears in the center of the seat under use. (Sag seats, of course, are not crowned.)

Lay the stuffing in place, weaving it together into a felted pad as before,

104 STITCHING EDGE ROLL

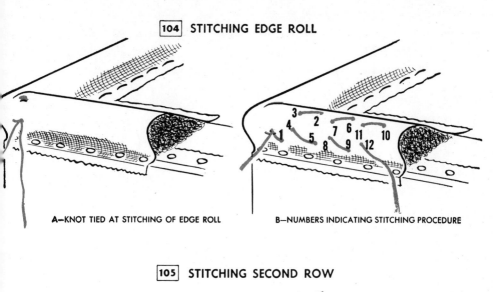

A—KNOT TIED AT STITCHING OF EDGE ROLL

B—NUMBERS INDICATING STITCHING PROCEDURE

105 STITCHING SECOND ROW

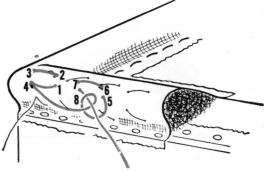

106 STITCHING LOOSE STUFFING

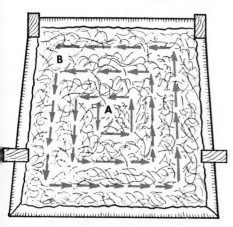

A—STITCHING A SEAT.

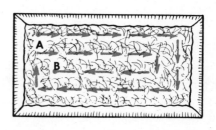

B—STITCHING STUFFING ON BACK OR RECTANGU-
LAR SEAT.

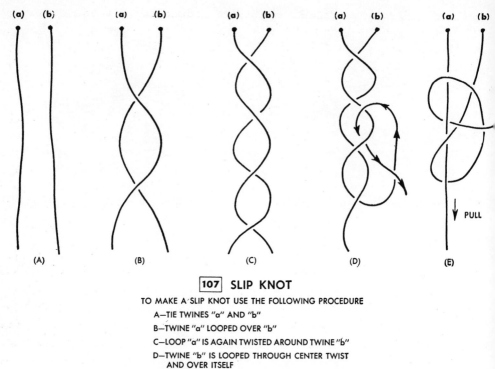

107 SLIP KNOT

TO MAKE A SLIP KNOT USE THE FOLLOWING PROCEDURE

A—TIE TWINES "a" AND "b"

B—TWINE "a" LOOPED OVER "b"

C—LOOP "a" IS AGAIN TWISTED AROUND TWINE "b"

D—TWINE "b" IS LOOPED THROUGH CENTER TWIST AND OVER ITSELF

E—PULLING "a," DRAWING KNOT TO BURLAP. KNOT IS TIGHTENED WITH A QUICK JERK WHEN IT IS AT SURFACE OF BURLAP

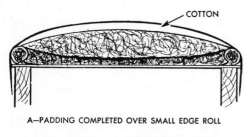

A—PADDING COMPLETED OVER SMALL EDGE ROLL

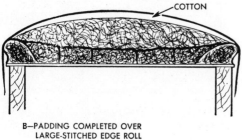

B—PADDING COMPLETED OVER LARGE-STITCHED EDGE ROLL

108 SECTION THROUGH PAD

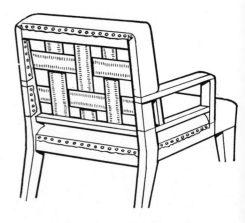

109 MUSLIN TACKED ON BACK

MUSLIN IS TACKED ALONG BACK SIDE OF TOP RAIL AND ALONG INSIDE OF POSTS AT SIDE. AT THE BOTTOM, MUSLIN IS TACKED TO BACK SIDE OF BACK LINER

taking care to build the center higher than the edges. Do not allow loose fibers to overhang the edge roll. This top stuffing may be built up to two or three times the desired finished height of the seat, for the cover will compress it.

The pad can now be covered with a layer of upholsterer's cotton large enough to overhang the edges slightly. Here again, however, you may prefer to cover the loose stuffing with the muslin first and lay the upholsterer's cotton between the muslin and final cover. Fig. 108A illustrates a section of padding as it is completed over a small edge roll, and Fig. 108B shows a padded section over a large stitched edge roll.

Padded Backs: When the seat has been covered with muslin, work on the back should be started. Stuff the back as you did the seat, and where there is a cavity between the edge roll and vertical webbing, stuffing should be applied until the entire surface is even with the outside of the edge roll. Then stitch the stuffing in place. Next apply the top stuffing, crowning it as you did the seat. The back is then ready to be covered with cotton and muslin.

SAG SEATS

The burlap-cover piece should be spot sewed to the webbing on a sag seat before it is tacked to the rails. Do not stretch the burlap too tight, for the weight of the seated person should be on the webbing, not on the tightened burlap. Build a ¾ to 1-inch edge roll around the seat edges. The first stuffing that is to be stitched in place should be about 1 inch deep. The second layer of stuffing should be 1 inch deep before compression. *Do not*

crown stuffing on sag seats. Place a layer of upholsterer's cotton so that the edges of the seat are slightly covered.

Laying Upholsterer's Cotton: Always tear the upholsterer's cotton to the general size needed and center the cotton on the pad to be covered. Once the cotton has been placed it may be torn to the size and shape of the pad. Split the cotton to fit it around the arm stump. Tear out corners for the back posts. While the cotton should extend over the edges somewhat, it should not interfere with the placement of the covers.

Muslin Cover: Cut the muslin large enough to cover the pad, allowing several inches on each side for tacking. Center the muslin over the pad, drawing it taut to compress the cotton, and slip tack it at the center of the front and back rails. Pull the muslin to each side and chalk mark the cutting lines for the arm stump, post and arm-board fittings. Cut the muslin along the chalked lines, stretch it from side to side at the center and slip tack it to the sides. Slip tack the muslin from the center to the four corners, working on all four sides together. Take care to avoid drawing the stuffing over the edge roll.

When finishing the corner, cut the muslin and gather and form into neat pleats, which should be tacked in place. Check the cover for pull marks and wrinkles, and if pull marks are noticed, knock out the slip tacks causing the strain and retack. When the muslin cover is satisfactorily placed, drive the tacks permanently in place. Trim off the surplus muslin at the bottom.

On the backs, the muslin is tacked along the back of the top rail, along the inside of the posts at the sides and to the back of the liner at the bottom. Fig. 109. Trim all surplus muslin off so that it will not interfere with applying the final cover. If buttons are desired, mark their locations on the muslin and proceed to install the final cover.

Lesson Four — SPRINGING

THE COMFORT of spring seats depends upon the resiliency of the springs used in the upholstering. The type, size, number used and the arrangement of the springs in the seat, together with the way they are tied and compressed, determines the soft or firm quality of the seat. The pad built over the springs is used to eliminate the feel of the springs and produce a smooth surface. Even the shape of the seat depends on the spring arrangement and the method used in tying them down.

The two basic methods of mounting springs may be classified as follows. In *tight seats* the springs are tied directly to the top edge of the frame. On *spring-edge seats* the springs on the exposed edges ride comparatively free above the rails. Spring edges are usually used on either one or three sides of a seat. They are difficult to build, but the end result is a most comfortable seat. All easy chairs are made with a spring edge so that there will be a flat platform on which a loose cushion or a second set of springs may be retained. Wherever possible, the webbing foundation in a seat to have spring-edge construction should be planned so that the springs can be placed over the bands of webbing. When the frame is webbed, or a solid base has been built into the frame, the springs may be mounted.

TIGHT-SPRING SEATS

Planning: If the piece to be upholstered has a closed back and the liners are in place, the height of the springs to be used will be equal to the distance between the webbing and the underside of the liners. When the piece has an open back, or lacks liners, the following method is used to determine the needed spring height: subtract from the desired seat height the distance between the webbing and the floor at the front of the seat; from this figure subtract 1 inch to allow for the pad. For instance, if the desired seat height is 17½ inches and the webbing is 10½ inches from the floor, the difference is 7 inches; now, subtracting the 1 inch allowed for the pad, the result indicates that the spring height will be 6 inches—a No. 0 medium or No. 1 soft spring. If the height of the front rail is 3 inches, either of these spring sizes will be well suited.

The seat springs should project at least 3 inches, but not more than 4½ inches, over the rail when tied down. Usually about one half of the spring height should project above the frame. The higher the springs are above the seat rail, the more difficult it is to keep them in an upright position. See the spring chart, Fig. 57, for the size and working height of various springs. The less the normal height of the springs is compressed, the more effi-

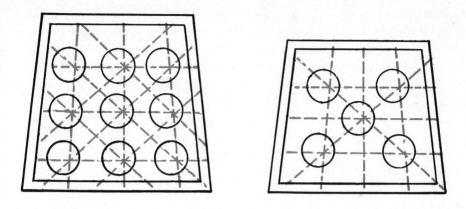

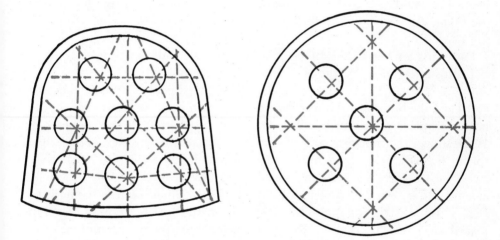

110 SPRING PLACEMENT

cient and resilient the seat will be.

Use soft springs wherever possible, but if the springs must be widely spaced, use harder springs. When springs of the desired size cannot be purchased, get the next size smaller and firmer, or the next size larger and softer.

Placement of Springs: The top side of a seat spring is the end which has the coil tip bent down and toward the center of the spring. The coil is bent down in this way so that the tip will not wear a hole in the burlap through which the stuffing might escape. When the springs are mounted, the bent tips should all face toward the center of the seat. The closed side is stronger and will help build a firmer edge than the open end.

Fig. 110 illustrates the various ways in which springs may be placed. Springs placed close together at the center of the seat will make a harder seat than springs more widely spaced. The springs should be arranged so that there will be at least 1½ inches between the coil tops. There should be a 2-inch space between the inside seat rails and coil tops along seat edges that are exposed. When the back and arms are closed, the coil tops should be 1 inch in from the inside of the back and arm liners.

To avoid trouble when tying down the springs, keep them in straight lines and rows. When the spring arrangement has been planned, chalk-mark the foundation to show the spring positions desired.

Fastening Springs to Solid Base: Fig. 111 illustrates three methods of fastening coil springs to a solid base. In Fig. 111A the bottom coil of the spring is held in place with four staples. Fig. 111B shows the bottom coil of the spring held in place with four small strips of webbing or leather looped around the coil and tacked down. In Fig. 111C a strip of webbing was placed over the bottom of the coil and tacked down on the inside and outside of the two sides of the coil. This method requires no insulator. A wad of cotton placed as shown in Fig. 111D should be used when springs are mounted as shown in Figs. 111A or B, or the spring will rattle as the coil strikes the wood frame.

Sewing Springs to Webbing: When the springs are placed, they should be sewn to the webbing. Thread a double-pointed straight needle with stitching twine. Work from the top side of the frame so that the location of the coils can be seen and care taken to avoid moving the springs as they are being sewn. Take four stitches, planning them so that the last stitch will be at the nearest point to the next spring. Start by putting the corner spring in place, bent-coil end up, facing toward the center. When necessary, to keep springs in line, the bottom coil of the corner spring can be pushed under corner blocks. Push the needle through the webbing from the underside close to the coil, and down on the other side, looping the coil. Tie the first stitch. Take the next stitch as illustrated in Fig. 112, continuing the stitching until the coil is stitched at four points and tying the last stitch on the coil. The twine running between the coils is under the webbing. Stitch the coils down tight so that they will not fall over.

Tying Springs: When the springs are sewn in place, their tops should be tied in position to the proper height. See that the springs stand upright when they are tied, and that they do not slip on the twine.

The resiliency of the spring is taken up in the first inch or so of compression. If the springs are pulled and tied down too low, the resiliency will be taken away and the seat will be hard. Springs tied at their maximum height give the most resilient seat. To avoid having the twine bear the strain when the springs are compressed, do not tie them to less than 3 inches over the rail.

Two of the ways of tying down springs are the two-way tie, Fig. 113, and the four-way tie, Fig. 114, also often called the eight-way or diagonal tie. The two-way tie produces a more resilient seat than does the four-way tie, for a seated person compresses

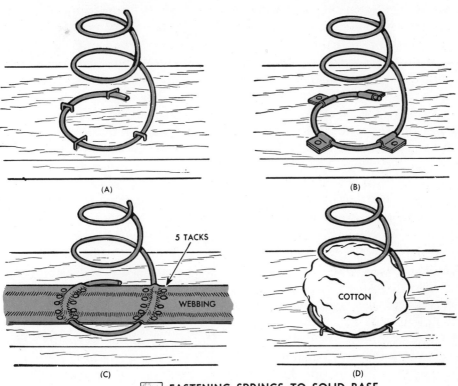

(A)   (B)

5 TACKS

WEBBING

COTTON

(C)   (D)

111 FASTENING SPRINGS TO SOLID BASE

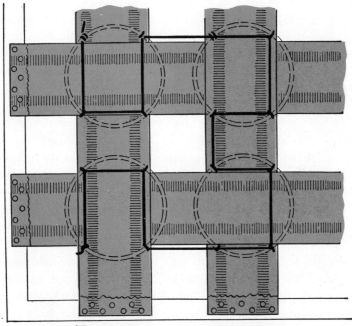

112 SEWING OF SPRINGS TO WEBBING

more springs when they are tied four ways. Each individual spring takes full compression when tied two ways.

Springs are usually tied two ways in rounded seats, but may be tied either two or four ways in flat seats.

Two-Way Tie: In making two-way spring ties for a rounded seat without return twine, first cut the twine for tying the springs. The length needed is determined by measuring the distance from the front to the back of the frame and then doubling that measurement. Cut as many lengths of twine as there are rows of springs.

Slip-tack a No. 8 or No. 12 tack on the top of the front and back rails at the center of each row of springs. Tie a simple knot at one end of each piece of twine, slip the knots over the tack heads and drive the tacks down, with the knots at the back side. Fig. 115A.

First tie down the center row of springs. Working from the back, loop the twine around the back and front side of each coil, working forward until each coil has been looped at its back and front. Fig. 115B. Pull the twine down until the springs are at the desired height, adjusting the springs back and forth along the twine to keep them standing upright. When the springs are properly compressed and adjusted, tie the twine to the front slip tack with a simple knot and drive the tack down. Fig. 115C. Repeat this procedure on each spring row, making sure that each row is tied at the same height.

Now cross-tie the springs. Cut the twine to size (double the distance across the frame plus a few inches extra to allow for knots), and drive slip tacks on the top side of the side rails. Once again these tacks should be cen-

tered on each row of springs, and one of the twines should be tied to each slip tack on one side and the tacks driven down. Tie down the center row of springs first; bring the twine to the first spring, push it down slightly and knot the twine to the nearest coil. The knot should be made by looping the twine over the coil, bringing the twine up and around again on the other side of the twine and passing the twine end through the loop formed. Fig. 116. Next tie the front-to-back twine with the same type of knot at the center. Then knot the twine inside the edge of the coil and over to the next coil. Keep repeating this operation, knotting the twine at both sides of the coil and to the front-to-back twine, allowing no slack between the springs. When the last coil has been tied, pull the twine down in place and knot it to the slip tack. Drive down the tack. Take care to avoid pulling the front-to-back row of springs out of line as you cross-tie, or pulling the cross twine down so tightly as to pull the front-to-back twine slack. Complete this cross-tying operation to the other rows of springs. Fig. 113.

If the twine is under a strain, the tacks should be reinforced by driving a second tack beside each existing tack, placing the second tack so that its head will overlap the head of the first tack.

Four-Way Tie: This tie is used to strengthen the spring structure and prevent horizontal movement of the springs. The four-way tie produces a harder seat because it distributes the load of the seated person over more of the springs. Back springs should never be tied four ways.

The twine is tied in the same way as were the cross ties on two-way tying.

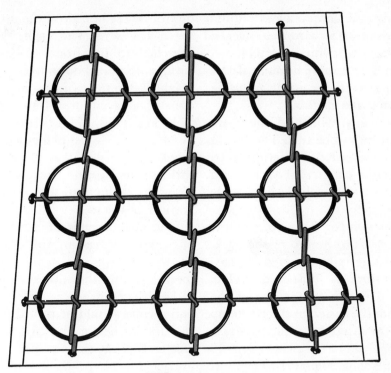

113 TWO-WAY TIE

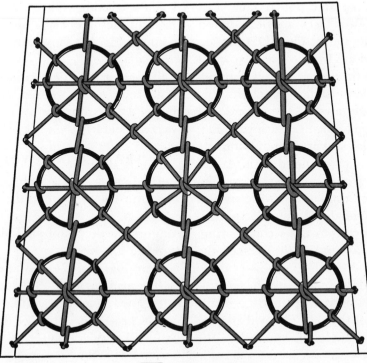

114 FOUR-WAY TIE

Here again take care to avoid pulling the springs down so hard as to slacken the existing tied twines. Fig. 114.

Return Tie: A more durable, flatter spring surface can be made by using the return-twine method.

Cut as many twines as there are rows of springs to be tied. The length of the twines needed is determined by measuring the length of the frame and cutting the twines a little over three times that long.

Slip-tack two No. 8 or No. 12 tacks ½ inch apart on the top of the back, front and side rails, centered on each row of springs as illustrated in Fig. 117A. Slip a loop of one end of the twine from the inside of the frame up between the slip tacks on the back rail, leaving one end of the twine about 15 or 20 inches long. Fig. 117B. The short end of the twine is called the *return twine*. The loop is now turned over the slip tacks and pulled taut. Fig. 117C. The slip tacks are next driven down on the twine. Fig. 117D.

The center front-to-back row of springs should be tied first. If a rounded seat is desired, start by looping the longest twine around the second coil from the top of the nearest spring. Fig. 118. If a flat seat is desired, loop the longest twine around the third coil from the top of the nearest spring. Fig. 119. Proceed to loop the twine around the far side of the top of the coil, carrying the twine to the second spring, looping it around both sides of the top coil, and continuing this practice until the last spring in the row is reached. At the last spring, the inside of the top of the coil is looped and the twine is brought down inside the spring and looped around the outside of the second coil for a round seat, or around the outside of the third coil for a flat seat. The twine is then stretched to the front rail and the springs are pulled down to the desired height. Loop the twine around one of the slip tacks and drive down the tack as in Fig. 117E. This permits adjustment of the loose twine while the other tack holds the springs. The springs are slipped back and forth along the twine until they are all in a vertical position.

The outside ends of the top coils of the end springs are still loose. Now the short ends of the twine should be looped around the slip tacks and the tacks driven in place, and next the end springs should be pulled down to the desired height and tied with the free ends of the short twine.

Each row of springs should be tied the same way with the front-to-back twines.

Then, starting with the center row, the cross-ties are made in the same manner. Fig. 113 shows how these ties are made.

If the seat is subject to heavy wear, or a firmer seat is desired, the spring should be reinforced by tying four ways. Fig. 114.

SPRING-EDGE WORK

Another way to tie springs, and the way to utilize the springs to their fullest extent and so produce the most comfortable type of upholstery, is to make a *spring edge*.

Planning: Fig. 121 illustrates several spring arrangements for spring-edge seats. The frame to be upholstered will decide how many spring edges there will be. Edges surrounded with closed arms and backs do not have spring edges, and are therefore tied as flat

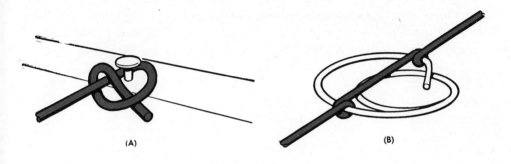

(A)   (B)

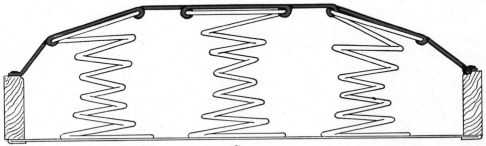

(C)

115   SPRINGS TIED FOR ROUND SEAT

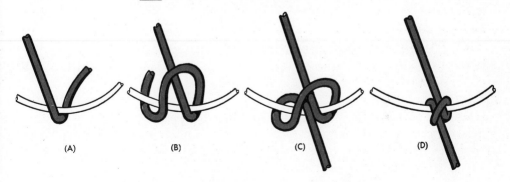

(A)   (B)   (C)   (D)

116   SPRING KNOT OR CLOVE HITCH

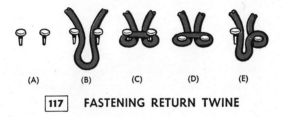

(A)   (B)   (C)   (D)   (E)

117   FASTENING RETURN TWINE

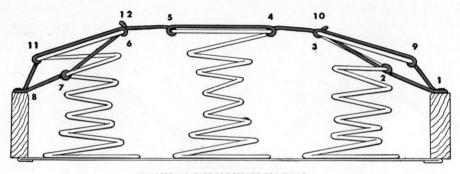

NUMBERS INDICATE PROCEDURE FOR TYING
SPRINGS. RETURN TWINES ARE TIED AFTER
SPRINGS ARE TIED IN UPRIGHT POSITION. ON
A ROUND SEAT THE TWINE IS TIED TO SECOND
COIL FROM TOP

118 **RETURN TWINE TYING OF ROUND SEAT**

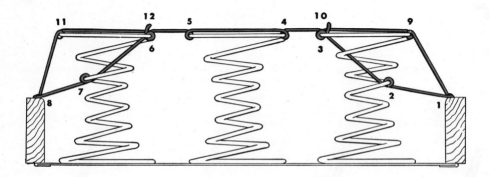

NUMBERS INDICATE PROCEDURE FOR TYING. ON
FLAT SEATS TWINE IS TIED TO THIRD COIL
FROM TOP

119 **SPRINGS TIED FOR FLAT SEAT**

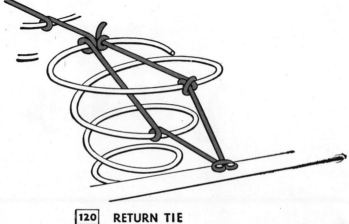

120 **RETURN TIE**

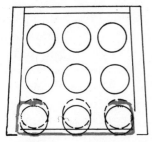

A—EDGE WIRE ALONG FRONT EDGE
BETWEEN ARMS

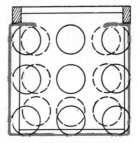

B—EDGE WIRE ON FRONT AND
SIDE OF OPEN SEAT

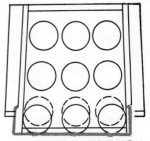

C—EDGE WIRE ON FRONT AND
RETURNING ALONG SIDES
TO SET BACK ARMS

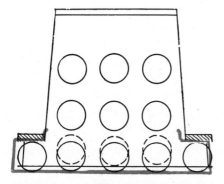

D—EDGE WIRE ALONG FRONT, RETURNING ALONG
SIDES AND AROUND BACK OF SPRING, FASTENING
ALONG SIDE ARMS ON A T-SEAT

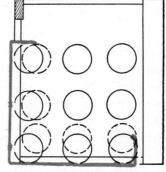

E—EDGE WIRE AT FRONT
AND ONE SIDE ON A ONE-ARM SEAT

COLOR LINES INDICATE SPRING EDGE WIRE

121 PLACING OF SPRINGS

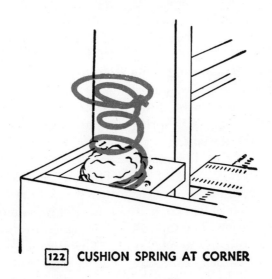

122 CUSHION SPRING AT CORNER

seats with return ties. Only exposed edges are built with a spring edge. It is not advisable to build a spring edge on four sides of a seat, because it will then have too much horizontal movement. Spring edges are usually built on either one or three sides of a seat.

The springs should be tied as nearly to their full height as possible to take advantage of their maximum resiliency. On seats not having a loose cushion or a second set of springs, the springs should be tied from 15½ to 16½ inches from the floor. Seats that have a loose cushion or a second set of springs may be tied 12 inches from the floor. The springs should project at least 3 inches over the front rail. On frames having back and arm liners, the spring height will be the distance from the webbing to the bottom side of the liners. Here the springs should never be tied down more than ½ inch below the liners.

It is often necessary to use a cushion spring at the corners in front of the arms because seat springs will not fit. In cases such as this, a platform is built in front of the arm over the corner block, and the spring is stapled in place. A wad of silencing cotton is placed between the coils of the spring. Fig. 122.

Bending Springs: The springs along exposed edges must be pulled out of vertical position in order to reach the outside of the rails to support a spring edge. The top coil of the spring is enlarged by pulling it out all around. Fig. 123A. Next form the end of the coil into a hook and hook it into the second coil. Fig. 123B. Then tie it in place with sewing twine. The top coil should then be bent up at the side opposite the knot. Fig. 123C. Take care to bend all the springs uniformly to

avoid producing an irregular seat edge.

When the webbing has been tacked to the underside of the frame, the springs are sewed in place. The springs along the rails that are to have spring edges should be sewn down as close to the rail as possible. The nearest coil of the spring along the edge should be about ½ inch from the rails. The tipped-up edge of the coil on top of the spring should face the rail. The remainder of the springs should be sewn in straight rows so that they will be simple to tie.

Bending Spring-Edge Wire: A No. 9 or No. 10-gauge spring wire is used for a spring edge. The wire must be bent to the exact shape of the frame before it is attached to the springs. The wire can be held and bent with two pairs of pliers; however, it is simpler to run the wire through a ½-inch pipe about 8 inches long and then bend the wire over the edge with pliers. Fig. 124A. To bend the wire to a curve, lay the wire on a block of wood and strike it with a hammer until the wire has been formed to the desired shape. Fig. 124B. It is necessary to bend the ends of edge wire down to prevent them from making holes through the burlap over the springs. The twist must be taken out of the edge wire after it has been formed, so that it will lie flat.

Fastening Wire Edge: The edge wire is fastened to the frame with a piece of webbing looped around the wire. The tab is tacked to the frame. When the edge wire must be fastened to the frame, this fastening is done before the springs are tied to the edge wire.

The edge wire can be fastened to the springs with metal clips, using spring-clip pliers or ordinary pliers.

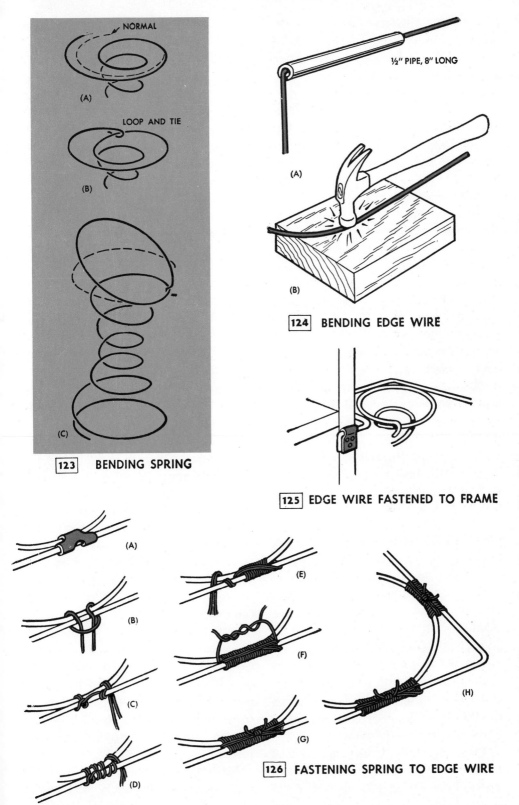

NORMAL

(A)

LOOP AND TIE

(B)

(C)

123 BENDING SPRING

½" PIPE, 8" LONG

(A)

(B)

124 BENDING EDGE WIRE

125 EDGE WIRE FASTENED TO FRAME

(A)

(B)

(C)

(D)

(E)

(F)

(G)

(H)

126 FASTENING SPRING TO EDGE WIRE

85

Fig. 126A. Another method of fastening springs to edge wire is to tie them with a 15-inch length of sewing twine. Fig. 126B through 126G. When the springs touch two or three sides of the edge wire, the spring must be fastened to the wire at each edge. Fig. 126H. Care must be taken to so fasten the springs to the edge wire that they will not be pulled out of place when the springs are tied.

Tying Springs: The same procedure as is used in tying a flat seat, using a return twine, should be followed in tying down springs on a spring-edge seat. Fig. 127. It is important that the spring edges are drawn into proper position before tying the knots. Each row of springs must be tied to the same height as the first row in order to keep the deck as flat as possible.

All spring-edge seats should be tied four ways. The diagonal twines are not attached to the edge wire, but are brought directly from the springs to the top edge of the rails.

Before the back springs are stitched and tied in place, pad and muslin-cover the seat.

SPRING BACKS

Back springs are made of lighter-gauge wire than seat springs, and so produce a softer back. These springs are knotted on both ends. Back springs are tied with a lighter-weight and softer twine than that used on seats, and should be tied two ways only. A four-way tie would make the back too firm and necessitate placing too much padding over the springs to eliminate feeling the knots.

Planning: The front edge of the back liner outlines the depth of the seat. The padding will extend about 1 inch beyond the liner. The first back springs should project about 2 or 3 inches over the front edge of the back liner. The springs should be set from 2 to 5 inches apart. When the springs are set too close together, they are difficult to tie, and when they are too far apart, the back is apt to be weak. Fig. 128 illustrates placement of back springs and webbing. The bottom row of springs should be mounted from 3 to 5 inches above the back liner.

Webbing: The upright webbing on the back should be centered to be under the planned spring rows. This webbing should be tacked at the back side of the top rail and the back side of the back liner. The crossband webbing should be tacked to the front side of the back posts or to the front side of the back slats, if slats are used. The cross webbing should be placed in back of the upright webbing and tack-stitched at intersections.

Stitching Springs: The piece being upholstered should be laid on its back and the springs sewed in place. The sewing procedures are the same as those involved in sewing seat springs.

Tying Springs: Backs with rounded or knife edges are two-way tied. No return twines are needed. Fig. 129. For knife edges, the springs are compressed more along the edges than are those installed on round-edge backs. The backs are tied the same as are those in a two-way-tie seat. The upright twines are tied first, looping the tops of the coils, starting with the center row of springs. The tops of the coils and twine intersections are knotted on the side-to-side rows of springs.

Filler Tie: Filler ties are used on backs to build a firmer foundation for

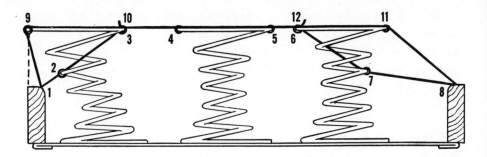

127 TYING SPRING EDGE

128 PLACING BACK SPRINGS

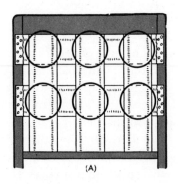

(A)

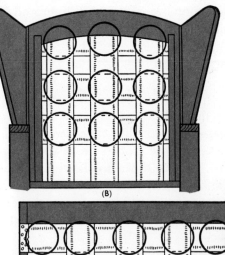

(B)

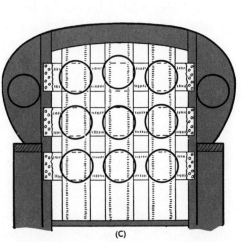

(C)

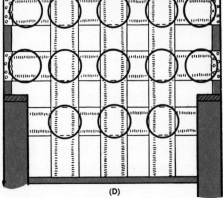

(D)

stuffing. This is done by tying twine between the vertical and horizontal rows of springs. The filler ties should be knotted over each intersecting twine. Fig. 130.

SPRING-EDGE BACKS

These backs are tied in the same way as are the spring-edge seats. Two-way tying will be required on the backs. Fig. 131 illustrates how to place and tie the springs. In Fig. 131A the numbers indicate the tying procedure. In Figs. 131B and C, the dark line indicates spring-edge wire around the back. This wire should be 12 or 14 gauge. Filler ties are placed between the rows of springs. These ties are terminated by tying the filler-twine ends to the edge wire. Fig. 132 shows how the edge wire on the back goes to the front side of the back liner and is there held in place with a strip of burlap looped over the wire and tacked down.

MARSHALL-UNIT BACKS

On chair backs that are to have marshall units, the vertical webbing is tacked to the front side of the back-rail top and down to the top side of the back liner parallel to the front of the back posts. The horizontal webbing is tacked to the front side of the back posts.

The bottom marshall-unit springs should project 2 inches over the front edge of the back liner. As you make up the marshall unit, allow 1 to 2 inches of frame exposure along the top and sides, and mount the unit 2 to 4 inches above the back liner.

Before the marshall unit is set in place, tack burlap over the webbing. Spot-sew the marshall unit to the bur-lap and webbing, making sure that only the bottom coils of the marshall-unit springs are caught in the stitches.

BARREL-BACK SPRINGS

Springs in barrel backs should be tied vertically only, because the top coils of the springs are closer together than are those at the bottom. Fig. 133A. If these springs were cross-tied and then placed under pressure, they would lock into each other and damage the springs, burlap and padding.

Only vertical webbing is used on the backs of barrel chairs, and it should be placed in accordance with the spring-placement plan. The webbing should be placed on the chair arms also, as springs are usually used in the arms of barrel chairs. Then stitch the springs in place on the webbing and tie them down to height.

Next cut the burlap piece required. It should be cut long enough to reach from the bottom of the back liner up over the tops of the springs so that it can be fastened to the top rail, and wide enough so that when it has been pushed down between the springs to the face of the rail and the face of the liner it will cover the springs from side to side. Add a few extra inches each way to be sure of having plenty of material. The excess can be trimmed away after the burlap has been tacked.

Tack the center of the burlap to the top rail over the center row of springs and pull it down tight. Tack the burlap to the front edge of the back liner. Push the burlap down between the center row of springs and tack it to the back liner at the bottom. Draw the burlap taut between the springs and tack it at the top rail. Re-

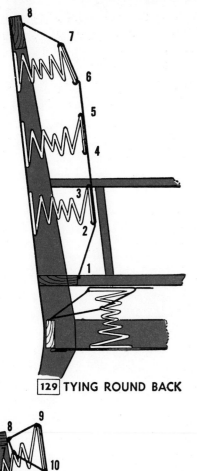

129 TYING ROUND BACK

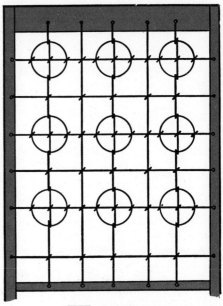

130 FILLER TIE

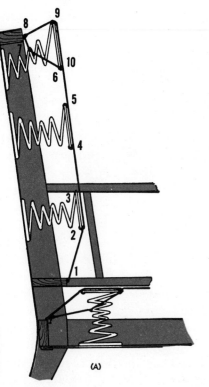

(A)

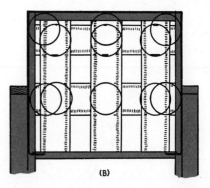

(B)

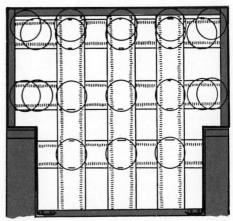

(C)

131 SPRING-EDGE BACKS

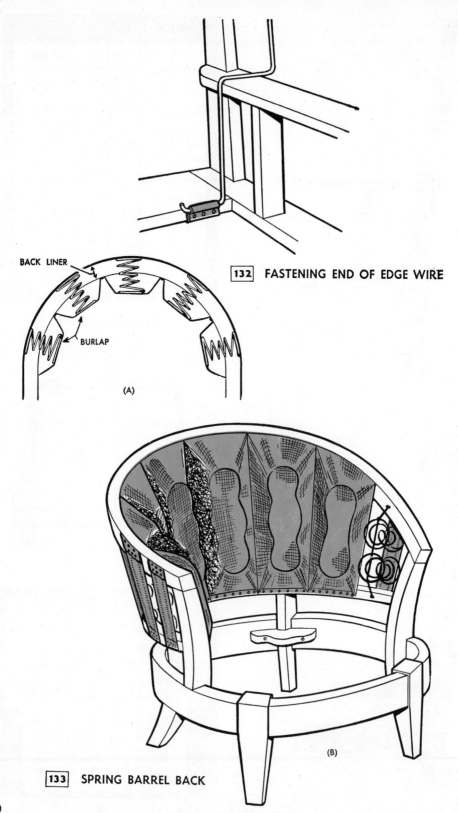

BACK LINER

BURLAP

(A)

132 FASTENING END OF EDGE WIRE

(B)

133 SPRING BARREL BACK

peat this operation on the other side of the center row of springs, and on each row of springs until all rows are covered with burlap. Finish by tacking the burlap over the spring centers on the front edge of the liners and on the top rail. Fig. 133B.

To avoid having the burlap shift, stitch it to each row of springs. Fill the troughs between the springs with sisal or moss so as to force the burlap under the top coil of the springs. The stuffing should be firm but not hard enough to interfere with the action of the springs.

No additional burlap is required. Spring-back barrel chairs are usually channeled.

Lesson Five — PADDING OVER SPRINGS

PADDING IS USED over spring seats and backs to eliminate the feeling of the springs and to give the final contour to the seat and back. The springs, not the padding, give the seat and back the desired resilience.

An edge roll or stitched edge is used to give the exposed edges of the seat their contour. Spring seats and backs require a larger edge roll or stitched edge than do pad seats and backs because of the height of the springs over the rails. The difference in height between the springs and the rail is eliminated through the use of an edge roll or stitched edge. Thus the seat top will flow smoothly over the edge.

Burlap Over Seat Springs: Here again burlap is used over the springs to prevent having the stuffing fall through. Heavy-weight burlap should be used over all spring work.

Estimate the size of the piece of burlap needed by measuring as follows: for the front-to-back length, measure over the spring from the top of the back seat rail to the top of the front seat rail, and add to that total 1 inch for each side not having an edge roll and 10 inches for each side having an edge roll. For the width, measure from the top of one side seat rail to the top of the opposite seat rail, again adding 1 inch to each side for tacking and 10 inches to each side where an edge roll is to be used. The back should be measured from the back edge of the back liner over the springs to the top of the top rail. The side-to-side measurement of the back is made over the springs from the outside edge of the back posts. Add 1 inch to the measurements for tacking and 10 inches for the edge roll if one is to be used.

Then cut the burlap to size and center it over the seat or back. Slip-tack it at the centers on four sides, drawing the burlap taut. Next, pull the burlap to each side and mark it for the arm stump, post, corner and arm-board cutouts. Fig. 96. Cut the burlap as you have marked it. Now slip-tack it, working to all four corners at once, drawing the material tight all the way around. Fig. 134. Note that it is to be *slip-tacked* only, because the tacks are to be knocked out after the springs are stitched to the burlap.

Stitching Burlap to Springs: Thread a small curved needle with stitching twine, make two simple knots in one end of the twine, and, starting at the

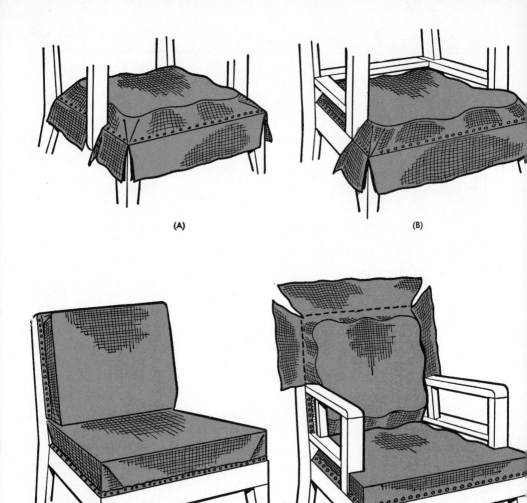

(A) (B)

(C) (D)

134 TACKING BURLAP OVER SPRINGS

corner, stitch the burlap to the springs. Pierce the needle through the burlap and catch the top coil of the corner spring as you take the stitch. Proceed in that way, taking three stitches in the top coil of each spring, making the last stitch close to the next coil. Fig. 135A. Each stitch should be locked as illustrated in Fig. 135B. Tie off the last stitch of twine and the last stitch on the coil with two simple knots. Take care to stitch only the top coil of each spring, for if the lower coil is stitched it will wear the twine to the breaking point and thus loosen the burlap from the springs.

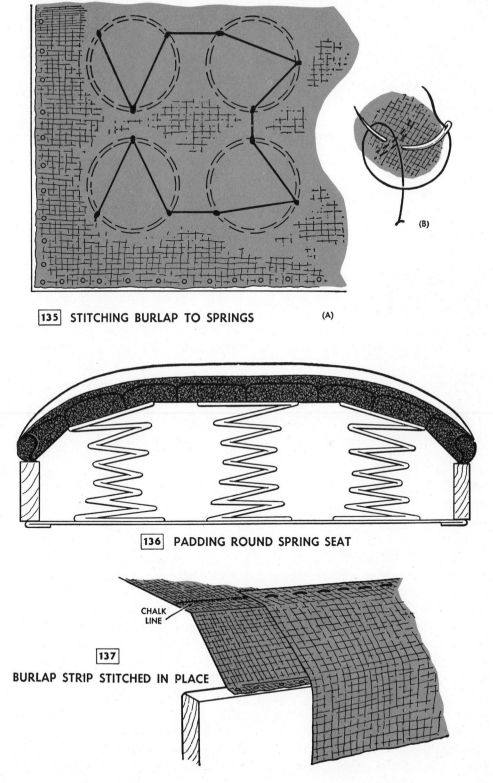

135 STITCHING BURLAP TO SPRINGS   (A)

(B)

136 PADDING ROUND SPRING SEAT

CHALK
LINE

137
BURLAP STRIP STITCHED IN PLACE

Release the burlap at this point by knocking out the slip tacks. Now retack the burlap, leaving it slightly slack so that there will be no strain on it. Turn the burlap under or up on the edges where an edge roll is not planned, and let the surplus material overhang the edge.

Edge Roll for a Rounded Seat: After the burlap has been fastened over the springs, the next step in building a rounded spring seat is to form an edge roll along the exposed edges. The height of the top coils of the springs along the front edge, and the amount of roundness desired on the seat or back will govern the size of the edge roll. For most upholstered pieces, the edge roll ranges between ¾ of an inch and 1½ inches.

Edge rolls are made the same for both spring seats and pad seats. A quantity of tow is cleaned and fluffed free of foreign matter and lumps. The roll is then stuffed by placing sufficient tow along the burlap to build a roll of the required size. Draw the burlap strip over the tow, shaping the roll with a kneading motion, until it is firm. Fig. 136. Keep the burlap tight and free of wrinkles; the roll uniform in diameter and free of lumps and hollows. Tack the burlap down at the inside of the roll, allowing the roll to overhang the rails a little. The amount of stuffing needed to form the roll can be found only by experimenting. Use a stuffing regulator to straighten out any irregularities which might appear in the roll.

The corners are formed last and should be full and firm. Miter the burlap at the corners and place a tack squarely in the corner on the back side of the roll. The corner is then stitched closed, using a small curved needle.

When the edge roll finishes against the frame, tack the burlap against the frame so the stuffing will not come out.

Stitched Edge Roll for a Flat Seat: When a flat seat is desired, a large edge roll is needed. Start this roll by sewing a strip of burlap to the burlap over the springs. The width of the strip should be equal to the distance from the edge of the springs to the front of the rail, plus the distance from the top of the rail to the top of the spring, plus 2 inches for sewing and tacking. Cut the strip along the thread of the weave to let the weave be a guide in forming a uniform roll, tacked and sewn straight.

Chalk mark the burlap ¾ of an inch in from the front edge of the springs. Thread a small, curved needle with stitching twine and sew the burlap strip to the burlap over the springs along the chalk line. Keep the stitches straight with the thread of the burlap. Fig. 137. Make pleats at the corners to allow for fullness in the edge roll.

Prepare a quantity of tow for stuffing the edge roll. Then place the stuffing under the burlap strip, working it in smoothly, slip-tacking the free end of the burlap as the work progresses. Working toward the corners, remove two or three slip tacks at a time on each side of the centers. Adjust the edge roll for firmness and uniform size and then turn the burlap strip under and tack it to the top edge of the rail before removing more slip tacks. By following the thread of the burlap strip as you tack, it will help to keep the roll uniform. Fig. 138A. Care should be taken to make the corners full, firm and square.

Use the regulator to work the stuff-

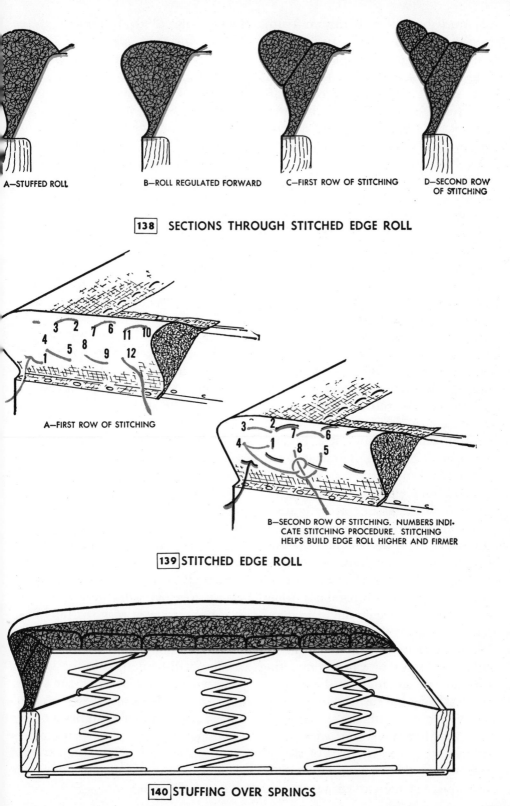

A—STUFFED ROLL   B—ROLL REGULATED FORWARD   C—FIRST ROW OF STITCHING   D—SECOND ROW OF STITCHING

138   **SECTIONS THROUGH STITCHED EDGE ROLL**

A—FIRST ROW OF STITCHING

B—SECOND ROW OF STITCHING. NUMBERS INDI-CATE STITCHING PROCEDURE. STITCHING HELPS BUILD EDGE ROLL HIGHER AND FIRMER

139 **STITCHED EDGE ROLL**

140 **STUFFING OVER SPRINGS**

ing into the roll smoothly and uniformly. Now draw the stuffing forward and up to the front edge with your fingers and the regulator until it is shaped as shown in Fig. 138B. The rolled edge is then stitched with one or two rows of stitching depending on the height and firmness desired. Figs. 138C and D.

Thread a double-pointed straight needle with a length of stitching twine. Start sewing the roll at the left-hand corner, piercing the needle through the roll at the front, slightly above the rail, and pulling it through. Pierce the needle back through the roll and tie the first stitch. When tying the knot, shape the roll by squeezing the back of the roll *forward* to take out the slack, and pressing the front edge at the rail *back* so that the roll projects just slightly over the rail. Now stitch the roll as shown in Fig. 139A. Pierce the needle through at point 1, bringing it out at 2. Enter it again at 3, bringing it out at 4 and pulling the stitch tight as you shape the roll. Pierce the needle through at point 5, bring it out at 6; enter it again at 7, bring it out at 8, pulling the stitch tight and shaping the roll. Continue this operation, working to the right, making each stitch 1 to 1½ inches long. Use the regulator whenever necessary to keep the roll smooth and even. Knot the end of the twine to the last stitch when the twine becomes too short or when completing the row of stitching. Take care to avoid pulling the corners out of shape as you proceed with the stitching.

If a higher and firmer edge roll is desired, take a second row of stitches just above the first row. Start by threading a large curved needle with

twine. Fig. 139B. Beginning at the left-hand corner, pierce the needle through at point 1, bring it out at 2, enter it again at 3 and pull it out at point 4. Tie the loose end of twine at point 1 with a slipknot around the twine at 4, pulling the stitch tight and shaping the roll between the thumb and fingers, pulling the roll forward. Pierce the roll at 5, coming out at 6; pierce at 7, coming out at 8. Then loop the twine hanging from 5 around the needle and pull through, tightening stitch by pulling to the right. Now shape the roll, and then repeat this process, making the stitches from ¾ to 1¼ inches long, connecting each stitch at the front and pulling to the right to tighten the stitches. The needle should be pierced through the roll at right angles. The stitches are not connected at the back side of the roll. Regulate the stuffing as the stitching progresses and again tack the end of the roll to the frame when it finishes against the frame.

First Stuffing: Tow is the best material to use first over the burlap-covered springs, as it will best disguise their presence.

Pick, fluff and shake free of foreign matter a quantity of stuffing. Lay the prepared stuffing over the burlap, matting it together with the fingers until it is built up even with the top of the edge roll. Keep the stuffing level and free from lumps and hollows. Extra stuffing will be needed in the hollows between the edge roll and the spring tops on rounded seats. It is good practice to sew this stuffing in place before building the rest of the stuffing. Stitch the stuffing in place, taking care to avoid catching the spring coils in the stitches. Fig. 106.

Top Stuffing: A quantity of hair or moss should be prepared for use as top stuffing. Place it over the first stuffing in thin layers, weaving and felting each layer together with the fingers. The center of the seat should be crowned slightly and care taken to avoid having loose fibers overhang the edge rolls. Use the palm of your hand to test the stuffing, making sure that enough was used so that you cannot feel the springs. Fig. 140.

Next apply the cotton pad and muslin cover in the order you prefer.

Marshall Unit Over Spring-Edge Seat: When a marshall unit is to be built over a spring-edge seat, the arms and back of the piece should be upholstered before the seat.

First cover the spring-edge seat with burlap and a thin layer of stuffing. Fig. 141A. Then sew the spring together on both sides, making a unit that will leave a ¾ to 1½-inch border on all sides when centered on the seat. (See Part 3, Lesson 7, for instructions on sewing marshall units.) Next spot-sew the unit to the burlap over the seat springs.

Tear strips of cotton as wide as the height of the marshall coils. Place these strips around the edges of the marshall unit, tightly filling the openings between the marshall unit and the back and arms. Place more cotton strips around the outside of the exposed edges until they are built slightly over the outside edges of the spring seat. Be sure to build the corners full. Now place a layer of cotton over the top of the seat to the edges of the marshall unit. Two more layers of cotton are placed in the same way filling the seat to the back and arms. The top cotton should project slightly over the cotton on the exposed edges. Finally, apply muslin cover. Fig. 141C.

Spring Edge Roll: The roll on spring-edge work lies directly over the springs along the exposed wire. The size and shape of the roll will depend upon the shape of the edge, and the type of seat desired. If a flat, padded seat or back is desired, the spring edge roll will not be as high or deep as those needed on a seat that is to have a loose cushion. The spring edge roll is usually built flush with the edge wire on the back of the chair. The roll usually projects ½ to ¾ of an inch over the edge wire on the seat. A spring edge roll from ¾ to 1 inch high and built from 2 to 2½ inches over the springs is usually sufficient on backs and seats to be padded. A roll 1¼ inches high and built from 3 to 4 inches over the springs will be adequate on seats which will have a loose cushion.

A strip of burlap 8 inches wide and long enough to allow a 4-inch overlap over the ends of the spring edge should be cut, following the thread of the weave. If the edge roll returns around the sides, cut burlap strips for the sides, again allowing 4 inches on each end—for finishing against the frame and overlapping the front of it. Chalk mark the burlap over the springs a uniform distance in from the wire edge to the width of the edge roll desired. Lay the strip of burlap over the seat or back and, following the thread of the weave, stitch the strip in place, allowing the seam to overlay the chalk line ⅝ of an inch to the outer edge. Fig. 142.

Prepare a quantity of stuffing for the spring edge roll, shredding and fluffing it free of lumps and foreign matter.

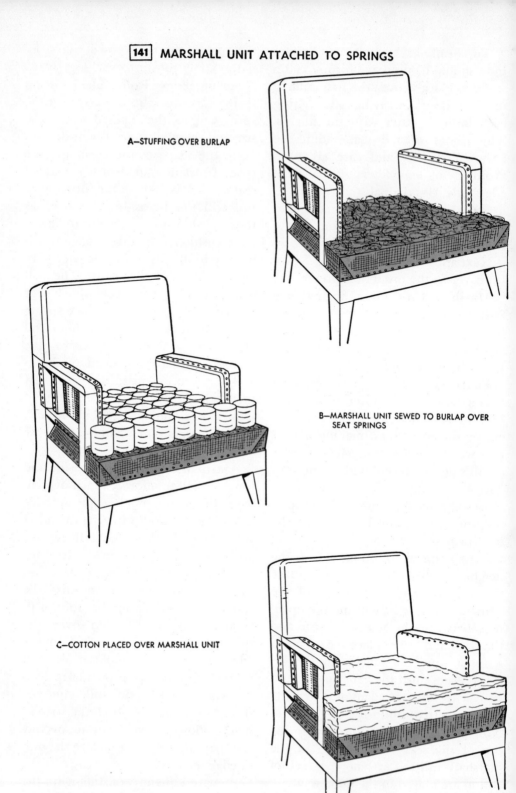

A—STUFFING OVER BURLAP

B—MARSHALL UNIT SEWED TO BURLAP OVER SEAT SPRINGS

C—COTTON PLACED OVER MARSHALL UNIT

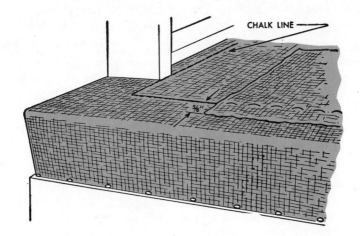

CHALK LINE

⅝"

142 BURLAP STRIP SEWED IN PLACE

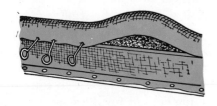

(A)

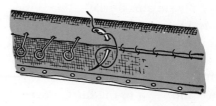

(B)

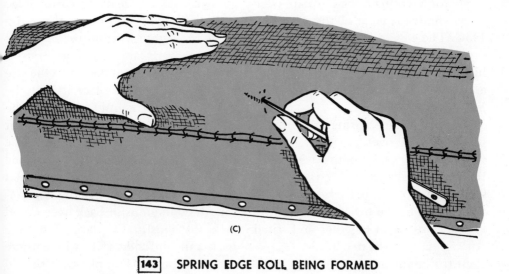

(C)

143 SPRING EDGE ROLL BEING FORMED

Use hair or moss for seat and back work, and tow for loose cushions. Place the stuffing along the edge and draw the burlap over it. The quantity of stuffing needed will depend upon the size of the roll desired. Fasten the burlap strip to the front edge with skewers just under the wire edge. Fig. 143A. Adjust the stuffing through the roll with a stuffing regulator. Then sew the burlap to the edge wire, folding the edge of the strip under. Fig. 143B. Each stitch is locked as illustrated in Fig. 143B. By following the weave of the burlap strip while stitching, the roll can be kept uniform and even.

The corners and ends of the roll should be full and well filled. Miter and sew the corners closed, cutting away the surplus burlap. The mitered corners are sewn together when the roll has been stitched. The burlap which overlaps the end of the roll finishing against the frame is turned down and sewn to the burlap over the spring.

Push the stuffing forward with a regulator, forming a high, square edge along the front edge of the roll. Fig. 143C. The edge roll is now stitched as previously explained. Fig. 144A. If a higher and firmer roll is desired, make a second row of stitches as shown in Fig. 144B.

If a ready-made spring edge roll is used, place it over the springs with the edge overhanging the wire edge the desired distance and sewn in place along the front and back edges. Cut the corners to the proper angle at the corner, butt them together and stitch with a small curved needle.

At this point the upholstering work is divided into two types: first, a platform upon which a loose cushion or cushions are placed; and second, a padded seat or back without cushion.

Platform Seat: The platform for a cushion seat is not deeply padded because the loose cushion provides the softness. The padding is used to build a flat and smooth deck for the cushion. The spring edge roll must come up high above the padding in order to keep the cushion in place. A light layer of tow—¼ to ¾ of an inch deep—is placed over the burlap in back of the spring edge roll on seats that are to have loose cushions. Sew the tow to the burlap, taking care to avoid looping the coils with the stitching twine. Use tow over the top to finish out any irregularities.

Cut the muslin cover for the seat so that it will cover the stuffing from the bottom side of the front rail to the top side of the back rail, allowing 4 inches for handling. Center the muslin over the seat and slip-tack it to four sides, making cutouts for the arm stump and back posts. When the muslin is slip-tacked smoothly in place, stitch it along the back edge of the spring edge roll, dividing the seat in two parts. Remove the slip tacks from the back rail and side rails and pull the muslin back. Tear a piece of cotton to the size of the platform and place it over the tow. The cotton should lap under the arm and back liners. When the seat has a spring edge roll at the side, the cotton should come up to the inside edge of the roll where the muslin is stitched down. After placing the cotton, draw the muslin back over it and tack the muslin in place along the back rail and side rails where there are closed arms. The platform should be smooth and free of wrinkles.

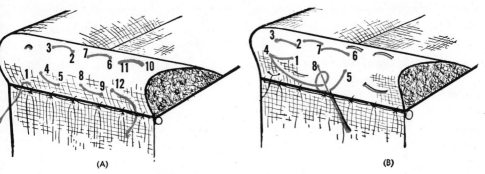

144 STITCHED SPRING EDGE

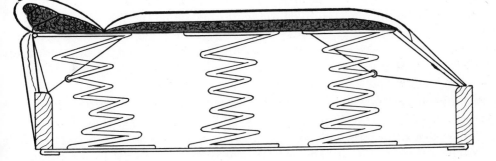

(A)

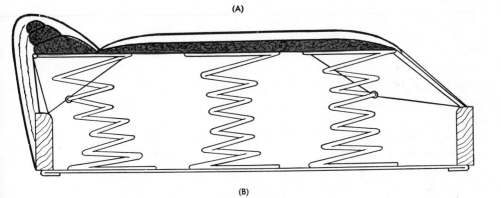

(B)

145 PADDING PLATFORM

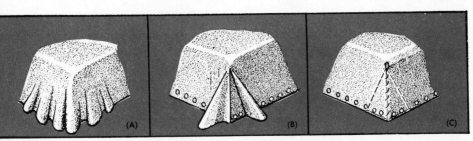

146 FORMING CORNER

Now remove the slip tacks from the front rail and the sides in front of the set-back arms, and draw the muslin back over the platform. Place a strip of cotton, the length of the front and sides having an edge roll, over the edge roll. This strip should be wide enough to cover the spring edge roll up to the wire edge as illustrated in Fig. 145A, or to the bottom of the rail as illustrated in Fig. 145B. In Fig. 145A the muslin is drawn under the edge roll and sewn under the edge wire. The muslin should be straightened and held in place with skewers before it is stitched. The space between the wire edge and the rail should be stuffed with one or two layers of cotton before the muslin is drawn down and tacked to the seat rail at the front and sides having the spring edge roll. This will help keep the cover from sagging when the platform is depressed. Take care to leave no wrinkles in the muslin cover. The outside corners should be tacked as illustrated in Fig. 146 and then sewn closed with a small curved needle.

Spring-Edge Seat Padding: Except for the spring edge roll, the pad of a spring-edge seat is built in the same way as is the pad over a flat spring seat. First place one or two layers of cotton between the edge wire and the top rail. Fig. 147. Now place a layer of cotton over the entire seat, overlapping the exposed edge to the top side of the rails.

Next cover the seat with muslin. Cut the muslin long enough to reach from the top of the back rail to the bottom side of the front rail, allowing 4 inches for handling, and wide enough to reach from the top of the side rail to the top of the rail on the opposite side, again allowing 4 inches for handling. Center the muslin over the seat and slip-tack it to the four sides, keeping it free of wrinkles and pull marks. Cut slits in the muslin for the arm stumps and back posts. When the muslin cover is in satisfactory order, drive the slip tacks in tight. Fold and stitch the corners as illustrated in Fig. 146.

Padding Spring Backs: Place burlap over the back springs as it was placed on the seat springs. Backs having round, scroll or knife-edge tops should be understuffed before edge rolls are formed along the posts at the sides.

Fig. 148A shows the back posts and top rail of a frame on which a scroll top is built. Note that the top rail is below the top edge of the posts. This difference is made up by stuffing the area with burlap-enclosed tow.

Cut a piece of burlap wide enough to permit tacking it to the front side of the top rail, over the post and down to the back side of the top rail, allowing 4 inches for handling. The strip should be long enough to reach from the outside edges of both posts, again allowing 4 inches for handling. Tack the strip to the front side of the top rail.

Prepare a quantity of tow for stuffing the area. Spread a layer of the tow over the top side of the rail and spot-tack it in place. Tack the burlap strip just over the top of the back posts at the sides and add more stuffing, packing the roll full and firm. Fig. 148B. Finish the tacking over the posts and tack the burlap strip along the back of the rail. Smooth out the stuffing with a regulator.

Understuffing will form the shape on the top of the back. A strip of burlap sewn to the burlap over the

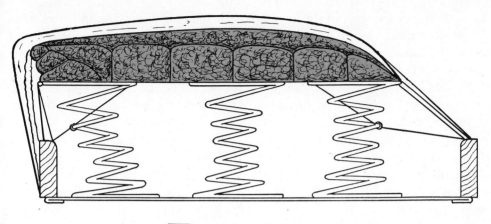

147 PADDING SPRING EDGE SEAT

A—BACK FRAME

B—FIRST UNDERSTUFFING

148 SCROLL SPRING BACK

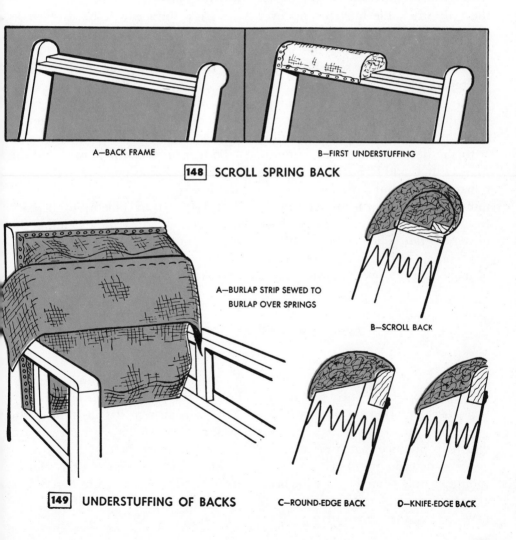

A—BURLAP STRIP SEWED TO
BURLAP OVER SPRINGS

B—SCROLL BACK

149 UNDERSTUFFING OF BACKS

C—ROUND-EDGE BACK

D—KNIFE-EDGE BACK

springs and then stuffed and tacked to the back side of the top rail constitutes the understuffing. With a steel tape measure, form the shape of the under-stuffing desired. Add to this total 4 inches for handling to determine the necessary width of the burlap strip to be used. The length of the strip will be the same as the width of the back from one outside-post point to the other, plus 4 inches for handling. If an edge roll is to be formed, allow 8 inches more on each side.

Mark a chalk line over the burlap-covered springs, parallel to the top of the rail. Stitch the burlap strip over the chalk line, allowing ⅝ of an inch for the seam and leaving the widest edge hang down to the seat. Fig. 149A.

Prepare a quantity of hair or moss for the understuffing. Place the stuffing over the top side of the springs and the front side of the top rail, building it to the desired shape and firmness. Figs. 149B, C and D. Stitch the stuffing down to help build the shape. Add more stuffing to form an even curve from the top of the springs to the back of the top rail. The stuffing should be firm enough so that it will not sag out of shape, but not uncomfortably hard.

Pull the burlap over the stuffing and tack it along the sides and back side of the back rail. Take care to avoid letting the stuffing work back and out from under the burlap. Use a regulator to even out lumps and hollows, and work the stuffing up to the top edge of the top rail.

If an edge roll is to be built around the outside edges of the posts, it should be added at this point.

When placing loose stuffing on the backs of chairs, fill the hollows between the edge rolls and springs first, stitching this stuffing in place so that the back surface will be as even as possible before the first stuffing is placed and sewn to the burlap. Crown the center of the back high, because the edges of back are compressed more than the center. The final cover will not fit smoothly if the center of the back is not highly crowned.

So that no gap will show, build the stuffing as close as possible to the arms and wings.

If the seat is to come up to the back liner, take care to avoid extending the stuffing under the back liner.

Once the back is completely stuffed, cover it with cotton and muslin.

Lesson Six — ARMS AND WINGS

IT IS BEST to build both arms of an upholstered piece at once, performing the same operation on each arm before going on to the next step. This will help produce matching arms.

Arms that do not have arm slats should be upholstered before the back. If they have slats, upholster the back first. Where the arms curve to form

a continuous line with the back, upholster the back and arms together. If there is an arm slat in front of the back post on chairs of this type, upholster the back before the arms.

The inside of closed arms should be webbed as explained in Part 3, Lesson 1. Then burlap is tacked over the webbing. Fig. 151.

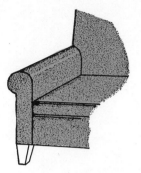
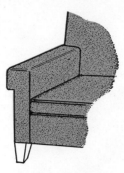
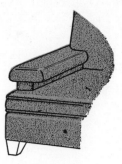

LAWSON OR SCROLL   SQUARE LAWSON   CHARLES OF LONDON OR T SHAPE

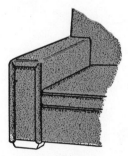
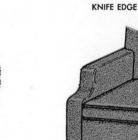

BLOCK MODERN   ROUND   KNIFE EDGE

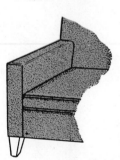

SQUARE FULL   SET BACK   RETURN

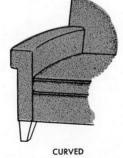

CURVED OUTSIDE   CURVED   CURVED

150 ARM STYLES

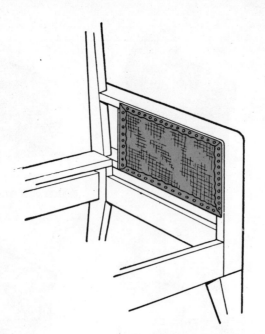

151 BURLAP OVER WEBBING

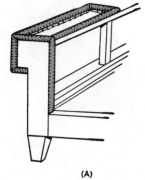

(A)

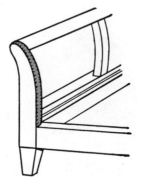

(B)

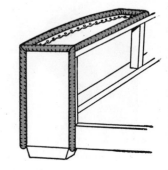

(C)

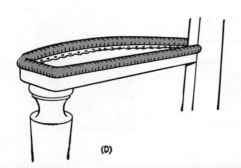

(D)

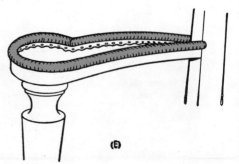

(E)

152 APPLICATION OF EDGE ROLL

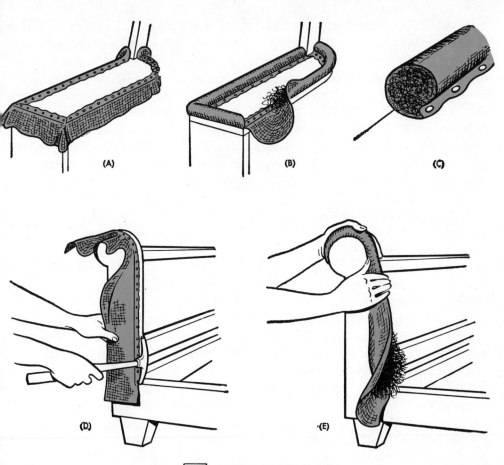

(A)   (B)   (C)

(D)   (E)

153   BUILDING EDGE ROLL

If welts are to be used along the inside and outside edges of the arm boards, the top of the arm is not added until final cover is applied.

Edge Rolls: Some arm boards and inside-front edges of arm stumps will have panels facing them when the final cover is applied. Here edge rolls should be built along the exposed-wood edges. Fig. 152. The edge rolls soften the hard edges of the wood and help prevent excessive cover wear. They also help keep the stuffing in place on the top of the arm boards and give shape to the edges. Edge rolls may be decorative, too, where a recessed-panel effect is desired.

Ready-made edge rolls are ideal for arm work, as they need only be tacked in place.

If you plan to make your own edge rolls, start by cutting a piece of burlap for each arm. Each piece should be 3 to 4 inches wide, depending on the desired size of the rolls, and as long as it needs to be to reach around the outside of the arm board. (Edge rolls on arms are built from ½ to ¾ of an inch in diameter.) Cut the burlap straight with the thread so that the weave of the cloth will serve as a guide in forming and tacking the rolls.

Lay a cardboard strip over the burlap along the edges and tack the burlap in place. At corners or on a curved or round edge, pleat the burlap strips to allow for fullness in the rolls. The number and size of the pleats will depend on the curve of the wood and the size of the rolls. Fig. 153A.

Inasmuch as it is difficult to build edge rolls to the top of the front seat rail, the edge rolls on lawson-type arm stumps should be built before the seat is started.

Prepare enough hair or moss for stuffing the roll on each arm. Place some stuffing under the burlap strip on one arm, kneading and twisting it into a roll and tacking it down through the burlap on the inside edge of the roll. Figs. 153B and C. Then repeat this procedure on the other arm. Take care to make the roll uniform in diameter and firmness.

The edge roll on square corners must be made full and square. Miter each corner with neat pleats and tack the pleated edge roll squarely in back of the corner on each arm. Use a twine-threaded, small, curved needle to stitch the corners together. When the rolls are finished, go over them with a regulator to even out any lumps.

Understuffing Arm Boards: Round-top arms, such as lawson-type arms, need to be understuffed because the arm boards are below the top edges of the arm stumps.

Prepare a quantity of tow for use as understuffing. If the arm boards are exposed in their entirety on the finished piece, plan to stuff them all the way to the back posts. If the arms will be overlapped by the back, end the stuffing halfway between the back posts and the planned front edge of the back.

For each arm, cut a piece of burlap wide enough to go from the bottom of the inside of the arm board, up over the roundness of the arm stump, down to the bottom of the outside of the arm board and then allow 4 inches for handling. Cut the strips long enough to reach from the outside edge of the arm stump to the outside of the back post, again allowing 4 inches for handling. Tack one side of each strip to the inside of each arm board.

Place a layer of tow over the arm boards, spreading it uniformly and spot-tacking it to the boards. Build the stuffing up to the proper shape. Fig. 154A. It should be firmly built in back of the arm stumps. Pull the burlap over the stuffing to determine the amount of additional stuffing needed. This should be done several times on each arm as the understuffing progresses so that they can be kept uniform. (Slip-tack the burlap to the outside of the arm boards for these checkups.) When the arm boards are adequately stuffed, tack the burlap to the outside of the boards, keeping the cloth wrinkle-free. At the front, tack the burlap to the top of the arm-stump wood or sew it to the edge rolls. At the back posts, cut off any excess cloth, turn an edge under and tack the burlap to the posts. Fig. 154B. If there are wings in front of the back posts, tack the burlap as illustrated in Fig. 154, details C and D. Use a regulator to even out any lumps or hollows, but take care to avoid pulling the stuffing out of place in back of the arm stumps.

Padding Arm Boards: After the edge rolls are built around the outer edges of the arm boards, build their centers up even with the tops of the edge rolls.

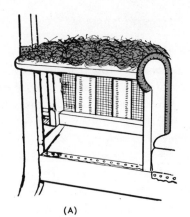

(A)

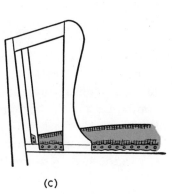

(B)

(C)

(D)

154 **UNDER STUFFING ARM**

Hair or moss, spot-tacked to the boards with No. 4 or No. 6 tacks, should be used here. A second layer of stuffing, built higher at the center than at the edges, should then be placed. Test the pads for softness as you build up the second layer of stuffing. They should be kept smooth and fairly firm.

Tack a piece of burlap just under the edge rolls on the inside of each arm board. Pull the burlap over the stuffing and tack it under the outside of the arm boards, under the edge rolls at the front, and at the back posts and back side of the arm boards. Use a regulator through the burlap to even out any irregularities in the pads.

Padding Inside of Arms: Build up the inside of the arms ½ to ¾ of an inch with hair or moss. The exact amount of stuffing required depends upon the size of the edge rolls used along the inside of the arm stumps.

To apply this stuffing, lay the piece to be upholstered on its side. Spread a layer of stuffing over the burlap on the inside of one arm, building the stuffing up layer upon layer, weaving it together with your fingers. When it is built up evenly to a little over twice the desired height, crown the center of the stuffed area. Take care to avoid having the stuffing fall over the edges of the liner, slat or edge rolls. Then stitch the fibers to the burlap.

Turn the chair to the other side and repeat this procedure.

To keep the arms evenly contoured,

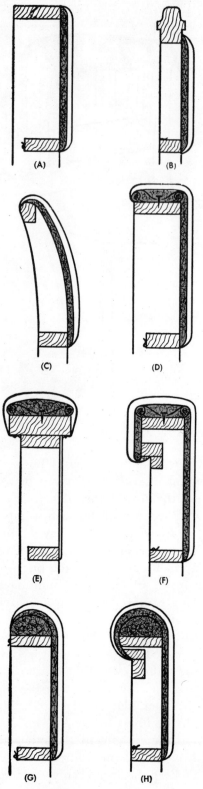

(A)
(B)
(C)
(D)
(E)
(F)
(G)
(H)

pad the inside, outside and top areas of both arms together. Fig. 155 illustrates various styles of arm padding. On square lawson-type arms, the outside of the arms must be covered with burlap or strips of webbing before stuffing the inside of the arm.

If there are arm slats in front of the back posts on a chair having arms that curve to form a continuous line with the back, upholster the back before the arms. If there are no arm slats, stuff the arms and back together in this type of chair. The back is usually padded at least twice as deeply as the seat. Stuff the arms and back to the depth of the desired arm padding. Sew this stuffing down. Now build up the back with more stuffing, tapering it out to the arms. Again stitch the stuffing. Now apply one more thin layer of stuffing to the back, but *do not* sew it down.

Muslin Cover: Place cotton over the loose stuffing. The cotton should overhang the edge rolls slightly, but do not let it project over the liners at the bottom or over the slats at the back of the arms.

Tack the muslin to the outside or top of the arm liners and pull it under the liners and out over the seat. Bring the muslin up over the inside of the arms. On arms like the one shown in Fig. 155A, the muslin is tacked to the top of the arm border. Arms that have show wood over the upholstery, as in Fig. 155B, have a groove under the show wood where the muslin should be tacked. Turn the muslin neatly on this type of work and keep the edges even and smooth. Fig. 155, details C, D and G, shows arms on which the muslin is tacked to the outside of the arm boards. On lawson-type arms, Fig. 155, F and H, the muslin is tacked to the underside of the tacking strip on the outside of the arms.

Tack the muslin close to the edge of the arm stumps or edge rolls, and at the back tack it either to the outside of the arm slats or to the front side of the back posts. On the top of the arms at the back side, the muslin is tacked to the posts and the back of the arm boards. Fig. 156.

Cut slits in the muslin for the arm boards and liners at the back. Then center the muslin on each arm, slip-tacking it at the center of each side. Keep the muslin smooth and free of wrinkles as you work toward all four corners of one arm. When the cover is slip-tacked in the same way on each arm, drive the tacks in place.

Take care to make neat pleats and miters at square corners and around curves on the face of the arm stumps. Fig. 157.

Armrest Pad: Some open-arm chairs require an armrest pad on the arm boards. The upholstery may be tacked on the rabbeted edges provided on these arms. Fig. 158A. Armrest pads are usually small, so care should be taken to keep the upholstery neat and compact.

Prepare a quantity of hair or moss and place some over each armrest, building it to the desired shape and size. Use a few tacks to anchor this stuffing at the center of the pads. Then cover each pad with a burlap strip 4 inches longer and wider than the armrest. Tack the burlap around the top edges of the armrest wood, driving the tacks in at an angle. Fig. 158B. Keep the burlap smooth by making as many small pleats as are needed. Use a razor blade to trim away any surplus burlap. Next bring the stuffing to the edges of the armrests with a regulator and stitch around the outer edges, forming a firm edge on each arm. Figs. 158B and C.

Spread more stuffing over the built-up edge, filling the centers and forming a crowned top on each arm. Take care to avoid having loose fibers overhang the edges. This stuffing is not sewn down.

Put a layer of cotton over each pad, letting it overlap the edges. Place the muslin cover, tacking it just under the burlap so that there will still be space for the final cover to be tacked in the rabbet. Do not let the stuffing work over the edges while the muslin is being tacked in place. Use as many small pleats as are necessary to keep the cover smooth and trim away the surplus muslin with a razor blade.

Upholstering Wing: Unless the wings are a continuation of the back, they should be upholstered before the back. When wings are part of the back, they are upholstered with it. When the inside of the wing frame is flush with the arm boards, the wings again should be upholstered with the arms. Here again the upholstery should be applied to both sides of the chair at the same time.

Fig. 159 shows various wing frames. Detail A shows a solid wood frame with a square edge; B shows a solid wood frame with a round or knife edge; C shows a straight open frame with a curved front edge, and D shows a frame that curves outward on the side and inward on the front. Open-frame wings require burlap tacked on the inside of the frame as shown in

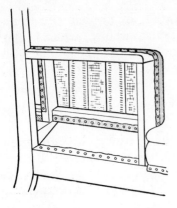

A—MUSLIN TACKED TO OUTSIDE OF BACK SLAT

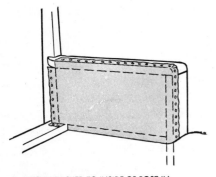

B—MUSLIN TACKED TO INSIDE OF POST IN
BACK. BACK SLAT LEFT OUT OF BACK
TO SHOW TACKING

156 MUSLIN TACKED TO ARMS

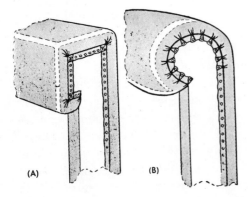

(A)   (B)

157 PLEATING MUSLIN ON ARM STUMP

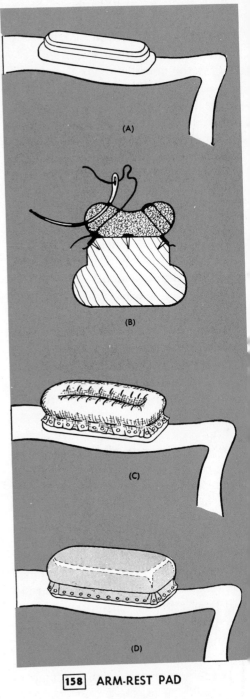

(A)

(B)

(C)

(D)

158 ARM-REST PAD

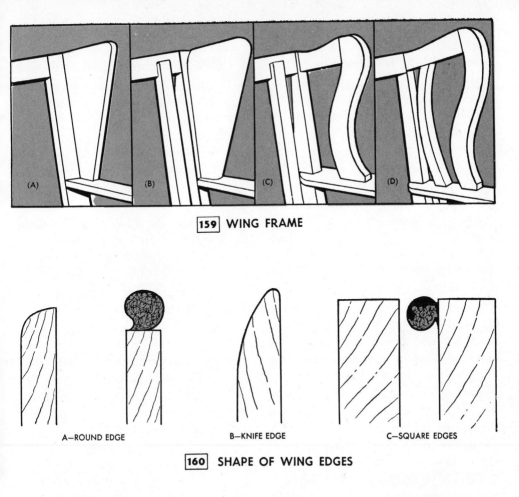

(A)   (B)   (C)   (D)

159   WING FRAME

A—ROUND EDGE   B—KNIFE EDGE   C—SQUARE EDGES

160   SHAPE OF WING EDGES

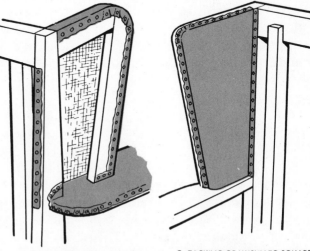

A—TACKING OF MUSLIN TO ROUND
OR KNIFE EDGE OPEN WING
WITH SLAT

B—TACKING OF MUSLIN TO ROUND
OR KNIFE EDGE OPEN WING
WITHOUT SLAT

C—TACKING OF MUSLIN TO SQUARE-
EDGE WING AND MUSLIN TO
INSIDE OF BACK POST

161   MUSLIN TACKED TO WING

Fig. 161. Cut this burlap to the size needed, allowing 3 inches extra for handling. If the frame is curved as in D, the burlap should be stretched only across the curve. Tack the cloth at the top wing rail, inside the edge of the wing post and inside the wing slat at the back. If there are no wing slats, tack the burlap to the back post. Pull the cloth tight across the frame at the bottom and tack it in place. It need not be tacked to the top of the arm board.

The amount of padding needed on wings depends on the size and proportions of the chair. If the chair and wings are small, only one or two layers of cotton need be placed over the inside of the wings. A ½-inch layer of moss is usually used on medium wings. Heavy chairs may have wings requiring a 1-inch layer of moss under the cotton. Knife-edge wings are not usually found on the heavier chairs, for where more than ½ inch of stuffing is used on the wing, an edge roll ½ inch in diameter should be built along the top and front edges of the wings. Fig. 160. Note that the edge roll should be placed directly on the *top side* of the wing frame with a round edge, Fig. 160A, but on a square

edge, Fig. 160C, the edge roll should be placed on the *inside* of the edge.

When round or knife edges are built, the muslin cover should be tacked to the *outside* of the front and top edges. Fig. 161A and B. The muslin should be tacked right *on* the edges for a square edge. At the back of the wings, tack the muslin to the wing slats or to the inside or front of the back posts.

Place cotton over the wing stuffing and cut the muslin cover to size, allowing 4 inches extra on each side. Center the muslin over the wing, slip-tacking it in the center of the top, front and back. Pull the muslin down tight to the bottom and fold it under. Slip-tack the fold of muslin close to the bottom at the front and draw the fold tight at the back, where it should also be slip-tacked. Remove the slip tacks at the top and center of the front and back, readjust the muslin and replace the slip tacks. If the wing is curved, stretch the muslin across the curved part only. On flat wings, the muslin should be stretched from the top to the bottom and from the front to the back. Be sure that the cloth is smooth and free of wrinkles as you tack it around curved edges and corners.

Lesson Seven — LOOSE CUSHIONS

LOOSE CUSHIONS filled with cotton-padded innerspring units are the most pouplar. Fig. 162, details A, B and C, shows the nonreversible style used on inexpensive furniture. These cushions may, of course, be reversed if a solid-color cover fabric is used. They require less sewing than the true

reversible cushions shown in details D, E and F. But because a reversible cushion can be turned over regularly, the padding and innerspring unit, as well as the final cover, will prove to be more durable and show less wear. Cushions also may be filled with down and feathers.

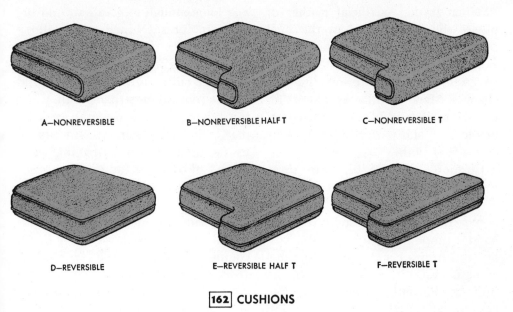

A—NONREVERSIBLE

B—NONREVERSIBLE HALF T

C—NONREVERSIBLE T

D—REVERSIBLE

E—REVERSIBLE HALF T

F—REVERSIBLE T

162 CUSHIONS

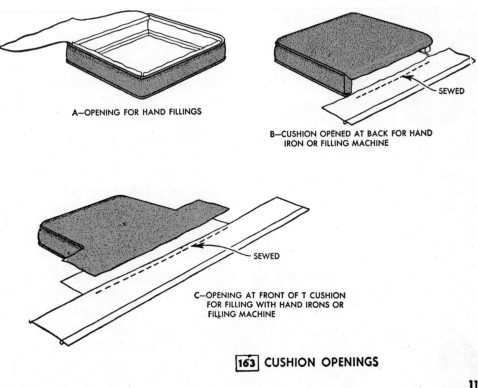

A—OPENING FOR HAND FILLINGS

B—CUSHION OPENED AT BACK FOR HAND
IRON OR FILLING MACHINE

SEWED

C—OPENING AT FRONT OF T CUSHION
FOR FILLING WITH HAND IRONS OR
FILLING MACHINE

SEWED

163 CUSHION OPENINGS

When leather, artificial leather or plastic sheeting is used as the final cover, make the cover in such a way as to allow air to be exhausted or taken in as the pressure on the seat changes. Metal ventilators may be fitted in the sides and back of the cover, or the back and part of the sides may be made of cloth.

Cushions may be filled in three ways—by hand, with hand irons or in a cushion-filling machine. The home craftsman will usually use the hand method, inasmuch as the cost of hand irons or a cushion-filling machine is prohibitive when use will be limited. Partially sewn extra-large cushion covers can be taken to a job shop for filling.

Measuring, Cutting, Sewing: All cushion covers are measured and cut in the same manner. Measure the depth of the seat from the extreme front to the back corner and add 2 inches for handling. Measure its breadth across the widest part of the seat front and again allow 2 inches extra. If a patterned cover fabric is used, center the main figure of the pattern in the planned seat-cover area. Cut the cover to size and center it on the seat. Be sure to cut the fabric in accordance with its up-and-down pattern and nap. Stretch the fabric over the seat smoothly and chalk-mark on it the outline of the back, arms and extreme front of the seat. Allowing ⅝ of an inch for a seam around the chalk line, cut the cover to fit. Now make a duplicate cover, again centering the pattern, for the other side. If you are upholstering a sofa, be sure to make all the cushion covers just alike.

For use as boxing, cut strips across the grain of the fabric 4¾ inches wide and long enough to go all around the cushion. This 4¾-inch width allows 3½ inches for the boxing itself, and ⅝-inch seams on both sides of the boxing. The cushion-front boxing should be one continuous strip of cloth, while the boxing for the other three sides may be made of remnants. If welts are to be used, 2-inch strips for them should also be cut at this time. See Part 4, Lesson 1, on how to make the welts.

Allowing a ⅝-inch seam along both outside edges, sew the welts or brush edging to the face of the boxing. Fig. 164A and B. If this sewing is to be done on a machine, use a cording foot attachment.

If the cushion is to be hand filled, sew the boxing-strip ends together at this point. Next pin the bottom cover to the front boxing, matching the corners and the fabric facing the inside of the cushion, and stitch the bottom cover and boxing together all the way around. Then sew the top cover to the front boxing, Fig. 163A. Turn the cover right side out and install the cotton padding and marshall unit.

If hand irons or a filling machine will be used, sew the cushion cover as follows: matching the corners and fabric facing the inside of the cushion, fasten the bottom cover to the boxing with skewers at the back and sides, but leave the front open; sew the back and side seams; turn the cover right side out and prepare to stuff it. Fig. 163B.

Both front and back seams should be left open on T cushions so that hand irons can be used. After a T cushion has been filled, stitch together the boxing and the back of the seat cover. Fig. 163C. Hand sew the front of the cover.

Building Marshall Unit: The marshall unit, or innersprings, should be about 2 or 3 inches narrower than the cushion cover. This permits the use of cotton to fill the sides of the cushion. It is usually possible to buy a marshall unit already made up to the size required. If, however, you are upholstering a piece styled with an irregularly shaped cushion, you will have to sew the innerspring coils together yourself. Innersprings are available sewn in a continuous strip of muslin. These strips may be cut to the number of springs needed in each row. The muslin should be cut through at the spring beyond the length you are going to use. Cut off and discard the spring that is no longer incased in muslin.

Using a small curved needle threaded with stitching twine, sew the spring rows together. Stitch through the muslin, connecting the top coil of the first and second spring and tie the end of the twine, drawing the top coils together. Carry the twine over to the opposite side of the second spring and stitch through the muslin, connecting the top of the second and third springs with a lock stitch. Continue this procedure until all the springs in each row are connected. Knot the twine at the last coil. Then turn the row over and stitch the other side.

When all the innerspring rows are stitched together, place them side by side, forming the size and shape unit needed. Next stitch together the entire unit, following the stitching procedure suggested for the individual rows.

Filling Cushion by Hand: Place two or three layers of upholsterer's cotton in the bottom of the cushion cover. Set the marshall unit over the cotton. Put cotton between the marshall unit and the cover sides, making sure that the corners are well filled. Fig. 165A. On top of the marshall unit lay the same amount of cotton as was placed in the bottom of the cushion. Fig. 165B.

Pull the top cover over the cotton and skewer-pin the cover to the boxing. Fig. 165C. Use as many skewers as are necessary to hold the cover and boxing together securely.

Make all adjustments needed in the cover, stuffing and border. Hand-sew the cover to the boxing, releasing the skewers one by one as the stitching progresses. Use a 4-inch straight, lightweight needle for this work. Keep the stitches small and close to the welt or brush edging.

Using Hand Irons: A set of hand irons will be a great aid in filling cushions and should be purchased if a quantity of work will be done. Cushions filled with hand irons will be firmer than those filled by hand, although the actual filling process is much the same.

Place the irons on a bench and into the lower iron place cotton, the marshall unit and more cotton around the sides and back and over the top just as described for hand filling the cover. Close the top iron over the stuffing. Hook the side piece on the bottom and press the top down, hooking it on the top of the side. Follow the same procedure on the other side. Now lay the filled hand iron on its side and press the top side down to the desired width of the cushion. Slip the cushion cover over the irons. When the cover is tight against the back of the irons, lay the covered irons flat on the bench and, with a pliers, pull out the two

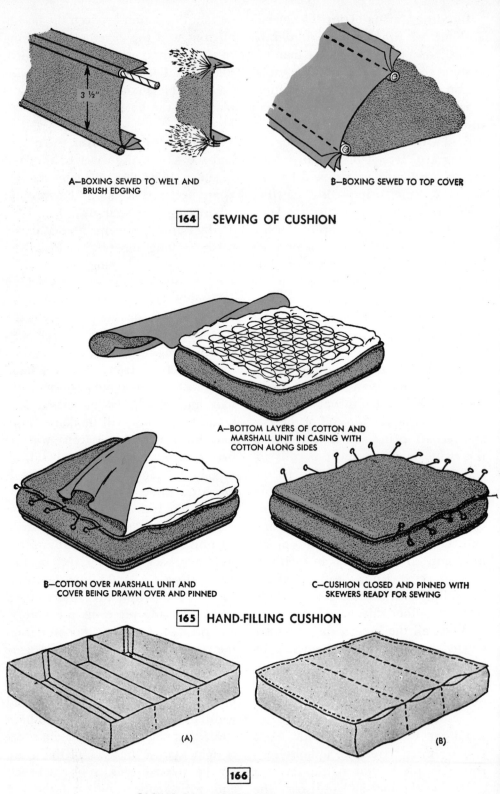

3 ½"

A—BOXING SEWED TO WELT AND
BRUSH EDGING

B—BOXING SEWED TO TOP COVER

164 **SEWING OF CUSHION**

A—BOTTOM LAYERS OF COTTON AND
MARSHALL UNIT IN CASING WITH
COTTON ALONG SIDES

B—COTTON OVER MARSHALL UNIT AND
COVER BEING DRAWN OVER AND PINNED

C—CUSHION CLOSED AND PINNED WITH
SKEWERS READY FOR SEWING

165 **HAND-FILLING CUSHION**

(A)

(B)

166

CASING FOR DOWN AND FEATHERS

side pieces. Hold the filling material firmly in place and remove the top and bottom sections of the irons.

Make the corners square and firm by using a stuffing regulator. If more cotton is needed it should be added *under* the cotton already in place.

Pin the open end closed with skewers and adjust the stuffing as needed.

Here again use a 4-inch straight, lightweight needle and take small stitches close to the welt or brush edging along the top to sew the end closed. The raw edge of the boxing at the corners should be turned under and the seams pinned with skewers. Sew them closed with a curved needle.

Filling Machine: When a volume of cushion work is to be done, a cushion-filling machine should be part of the upholsterer's equipment. These machines all work on the same principle, whether foot or electrically powered.

FIG. 168. Closing box over stuffing in machine

Cushion-filling machines operate a plunger which pushes the padding and marshall unit into the cover. The machine shown in Fig. 169 is foot powered, which means that pumping the foot lever activates the plunger.

Finish and sew the cover by the same procedure suggested at the close of the section on using hand irons.

Down and Feather Filling: When making the finished cover for a cushion that is to be down and feather filled, only the seam joining the bottom of the boxing to the cover at the back should be left unsewed.

Using ticking or heavy sateen, prepare a casing for the down and feathers. This casing should be cut 1 inch wider and deeper than the outer cover so that all the corners of the cushion will be full when the pillow is inserted. Keeping this in mind, cut the two sides of the casing 1 inch larger all around the required size of the finished cover. This allows ½-inch seams and ½ inch for fullness on each side. Cut a border 4½ inches wide and long enough to go around the top and bottom of the casing. For use as dividers,

FIG. 167. Placing stuffing in filling machine

Place the cotton and marshall unit in the metal box just as it would be placed in a hand iron. Fig. 167. Close the box and, using the wheel on the side of the machine, adjust the filling to the width of the cover. Fig. 168. Slip the cover over the box end. Fig. 169. Hold the cover firmly and directly in front of the metal box.

FIG. 169. Cushion cover being filled by filling machine

cut two pieces 4½ inches wide and as long as the casing is wide, plus 2 inches for seams and fullness. These dividers are used to prevent the front-to-back shifting of down and feathers when the seat is in use.

Divide the top and bottom of the casing into three equal parts, chalk marking the divisions to guide you in placing the dividers.

Sew the border to the casing top with the face sides of the pieces together. Turn the casing right side out, leaving the seams inside the casing. Now, using the chalk guidelines, sew the dividers in place in the casing, stitching along the bottom and up the sides. Next sew the other side to the dividers, again following the chalk guidelines as you stitch. Sew the border to the side last attached, allowing a ½-inch seam outside the casing. Leave one side, or front-to-back cushion seam open so that the down and feathers can be placed in the three divisions of the casing. The seams are shown in Fig. 166B.

Put the down and feathers in by handfuls, stuffing the front compartment quit firmly, the middle not quite so solidly, and the back compartment even more loosely. This procedure results in a better shaped, more comfortable seat.

Now stitch the casing closed, insert the pillow in the finished cover and complete any hand sewing required to finish the cushion.

PART FOUR

Trim and Final Cover

Lesson One — TRIM

TRIM IS FUNCTIONAL as well as decorative and must be taken into consideration when planning the final cover. Welts, for example, help hide seams and prevent excessive cover wear. Gimp and decorative nails finish ragged edges attractively. Overlay panels are used to finish hard-to-cover surfaces. Fringes and edgings tastefully placed may turn an otherwise ordinary piece of furniture into something different and distinctive.

Welts: As mentioned above, welts serve a two-fold purpose. They help conceal and reinforce seams and make a cover more durable. Welts are used extensively when the finished upholstered pieces must appear neat and tailored. Ready-made welts in a variety of colors, textures and fabrics are available, and the home upholsterer will do well to take advantage of this, particularly when plastic welts are needed. These are very hard to sew on a domestic-type sewing machine.

If you plan to make the welts yourself, start by cutting long strips of the cover fabric. These should be 2 inches wide and cut with the grain of the cloth. Do not use pieced-together remnants for making welts, as seams in welts always leave lumps.

Using a sewing machine equipped with a cording foot, sew a welt cord in the center of the strips. Fig. 170. Make the stitches close to the cord. Take care to keep the welt centered and the seam straight and untwisted. Welt cords ⅛, ⁵⁄₃₂ and ³⁄₁₆ of an inch thick may be obtained. Soft cords of cotton or cellulose tissue are used for welts along flexible edges such as those on loose cushions and spring edges. Hard cords made of kraft paper, craft cord and spring twine are used in welts along arms, borders, backs, rails and in back of panels. Depending on the size of the welt cord used, there will be from ⅝ to ¾ of an inch fabric edge outside the welt, which facilitates sewing the welt to adjoining fabric or tacking it in place.

Brush Edging: When a more decorated appearance is desired, brush

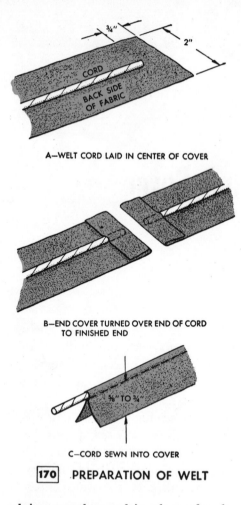

A—WELT CORD LAID IN CENTER OF COVER

B—END COVER TURNED OVER END OF CORD
TO FINISHED END

⅝" TO ¾"

C—CORD SEWN INTO COVER

170 PREPARATION OF WELT

Gimp: Edges that might otherwise appear unfinished may be covered with gimp. It is a ½-inch band made of cotton, rayon, silk, leather, artificial leather or plastic, and comes in a wide variety of styles and colors. Fig. 173.

To apply gimp, spread prepared glue over the fabric along the edges, locate the gimp and tack it in place with gimp nails until the glue is dry. Do not use too much glue, for if it soaks through, it will stain the cover fabric and the face of the gimp. On flat corners, miter the gimp as shown in Fig. 174A. On round and curved edges pleat it as shown in Fig. 174B.

Fig. 171. Brush edging

edging may be used in place of welts. These edgings are made of cotton or rayon yarns or a combination of the two, and come in varying lengths and thicknesses. Fig. 171. Available in mixed or combination-colored as well as a wide variety of solid colors, brush edgings usually can be matched exactly to the cover fabrics.

Boucle Edging: Similar to brush edging except for having looped instead of cut ends, boucle edging may serve the same function. Fig. 172. Made of rayon, silk or nylon, it is more durable and lustrous than brush edging and comes in the same range of colors.

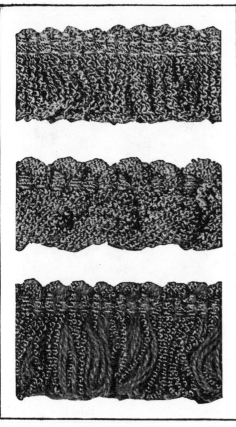

FIG. 172. Boucle edging

Skirts: The bottom edges of upholstered pieces may also be finished off with skirts made of the cover fabric. Fig. 176, details A, B, C and D, shows several skirt styles, their dimensions and circumference allowances. These dimensions can be varied in proportion to each other using the same circumference allowances.

The skirt will be fastened ¾ of an inch above the edge of the bottom rail at the front and should hang to within ½ inch of the floor. Note the fabric width required to do this and add to that total the hem width required. Heavyweight fabrics should have ½-inch hems; middleweight fabrics 1-inch hems and lightweight fabrics 1½-inch hems. Finally, to that total add ⅝ of an inch for tacking at the top. The result is the required width of the skirt fabric.

To determine the length of fabric

Decorative nails are often used over the gimp for additional decoration. Fig. 174C shows how the gimp-nail heads are covered by the trim nails.

Bullion Fringe: Used as trim along the bottom edges of upholstered furniture, this fringe comes in 3, 4, 4½, 5, 5½ and 6-inch-wide rolls, or can be made to order in any width. It is made of cotton, rayon, silk or a combination of the three and is available in many colors, styles and textures. Fig. 175.

After the dust cover is tacked to the bottom of the piece being upholstered, blind-sew the bullion fringe along the bottom. Place the stitches ¾ to 1 inch apart using a lock stitch. The bottom of the fringe should be ½ inch above the floor.

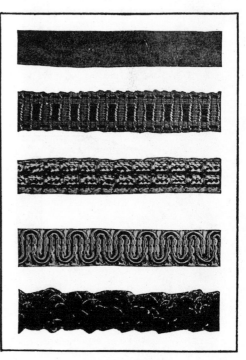

FIG. 173. Gimp

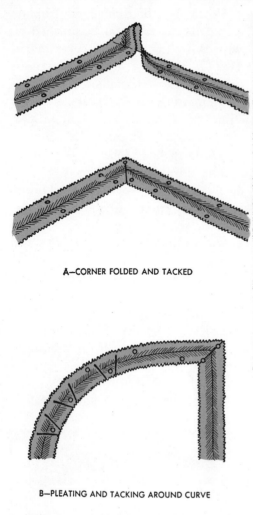

A—CORNER FOLDED AND TACKED

B—PLEATING AND TACKING AROUND CURVE

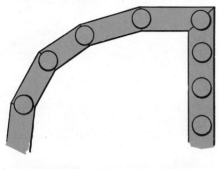

C—LEATHER OR PLASTIC GIMP PLEATED
AND TACKED WITH ORNAMENTAL NAILS

174 TACKING OF GIMP

Fig. 175. Bullion fringe

needed, measure the distance around the upholstered piece, add the pleat allowance and include 1 inch extra for closing the seam at a back corner.

Cut the cloth to the needed size and hand-sew the hem. Steam-press the finished hemline. Make the necessary folds for the pleats and sew them along the top edge. A piece of cardboard cut to the width of the pleats will serve as a guide in keeping the pleats uniform. Steam-press the pleats on the back side of the fabric. If a heavy fabric was used it may be necessary to tack-sew the pleats together at the bottom. (These stitches can be cut loose after the skirt has been hanging for two or three weeks.)

Make a welt long enough to go around the piece with the welt cord sewn ⅝ of an inch in from the top. Sew the welt to the front of the top edge of the skirt.

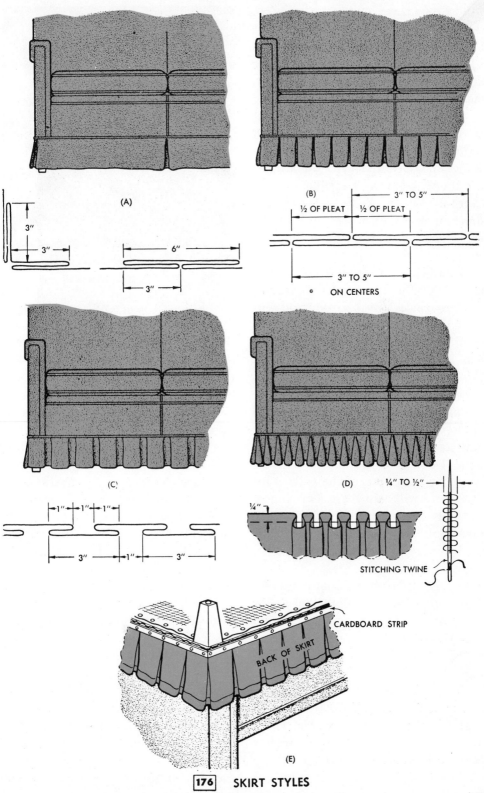

(A)

(B)

3″

3″

6″

3″

3″ TO 5″

½ OF PLEAT | ½ OF PLEAT

3″ TO 5″

ON CENTERS

(C)

(D)

¼″ TO ½″

¼″

STITCHING TWINE

1″ 1″ 1″

3″ 1″ 3″

CARDBOARD STRIP

BACK OF SKIRT

(E)

176 SKIRT STYLES

The dust cover should be tacked to the bottom of the seat before the skirt is fastened in place.

Turn the upholstered piece upside down and, starting at the back corner, tack the skirt in place. The face side of the skirt should be against the seat rails and the bottom of the skirt should hang towards the seat. Fig. 176E. Spot-tack the skirt all around the frame. Next lay a cardboard strip over the row of tacks and drive tacks at short intervals all around the frame. Hand-sew the seam closed at the back corner and trim off any surplus fabric.

Ornamental Nails: To hold down fabric along edges where nails are difficult to conceal, or to avoid hand-sewing edges, use ornamental nails. Aside from such functional uses, these nails may be used for decorative purposes. Ornamental nails come in various sizes, shapes and finishes. Fig. 177.

Cut a cardboard strip to the width of the centers desired and mark the nail center line and edge line on the strip. Use this cardboard as a guide in setting the points of the nails. This procedure will assure even spacing of the nails. Do not drive the first nail in place until the second one is set. Proceed this way all around the edge being nailed.

Panels: Used functionally to face arm stumps and back posts that might otherwise be difficult to cover, panels may also be used decoratively.

Overlay panels may be wood carvings, or ½ or ¼-inch plyboards covered with the cover fabric. Their edges may be finished with a welt or brush edging or left untrimmed. Fig. 178A. Wood carvings should be completely finished before being applied.

To make a fabric-covered panel, cut

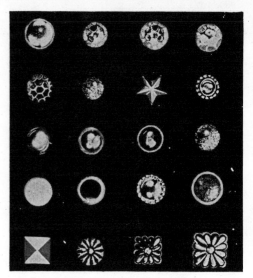

FIG. 177. Decorative nails

the cloth 1½ inches wider and longer than the wood panel and lay the material face down on a work surface. Center the panel face down over the fabric. Pull the cloth over the wood and tack it at the centers on all four sides. Here again, work from the centers toward all four corners and tack the fabric to the back of the panel. Make neat little pleats around curved edges. Fig. 178B.

If welts or brush edging are to be used, tack them to the panel back, letting only the welt or brush edging show in front. When the panel is to be mounted on an arm stump that is set back from the front rail, extend the welt or brush edging below the panel on the outside of the arm so that it will finish at the bottom of the side rail. Cut the welt seam just above the panel so that the welt can be finished on another surface. For panels mounted over arms on back posts, treat the welt or brush edging in the same way, finishing it at the top of the back leg.

To fasten the panel to the face of the arm stump or back post, insert a

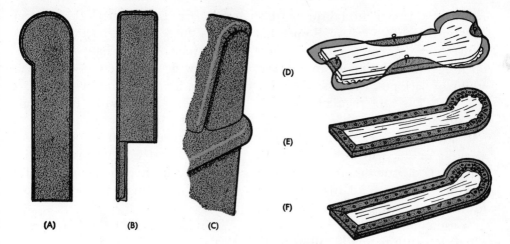

(A) (B) (C) (D) (E) (F)

178 OVERLAY PANELS

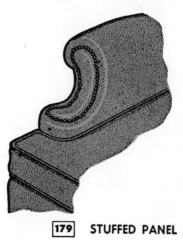

179 STUFFED PANEL

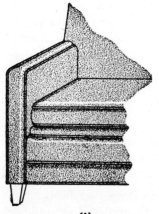

(A) (B) (C)

180 BORDERS

regulator through the fabric in front of the panel and form small openings between the threads. Through these openings, nail the panel to the arm stump or back post with a small finishing nail. Use the regulator to pull the threads back together.

If leather, artificial leather, plastic sheeting or silk will be used to cover the panels, a little different procedure is required. First of all, drive two-penny nails through the panels into the arm stump or back post. Next remove the panels with the nails still in them. Then cover the panel and spot-glue the panel on the back side. Next push the nails in the panel back into the same holes in the arm stump or back post, lay a piece of wood over the panel and drive it back in place.

Making a Stuffed Panel: If the arm stumps of an upholstered piece have an irregular shape, the face of these stumps should be covered with a stuffed panel. Fig. 179. Draw a chalk line around one arm where the panel will be placed. Make a paper pattern the size of the outlined area. Lay the pattern on the other arm and draw a chalk line around it. Now use the pattern to cut the panel fabric. Cut the fabric ¾ of an inch larger all around than the pattern. Follow the chalk line and tack one side of the fabric with slip tacks 2 or 3 inches apart. Lay cotton stuffing over the panel area. Fold the fabric under all the way around and, following the chalk line, slip-tack the fabric panel to the arm. Use a stuffing regulator frequently.

Finally ornamental nails of the desired size and design are driven in around the stuffed panel. Follow the chalk line and place these nails next to each other, head to head. using a

cardboard spacer. Knock the slip tacks out as the work progresses.

Borders: When chair arms are 4 inches wide or narrower, borders are used to hold the cotton padding in place. They may also be used to give interest to the large area below the seat. Fig. 180A. Each side of a border should have a welt or brush edging. Borders and border trim are often sewn to adjoining seat and arm-cover fabrics.

The first edge of the border seam is always blind-tacked in place with a strip of cardboard. Take care to tack the edges straight. Stuff the border with two layers of upholsterer's cotton and slip-tack it to the outside of the arm or bottom of the rail. Fig. 180B. Use a regulator to distribute the cotton through the border. (Be sure to use the regulator *under* the cover, so that no holes are poked in it.) When the cotton is satisfactorily distributed, drive the slip tacks in place.

Trapunto is a raised-applique decoration used on flat-cushion backs covered in plain or almost patternless fabric. Fig. 181A shows two designs.

After the cover has been sewn together and fitted, use chalk to draw the chosen design on the back side of the cover. Cut a strip of muslin 1½ inches wider than the design. Tear cotton strips the same width as the muslin. Place the cotton behind the design, between the back of the cover and the muslin strip. Use skewers to pin the cotton and muslin in place behind the design. Sew the design on a sewing machine using the same color thread as the cover fabric. When the sewing is completed around both sides of the design, remove the surplus cotton. Fig. 181B.

Buttons are used not only for decorative effects but also to hold the stuffing in place. Buttons which are used in upholstery work usually are covered with the same material as is being used to cover the piece. There are home button-making kits available which may be used if the fabric is not too heavy, or, the buttons and material can be taken to a department store, a sewing center or sent to a mail-order house to be covered. The button backs come in the styles illustrated in Fig. 182A. Large odd-shaped buttons can be homemade. Use ¼-inch-thick plywood pieces cut to have at least a ³⁄₁₆-inch radius at the outside top edges. In these pieces drill holes through which twine may be passed to attach the buttons to the upholstered piece. Lay a thin layer of cotton over the face of the plywood. Cut the cover fabric 1½ inches wider and longer than the button and trim it to the general shape of the button. Take small stitches all around the cover ¼ inch in from the outside edge. Lay the button face down in the center of the back side of the button cover and slowly pull both ends of the twine used to stitch around the cover. Draw the twine close around the button, checking and adjusting the cover as it closes over the back side of the button. Fig. 182D. Tie the twine with two simple knots. Tack down the edges of the button cover with No. 1½ tacks.

Stitch the button twines through stuffing and webbing. Put cotton between the twines and tie a slip knot under the webbing, drawing the button to the proper depth in the seat, back or arm sides. Make a simple knot over the slip knot.

If buttons are to be used on seats

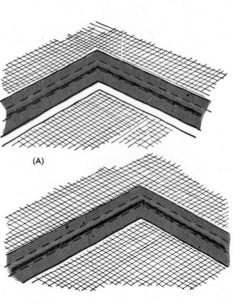

(A)

(B)

(C)

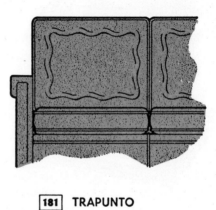

181 TRAPUNTO

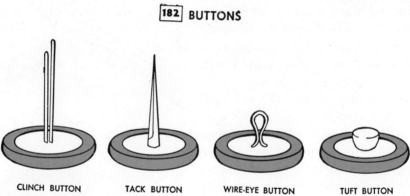

CLINCH BUTTON   TACK BUTTON   WIRE-EYE BUTTON   TUFT BUTTON

TYING DOWN BUTTON USING COTTON SUPPORT

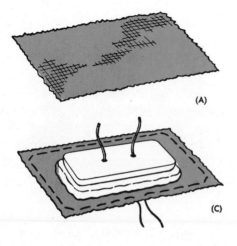

(A)

(C)

(B)

(D)

having a solid foundation, drill ½-inch holes where the buttons are to be placed. Drive a tack next to the hole and tie the button twine to the tack.

Take care to draw all the buttons down to the same depth—no more than the height of the button itself. When button twines must be passed through the spring area, pass the twines so that they will not rub against the spring coils or pull the springs down.

On scoop seats, tack front-to-back bands of webbing across the bottom of the seat. Center these bands under each row of buttons. Tie the button twines to this webbing.

Lesson Two — FINAL COVER

THE BEAUTY of an upholstered piece is largely dependent upon the fabric used for the final cover. The upholsterer should take great care in selecting the cover fabric, and should expect to pay more for this material than for any other single item needed in upholstering.

Tapestry, frieze, matelasse, damask, satin, brocatelle, brocade, velour, boucle, tweed and sail cloth are among the fabrics intended for use in upholstering. These fabrics are made 50 or 54 inches wide and can be had in a wide variety of modern and traditional designs, patterns and colors.

Drapery and slip-cover fabrics, which are made in 30, 36, 40 and 48-inch widths, should not be used on upholstered work. These fabrics, while attractive and apparently sturdy, will not prove to be durable upholstery coverings.

Color, texture and pattern are things to consider when selecting cover fabrics.

The color or colors of the cover fabric should always be in harmony with the other colors used in the same room. Neutral or subdued colors are best, for these will blend in with almost any surrounding. Bright colors can be very attractive when used with care; however, in a room furnished with pieces upholstered in subdued colors, one bright piece will stand out sharply and appear larger than it actually is.

If possible, it is good practice to take swatches of the rug material, draperies and other upholstery fabrics used in the room with you when shopping for cover fabrics, to aid in matching or harmonizing colors.

Rough-textured fabrics should be used only on large upholstered pieces. If they are applied to small chairs or sofas, these pieces will look too heavy for their size. They should be covered with smooth fabrics.

The pattern in the fabric should be in keeping with the period of the furniture on which it is used, as well as in harmony with any patterned rugs, draperies or other upholstered pieces in the room. Do not use large patterns on small pieces of furniture, for this will only further diminish their size. Stripes and geometric patterns should be used only on upholstered furniture with flat surfaces.

If the piece you are covering will be subjected to exceptionally heavy wear, choose a cover fabric known to be durable. Your salesperson should be able to suggest appropriate materials.

Leather is sold by the hide or the square foot, and is available in various grades, thicknesses and colors. Leather does not lend itself well to curved surfaces around which it would need to be pleated, for it neither folds nor stretches as readily as fabric.

Leather covers should be sewn only on industrial-type sewing machines. As the sewing progresses, lubricate the foot and needle frequently with paraffin to avoid having them stick to the leather.

Plastic-Coated Fabrics, sometimes called artificial leather, react to styling, sewing and use much like real leather.

These fabrics are made by coating a cloth base with pyroxylin, resin or vinyl plastic. They are made with highly polished surfaces, embossed grains and patterns, and come in various thicknesses and colors. The vinyl-coated fabrics are the most popular and are made 54 inches wide.

Plastic Sheeting is made from unsupported vinyl plastic. Finishes vary from simulated-leather grains and embossed designs to highly polished surfaces. This material is available in almost every color, and is becoming more and more popular.

A few precautions must be taken when working with plastic sheeting.

Use .012-gauge sheeting for covering pad seats, backs and arms, and .021-gauge or heavier sheeting over spring-based areas. Plastic sheeting thinner than .012 gauge is not suitable for upholstered work.

When cutting plastic sheeting, punch a ⅜-inch hole at the apex of all inside cuts and corners. Fig. 183A. A punch can be made from a 4 to 6-inch length of ⅜-inch I.D. pipe by grinding the outside edges at a 45-degree angle. Fig. 183B. Use a wood block under the plastic sheeting when punching the holes.

If buttons will be used, first mark their planned locations on the plastic sheeting. A black wax crayon should be used for any such needed markings on plastic. Next, punch holes at the markings to accommodate the button tabs. (NOTE: Large-diameter buttons with cloth tabs are best used on plastic work.) Finally, back each hole with adhesive tape. If these precautions are not taken, the material is apt to tear at inside cuts and around buttons.

Plastic sheeting should be machine sewn with a round No. 23 chrome needle. Use No. 16-4 or No. 20-4 mercerized cotton thread and set the machine so that it will make not more than 6 stitches per inch. Set the stitches at least ½ inch in from the outer edge of the plastic sheeting, and avoid double stitching.

Be sure to smooth off all sharp frame

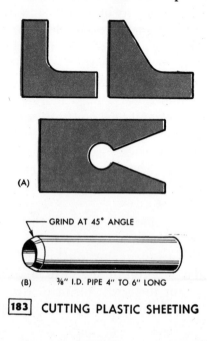

(A)

— GRIND AT 45° ANGLE

(B)   ⅜" I.D. PIPE 4" TO 6" LONG

183 **CUTTING PLASTIC SHEETING**

edges that will come in contact with the sheeting.

When this material will be tacked or stapled in place, fold the edges under and drive the tacks through the double thickness. Use ½-inch-long, round-shank billposter tacks with large, round, flat heads. Drive the tacks in straight, spacing them about 1½ inches apart. Do not drive the tack heads into the frame.

If necessary, heat plastic sheeting under heat lamps to make it more pliable. The material should be handled only when it is at room temperature (65 to 85 degrees Fahrenheit). This is especially true when stretching and pleating are required, such as around corners.

PLANNING AND CUTTING COVERS

Cover yardage needed can be determined in two ways. You can make a paper scale plan of the fabric (Fig. 184), and on this plan outline the shapes of the required pieces, or you can take careful measurements of all the pieces needed and make paper patterns. Patterns should be made of all the larger areas, especially if they are irregular in shape. In either case, remember that velours, mohairs and other pile-type fabrics should be planned and cut so that the nap will appear the same on all parts of the upholstered piece. The top end of these materials should be applied to the top of the back, arms and wings, and to the back side of the seat. The easiest way to tell the top end of a pile fabric is to rub a finger over the ends. At the top end an upward stroke will feel bristly, while a downward stroke will feel smooth.

Plan to use all of the cover fabric. Avoid wasting large areas of the material. Long strips should be cut along the edges wherever possible for use as welt covers. (NOTE: A piece cut too small is, of course, more wasteful than one cut with liberal allowances.) Allow ⅝ of an inch for seams, folds, blind tacking and turning under of edges. A 3-inch allowance should be made for handling (pulling and tacking down fabric when cover stretchers are not used). Allow 1 inch for making French seams and self welting.

Place the cover fabric face up on the cutting table. On it lay the patterns, or chalk mark the outlines indicated on the scale plan. Check each part carefully for size, nap and location of fabric design. Cut the material.

Cover Stretchers made of denim, muslin or other inexpensive materials may be used when large areas of the cover fabric are hidden from view under the liners or slats. They may also be made from the old cover fabric. Fig. 185 shows stretchers sewn on arm, back and seat covers.

These stretchers are merely extensions of the cover fabric. Their use avoids the unnecessary expense of using additional unseen cover fabric for tacking the cover in place. Be sure that stretchers are used *only* when they will be unseen. Use French seams when sewing the stretchers to the cover.

Notes on Cover Application: Take care to avoid depressing the springs when pulling down the covers. The stuffing will be packed down too hard, and the resulting excess strain on the cover will lessen its durability.

Keep inside covers smooth when pulling them around outside frame

CHAIR TO BE COVERED

COVERS REQUIRED

PIECES	ABBREVIATIONS	USE	WIDTH	LENGTH
1	S.	SEAT	30″	26″
1	I.B.	INSIDE BACK	28″	21″
1	O.B.	OUTSIDE BACK	21″	23″
2	I.A.	INSIDE ARM	20″	14″
2	O.A.	OUTSIDE ARM	18½″	13″
1	B.	BORDER	34″	3″
1	B.Bx.	BACK BOXING	41″	3″
1	W.	WELT	250″	2″

CUTTING PLAN

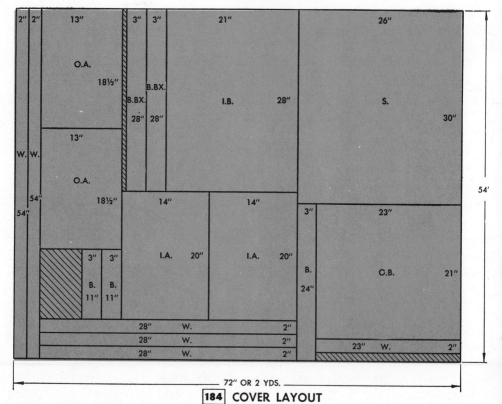

72″ OR 2 YDS.

184 COVER LAYOUT

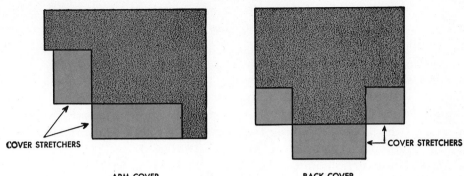

ARM COVER

BACK COVER

COVER STRETCHERS

COVER STRETCHERS

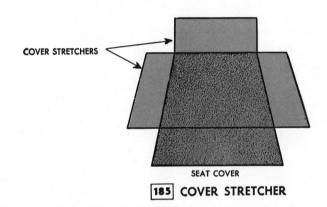

COVER STRETCHERS

SEAT COVER

185 COVER STRETCHER

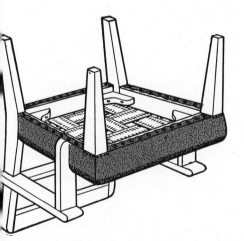

A—OPEN CHAIR SEAT COVER

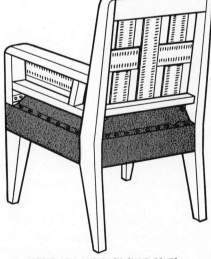

B—CLOSED ARM AND BACK CHAIR COVER

186 TACKING OF SEAT COVERS

members. Do not leave any large lumps when tacking these covers in place. Lumps not only will show through the cover, but will prevent neat fitting of covered panels on the arm stumps or sides of the back posts.

Covers must not be pull-marked. By tacking halfway between the existing tack and the hand that is pulling the cover taut, pull marks may be avoided. For complete instructions on this tacking procedure, reread *Muslin Cover, Part 3, Lesson 3* and note Fig. 93.

Pleats made in the final cover should be as small and uniform in size and spacing as possible. The fold of the pleats should always lie to the outside of the work on the front, to the back side of the piece at the sides, to the outside of the frame on the rail top, and face down along the sides of the posts.

COVERING SEATS

The seat of a chair is usually covered before the back. If the cotton has not been placed under the muslin cover, lay it in place over the muslin. Center the cover over the seat and drive slip tacks at the front, back and side centers. When edges will be exposed, tack the cover to the bottom edge of the seat rail or over the top edges of the show wood. Fold the raw edge of the cover under when slip-tacking over show wood. Fig. 186A. Tack the cover along the top edge of the seat rails on pieces built with closed arms and backs. Fig. 186B. Proceed to slip-tack all four sides of the seat as described in paragraph 3 under *Notes on Cover Application*. When the cover is tacked to within a few inches of the posts or arm stumps, fold and cut it to fit around these parts as

shown in Fig. 187. Do not make these cuts too deep, for that would spoil the cover. Turn the tabs under and tuck them in between the posts or arm stumps. Tack down the tabs.

Fig. 188A shows how the material should be cut and turned under at sharp corners. On round corners the material should be gathered into small neat pleats. Fig. 188B. The pleats should be laid back away from the front. Fig. 188C. If the cover finishes over the legs, cut it along each side and over the top of the leg, leaving a ½-inch tab. Fig. 189, details A and B. Turn the tab under and tack it down with gimp tacks. Fig. 189C.

When you are satisfied with the appearance of the cover, drive the slip tacks in place.

Welted Pull-Over Cover: When all sides of a seat are exposed, it is sometimes desirable to have the seat cover fit neat and tight against the posts and arm stumps. Fig. 190A. This fitted appearance may be achieved by sewing a welt around the cover openings for the posts and arm stumps. Make a paper pattern of the seat, fitting the pattern close around the posts and arm stumps. Mark the back and front centers on the pattern. Lay the pattern over the face of the cover and chalk mark the location of the welt on the cover. Trim the cutouts for the posts and arm stumps as shown in Fig. 190B. Cut slits at the corners. Sew a welt in place on the face side of the fabric as shown in Fig. 190C, following the chalk line with the inside edge of the welt cord.

The cover is now ready to install. Again, if the cotton has not been placed under the muslin cover, lay it in place now. Center the cover over

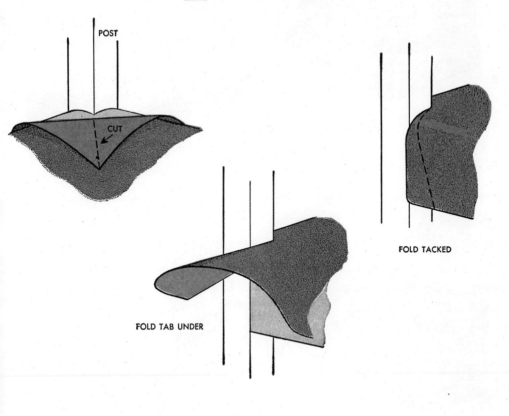

POST

CUT

FOLD TAB UNDER

FOLD TACKED

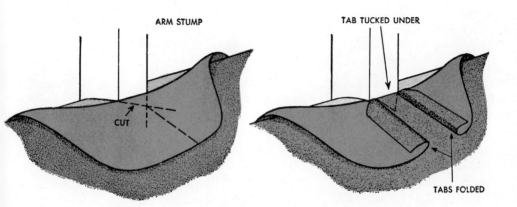

ARM STUMP

CUT

TAB TUCKED UNDER

TABS FOLDED

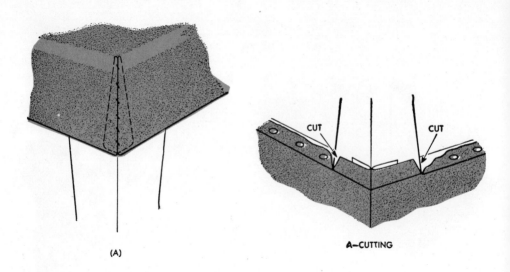

(A)

A—CUTTING

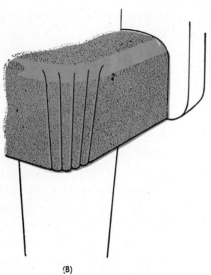

(B)

B—FOLDING TABS TO UNDERSIDE

(C)

C—TACKING

188 FINISHING CORNERS

189 FITTING OVER LEG

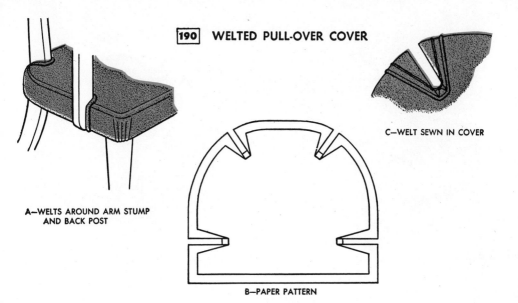

A—WELTS AROUND ARM STUMP AND BACK POST

B—PAPER PATTERN

C—WELT SEWN IN COVER

the seat and slip-tack the welt cords tight against the post and arm stumps. Slip-tack the cover around the bottom of the seat rails, adjust it satisfactorily and drive the tacks in place.

Banded and Boxed Covers are applied to seats and backs built with spring edges. Fig. 191A. These covers are cut and sewn like loose cushions, but have no bottoms.

Pinning the paper along the spring edge and allowing ⅝ of an inch for seams, make a paper pattern of the top of the seat or inside of the back. Fig. 191B illustrates the sewing of seat covers. When cutting these covers, be sure to leave an allowance for the tabs which will be tucked in around the arm stumps and posts.

Place the cotton if it is not already under the muslin. Center the cover over the seat or back, making sure that the cutouts for the arm stumps and posts are in proper position. Skewer the top welt to the spring-edge wire along the exposed edges. Make sure that the cover is tight, straight and free of wrinkles. Hand-sew the

welt to the burlap or muslin with lock stitches, using a small curved needle. Remove the skewers as the work progresses. Fig. 191C. Pull the cover taut and tack it along the edges that are not exposed.

On the frame sides mark the lower welt of the box. Use a few layers of cotton to fully pad the boxed edges. Placing the tacks about 6 inches apart, slip-tack the lower welt in place and adjust the cotton padding under the cover. When the padding is in satisfactory order, drive the slip tacks in place. Now tack a cardboard strip over the welt seam. Fig. 191D.

Place one layer of cotton below the welt and draw the cover over it to the bottom of the rails or to the back of the posts and rail, where the cover should be tacked. If the frame has show wood, fold the fabric under and tack it above the show wood.

Covering Platform Seat: The platform in back of the spring edge roll should be covered with denim or velourette of the same color as the cover fabric. Fig. 192A.

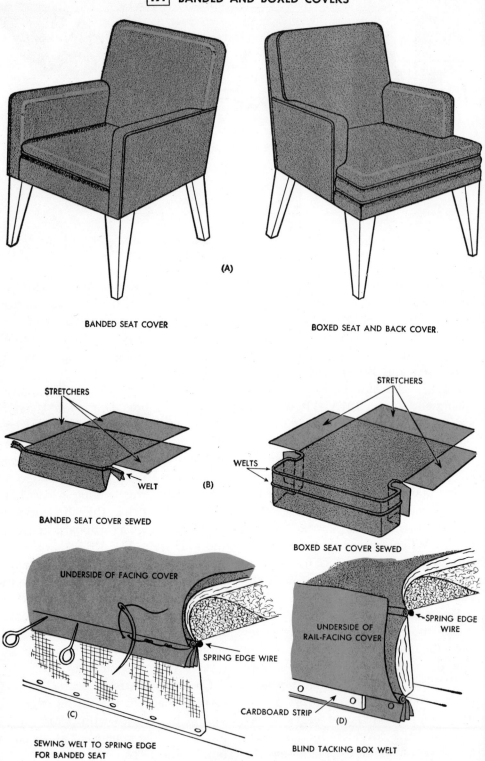

(A)

BANDED SEAT COVER

BOXED SEAT AND BACK COVER.

STRETCHERS

STRETCHERS

WELTS

WELT

(B)

BANDED SEAT COVER SEWED

BOXED SEAT COVER SEWED

UNDERSIDE OF FACING COVER

UNDERSIDE OF RAIL-FACING COVER

SPRING EDGE WIRE

SPRING EDGE WIRE

CARDBOARD STRIP

(C)

(D)

SEWING WELT TO SPRING EDGE FOR BANDED SEAT

BLIND TACKING BOX WELT

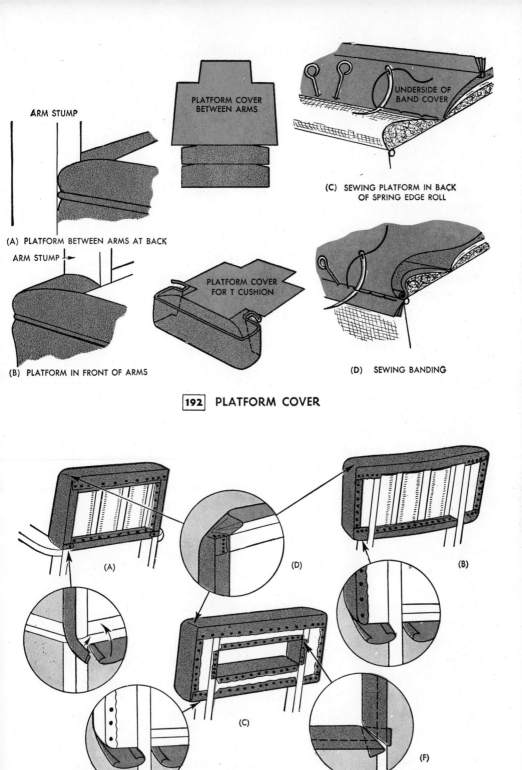

ARM STUMP

PLATFORM COVER
BETWEEN ARMS

UNDERSIDE OF
BAND COVER

(A) PLATFORM BETWEEN ARMS AT BACK

(C) SEWING PLATFORM IN BACK
OF SPRING EDGE ROLL

ARM STUMP

PLATFORM COVER
FOR T CUSHION

(B) PLATFORM IN FRONT OF ARMS

(D) SEWING BANDING

192 PLATFORM COVER

(A)

(D)

(B)

(C)

(E)

(F)

193 COVERING INSIDE OF OPEN BACKS

First make a banding wide enough to reach from the back edge of the spring edge roll forward to the spring-edge wire, allowing ⅝ of an inch at each side for seams. Make the band long enough to permit tucking it in around the ends of the spring edge rolls at the arm stumps. On T seats, fit, miter and pin the banding at the corners. Stitch the miter on a sewing machine. Sew a welt to the bottom edge of the band, letting the face of the cover fabric hang down over the seat rails. Fig. 192B. Sew the band to the platform fabric. If a border will be used at the bottom of the seat rails, sew it to the cover at this point. Sew a welt in between the cover and border. Wherever possible, match the cover and border fabric designs exactly so that they will appear to be a single piece of cloth.

Place cotton over the platform if it has not already been placed under the muslin. Center the cover over the seat, skewer-pin the front edge of the platform fabric to the back edge of the spring roll and slip-tack the fabric to the top edge of the side and back rails. When the fabric is satisfactorily placed, hand-sew the front seam of the platform fabric to the back edge of the spring edge roll, using a small curved needle. Remove the skewers as the work progresses. Fig. 192C.

If there is no cotton under the muslin over the spring edge roll, lay a piece over the roll at this time. Pull the banding over the roll and skewer the seam of the welt to the spring-edge wire. Straighten the welt and make sure that the padding is in good order. With a small curved needle, lock-stitch the welt seam to the muslin over the spring-edge wire. Remove the skewers as the work progresses. Fig. 192D.

Pad the cover facing the seat rails and tack it in place as described in the last paragraph of the section on banded and boxed covers.

COVERING INSIDE OF BACKS

Open Backs: An open back may be covered before or after the seat of the piece.

Apply the cotton padding if it is not already under the muslin cover. Do not let the cotton overlap the frame members.

Center the cover over the inside of the back and slip-tack the four centers. Wherever possible, tack the cover to the inside of the side posts, the top side of the back liner at the bottom and, if the rail is shallow, to the bottom of the top rail. If the rail is not too shallow, tack the cover along the back side of the top rail about ½ inch below its top edge. Fig. 193, details A, B and C, shows covers tacked to various types of open backs. Do not leave any lumps or wrinkles in the cover when tacking it to the back side of the frame. Slip-tack the cover all around, working toward all four corners at the same time. If the back being covered is curved or rounded, stretch the cover from the top to the bottom only and tack these edges in place before starting to tack the sides. Make small pleats at the corners. When the post is exposed along the side of a piece, as shown in Fig. 193A, the cover is folded under at the bottom along the side of the post. No tacking will be required at the post if the cover is pulled taut on the back side of the post.

When applying the cover to a back

like the one shown in Fig. 193B, tack the cover to within 3 inches of the posts or corners. Then make the cuts for the posts, and fold and tack the cover as shown in Fig. 193E.

If you plan to cover a chair back like the one shown in Fig. 193C, cut and sew the cover fabric before placing it on the back. Slip-tack the outside edges in place on the back, pull the cloth through the open part of the back and slip-tack it in place at all four centers. Fold the corner edges as shown in Fig. 193F. These folds should be hand-sewn after tacking the fabric in place.

After checking to see that there are no pull marks in the cover, drive in place all the slip tacks.

Closed Backs: These covers should be tacked in place like those on open-back pieces except at the bottom, where the cover is tacked to the top side of the back seat rail. Fig. 194A and B. If the piece being covered also has closed arms, tack their covers to the inside edge of the back post under the arm boards at the sides. Fig. 194C.

Cover stretchers are sewn to the bottom of inside back covers where the stretchers will be hidden by the back liner. Sew stretchers to the sides of inside back covers under the arm boards when covering closed-arm pieces. Fig. 194, details D and E, shows how to sew these stretchers in place. The final cover will overlap the top of the stretchers on the arms, and the surplus fabric should be folded and tucked in under the back upholstery over the arm board.

Scroll Backs: A different procedure is used when covering round or scroll-type backs or other backs topped with an overhanging edge roll.

When an edge roll has been tacked along the top of the back and the front edges of the posts, tack the cover fabric along the inside of the edge roll on the side of the posts. If the edge roll does not overhang the post, tack the cover ½ inch in from the post edges at their sides. Fig. 195A. Tack the fabric so that the covered panel will cover the tack heads.

On round or scroll-type back tops, trim the fabric at the top so that it will overhang the edge roll or edge of the post 2 inches. Taking ¼ to ½-inch-long stitches, twine-stitch the fabric ½ inch in from its edge. Make these stitches uniform, as each stitch will form a pleat. After the stitching is finished, draw together the pleats and tack down the twine ends. Fig. 195B. Arrange the pleats so that they are uniformly spaced and tack them in place. Then tack the cover between the pleats. Fig. 195C. Take care to place these tacks so that they will be covered with the panel to be placed later. The tacks holding the stitching twine are then removed and the stitching twine is pulled out.

Continuous Closed Back and Arms: Inside backs that flow in a continuous line with the arms are covered as one unit. So that the pattern on the inside of the arms will not appear to be slanted, it is necessary to cut three separate pieces of cover fabric to cover this type of back.

First place a piece of the cover fabric on the back, centering the pattern. Skewer the centered piece in place over the back. Fig. 196A. Chalk mark this inside-back-cover piece from the outside of the arms at the posts to the bottom of the back at each side. Take care to mark each side in the same

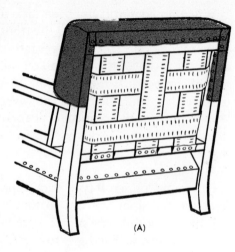

(A)

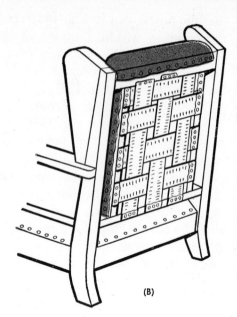

(B)

TACKING INSIDE BACK COVER AT BACK

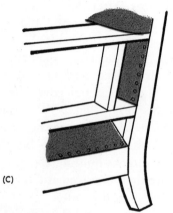

(C)

TACKING INSIDE COVER
'JN FRONT OF BACK POST UNDER ARM

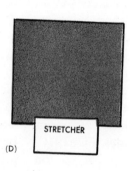

STRETCHER

(D)

ARMLESS CLOSED BACK CHAIR

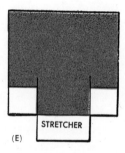

STRETCHER

(E)

BACK COVER FOR CLOSED
ARM AND BACK

194   COVERING INSIDE OF CLOSED BACKS

(A)

(B)

(C)

195   TACKING COVER ON SCROLL BACK

way. Following the chalk marks, cut the inside back cover. Allow ⅝ of an inch all around for seams.

Following the same procedure, center fabric on each arm and match the pattern to the back cover. Pin each arm cover in place with skewers, fold the cover forward and chalk mark the back of the fabric for cutting. Cut the arm covers, again allowing ⅝ of an inch for seams. Pin the back and arm covers together and make a French seam along the chalk guide lines. Welts sewn between the pieces can be used instead of French seams.

If cotton padding was not placed under the muslin cover, apply it now, taking care to avoid having it overlap the frame. Center the back-and-arm cover in place and pin it with skewers.

Next start slip-tacking the cover. Place tacks at the center of the back, on the back side of the top rail and at the center of the top edge of the back seat rail. Working from the center toward the arms, slip-tack the cover, pulling it tight from top to bottom. Place tacks all along the back to the posts, draw the fabric around the posts and slip-tack it to the inside of the posts above the arms. Draw the French seam or welt tight from top to bottom and tack it down. Continue along over the arms, slip-tacking the cover to the outside of the arm board and to the top side of the seat rail. Bring the arm covers around the face of the arm stumps at the front and slip-tack the fabric to the back side of the stumps. Fig. 196C. Tack the outside corners last, making neat and uniform pleats or folds. Make any necessary adjustments in the cover and drive the tacks in place.

196 CONTINUOUS INSIDE-ARM-AND-BACK COVER

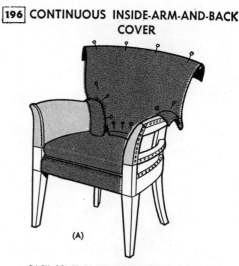

(A)

BACK COVER PINNED IN PLACE FOR MARKING

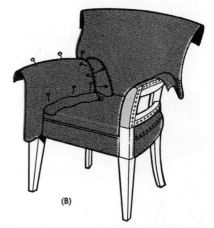

(B)

ARM COVER PINNED IN PLACE FOR MARKING

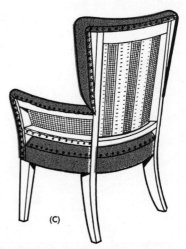

(C)

TACKING COVER ALONG THE OUTSIDE OF CHAIR

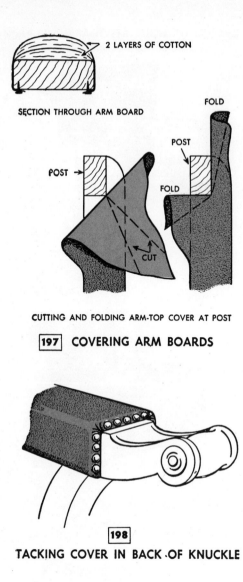

2 LAYERS OF COTTON

SECTION THROUGH ARM BOARD

FOLD

POST

POST →

FOLD

CUT

CUTTING AND FOLDING ARM-TOP COVER AT POST

197 COVERING ARM BOARDS

198

TACKING COVER IN BACK OF KNUCKLE

199

CAMBRIC TACKED UNDER ARM BOARD

COVERING ARMS AND WINGS

Covered Arm Boards: When there is no show wood on the arm boards their covers can be tacked along the bottom side of the arm boards. A few layers of cotton are usually sufficient padding on arms of this type. Fig. 197A. Do not let the cotton overlay the edges of the arm boards. Cut the cover at an angle to the corner of the back post. Fig. 197B. Turn the surplus fabric under the cotton and place tacks at the underside of the arm board. If the cover has been pulled taut enough no tacking will be required along front or sides of the posts. When arm boards end in knuckles at the front, turn the fabric under in back of the knuckles and gimp-tack the cloth in place. Fig. 198. Cover the tacks with gimp, or set decorative nails over the gimp-tack heads. Make neat small pleats at the corners in front of the arm boards.

When the cover has been tacked in place cut a piece of cambric 1 inch wider and longer than the arm board. Tack this cambric to the underside of the arm board ¼ inch in from the edge. Fold the strip under as the tacking progresses. This cambric strip is used to conceal the raw edges of the cover. If an arm stump divides the arm board, cut the cambric in two separate strips, one to overlap the other around the arm stump. Fig. 199.

When there is show wood around the side of arm boards or arm rests, turn under the cover fabric and tack it along the top edge of the show wood. This edge is then decorated with gimp or nails set head on head. Fig. 200.

Inside of Closed Arms: After the inside of the back has been covered, apply the covers to the insides of

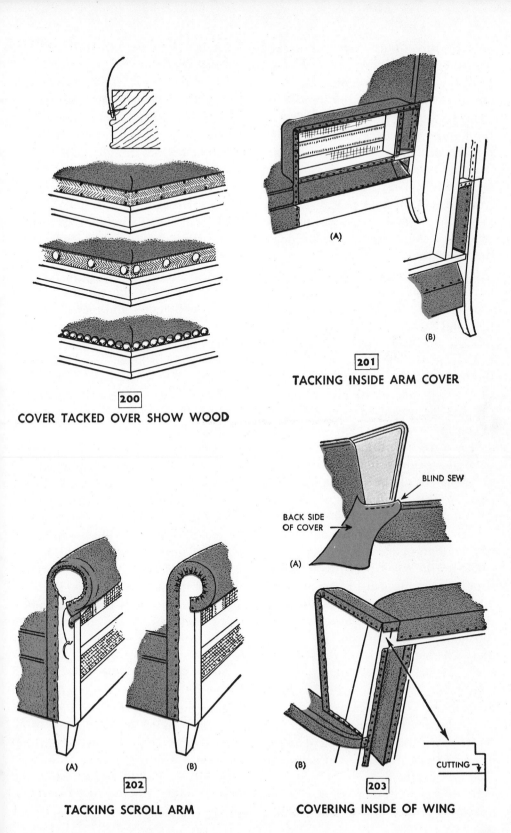

200
COVER TACKED OVER SHOW WOOD

(A)

(B)

201
TACKING INSIDE ARM COVER

(A)

(B)

202
TACKING SCROLL ARM

BLIND SEW

BACK SIDE
OF COVER

(A)

(B)

CUTTING

203
COVERING INSIDE OF WING

closed arms. This cover is tacked over the inside of the arms just as the muslin was tacked except at the back and bottom. (See Fig. 155 for tacking cover to the top side of the arms.) At the bottom the cover is tacked to the top side of the seat rail. If an arm slat is in place, bring the cover around in back of it and tack the fabric to the front edge of the back post. Fig. 201A. When the frame is styled without arm slats, tack the cover to the inside of the back post. Fig. 201B.

So that the cover will fit around the back post, mark a cut in the top of the arm cover at the back. Pull the tab taut and tack it on the inside of the post. If the back overhangs the arm board and the cover is pulled under the back and drawn taut from side to side, it will not be necessary to tack the cover on the top of the arm boards. When the back does not overlap the arm boards, tack the cover along the back edge of the arm boards. Sew cover stretchers to the bottom side and back of the inside arm covers low enough so that the stretchers will be hidden below the liners or behind the arm slats or back.

Center the cover over the arms and slip-tack it in place at the top and bottom centers. Work away from the centers toward the four corners on the top and bottom and pull the cover taut. The back and front edges of the cover are tacked last. When the cover appears to be satisfactorily adjusted, drive the tacks in place.

If a border is to be used over the top of the arms, machine sew it to the inside of the arm cover before placing the cover on the arm.

If no panels or borders are to be used on the face of the arm stumps,

bring the cover around and tack it to the inside of the arm stumps.

When tacking on the cover of scroll or round-top arms, start placing the tacks along the top, bottom and back side of the arms. Then tack the cover along the bottom straight edge in front of the arm stump. Fig. 202A. Next, trim the cover so that it overhangs the edge of the stump 2 inches. Taking ¼ to ½-inch-long stitches, twine-stitch the trimmed fabric ½ inch in from its edge. Make the stitches uniform in length as each one will form a pleat. After completing the stitching, draw the pleats together and tack down the twine ends. Fig. 202B. Arrange the pleats and tack them in place. Tack the cover down between the pleats so that the tack heads will be covered with the panel. Remove the tacks holding down the twine ends and pull out the twine.

Inside of Wings: After the arms are covered, tack the cover over the inside of the wings just as the muslin was tacked, but do not tack it along the back side.

Center the cover, skewer it in place, make any necessary adjustments in the placement of the cover and then remove all the skewer pins except those at the bottom. Turn the cover under at the bottom of the wing and blind sew it to the top of the arm cover. Fig. 203A. Once again pin the cover in place. Fold and tuck the cover under along the back side, pulling it close to the rail at the top. Fig. 203B shows how to cut and tack the fabric at the top. Take care to avoid pulling the arm cover away from the arm board as you stretch and tack the wing cover in place. Finally tack the front edge of the wing cover in place.

Outside of Arms: If the wings on the piece being covered are on a plane with the outside of the arms, cover the arms and wings together.

Trim away any surplus fabric on the outside edges of arms and wings so that this will not show as lumps under the outside arm and wing covers.

If a light-weight cover fabric is being used, or if the chair will receive any rough treatment, fill shallow arm cavities with cotton so that there will not be a hollow space behind the cover. If the arm cavities are deep, cover their sides with heavy-weight burlap or chip board. If chip board is used, place a thin layer of cotton over it to give a softer outline.

When welts or brush edging are to be used, tack these in place along the outside edges of the arms at this point.

Center the arm cover over the outside of the arm, fold the cover under about ⅝ of an inch along the top and pin it in place. Make sure that the fabric pattern runs vertical to the floor. If it runs vertical to the bottom of the seat rail or arm board, the piece will look as if it is tipping backward. When the cover is carefully pinned along the top edge, turn the fabric back over the inside of the arm and the folded-under seam and blind-tack the seam under a cardboard strip. Fig. 204A. Make sure that the cardboard strip is flush with the top edge of the wood of the arm board.

Bring the cover down over the side and slip-tack it at the center to the bottom side of the seat rail. Working from the center to the sides, slip-tack the cover in place.

Cut the cover in back of the front legs and in front of the back legs, fold under the surplus and tack the cover in place over the legs close to the bottom edge. Use gimp tacks here. Next slip-tack the cover to the back side of the back posts.

If the face of the arm stump is to be covered, fold the outside arm cover under and pin it in place so that the edge of the fabric is even with the front edge of the arm-stump wood. When the cover is in satisfactory order, sew it to the front cover fabric as in Fig. 204C.

When the arm-stump face will be covered with a panel, tack the outside arm cover to the face side of the arm stump. Fig. 204B.

If the piece being covered has show wood on the sides of the arm stumps, fold the outside arm cover under and tack it in place with gimp tacks. Fig. 204D. These gimp tacks should then be covered with gimp or decorative nails spaced head on head. Finally drive the slip tacks in place.

On chairs where the arms and back flow in a continuous curve, fold the outside covers under alongside the back edge in line with the back of the arm (usually over or along the side of the back post). Do not tack this back edge of the outside arm cover to the post. These edges will be sewn to the edge of the outside back cover when it is placed.

Outside of Wings: First tack in place any welts or brush edging to be used along the outside edges of the wings. Next center the cover and skewer it in place over the outside of the wings. When it has been correctly placed and pinned, trim the cover along the top and front edges, leaving ⅝ of an inch of the fabric project over the edges. Turn this edge under and sew it to the inside wing cover along

149

the top and front edges. If gimp or decorative nails will be used on these edges, turn the edge under and tack it in place with gimp tacks instead of hand-sewing it. This procedure is also acceptable when there is show wood along the edges.

Tack the outside wing cover to the back of the back post.

Turn the cover under along the bottom edge and sew it to the outside arm cover. Here again gimp tacks may be used instead of hand-sewing.

Whenever wings are a continuation of the back they are covered with the back-piece material.

COVERING OUTSIDE OF BACKS

If welts or brush edging are to be used along the back edges, tack them in place. Trim away any surplus inside cover fabric.

It is good practice to tack burlap or chip board over the open cavity of the back. If chip board is used, place a thin layer of cotton over it before applying the outside back cover.

If you are covering a love seat or sofa, the outside back cover will have to be pieced together. Make the necessary seams at the seat divisions. Use French seams.

Center the back cover and, turning under a ⅝-inch seam, skewer the cover in place along the top edge. If the top rail is straight, turn the cover over the inside of the back and blind-tack it in place under a strip of cardboard. Fig. 205A. Next pull the cover down over the back.

If the top edge of the back rail is not a straight edge, turn under a ⅝-inch seam and hand-sew or gimp-tack it in place.

The sides of the back then are folded under and hand-sewed to the inside back cover and outside arm cover as shown in Fig. 205B.

Tack the lower edge of the cover along the bottom side of the back seat rail. On open backs the covers are folded under and either hand-sewn or gimp-tacked under the back liner. Cut the fabric to permit tucking it under the cover over the legs. Gimp tacks should be used to tack the cover in place over the tops of the legs.

DUST PANEL

Turn the upholstered piece upside down, trim away any surplus cover fabric and tack a dust panel to the bottom to prevent loose stuffing and dust from falling out.

Dust panels are usually made of cambric. Cut a piece 1 inch longer and wider than the bottom of the upholstered piece. Center the cambric over the bottom and slip-tack it at the center of the four sides. Turn under ¾ of an inch all around the piece and, spacing the tacks about 1 inch apart, tack the cambric down about ¼ inch in from the outside edges of the seat rails. Here again, work from the four centers to the corners. Cut the cloth at each leg and tack it to the inside face of each leg.

If a fringe or skirt is used around the bottom, place it at this time.

The piece is now completely upholstered. Before bringing it into the room for use, go over the entire piece with a brush and vacuum cleaner.

CARDBOARD TACKING STRIP

COTTON

CHIP BOARD

(A)

(B)

(C)

(D)

204 COVERING OUTSIDE OF ARM

CARDBOARD TACKING STRIP

½"

(A)

(B)

205 COVERING OUTSIDE BACK

UPHOLSTERED PIECES that are to be channeled or tufted should be covered with plain or almost patternless fabric. The pattern in a fabric is distorted when pulled into channels or tufting and thus only detracts from the beauty of the technique. Fig. 206.

Channels and tufting are made directly over the unpadded burlap. Understuff the top of the back and arms on round or scroll-back pieces before making the channels or tufting. Edge rolls are not required on the edges of posts or arm stumps unless a panel will be used.

Muslin may be used to cover the channels and tufting before applying the final cover; however, it is a more common practice to place the final cover directly over the padding. This saves an extra covering operation, but means that great care must be taken in the work because a regulator cannot be used through the final cover to adjust the stuffing. It is not necessary to sew the stuffing down, for the channels and tufting themselves will hold it in place.

Channels are also called pipes or flutes. They usually run up and down except on fan or shell-back chairs where they must lay over to the sides. Up-and-down channels make a more comfortable back than channels run horizontally.

On straight backs and arms the channels are the same width from top to bottom. They are made wider at the top than the bottom on curved backs and arms, or at inside corners.

Narrow channels look full and deep but tend to make a piece appear high and slim. Wide channels look flat and tend to make a piece appear low and wide. Narrow channels are best used on chairs, and wide channels are most successfully used on love seats, sofas and chaise longues.

Channels are usually made from 3 to 6 inches wide at the bottom. Those that finish on the outside of an upholstered piece should be made a little narrower than the rest of the channels to avoid having them look unusually wide at the exposed end. Channels that finish in corners are made the same width at the bottom as the other channels on the piece.

When the size and number of channels required have been determined, chalk mark the outline of the planned channels on the bottom of the liners, along the top rail and down the burlap. Fig. 207. Center the crease of the channels over the springs on barrel-back chairs so that the cover can be stitched to the burlap.

The shape and fullness of the channels must be decided upon next. They should be at least 2 inches deep at the center of the channel, but may need to be thicker or thinner at the top or bottom of the back. Any such variation depends upon the desired profile of the back. Fig. 208. Irregularity of the surface over which the channels are placed may also cause variations in the thickness of the channels.

When you have determined the required depth of the channels at various points, bend steel tapes to the planned shape of the channels at these points and note the dimensions as shown in Fig. 209. Draw a full-size

206

EXAMPLES OF CHANNELS AND TUFTING

plan of the channels, allowing 2 inches for handling on the top, ⅝ of an inch for seams on each side and 1 inch for the stretcher seam on the bottom. Make a paper pattern for each channel that varies from the others. Allowances for pulling the cover around the chair-frame members should be made at the corners and ends.

Lay the paper pattern over the cover material and cut it to size. Cut as many covers from each pattern as needed. Center the pattern over the cover so that the pattern or weave of the fabric runs vertically to the center of the channel.

Sew the channel covers together. When channels of different sizes and shapes are marked off on the work, take care to sew the channels together in the proper order so that they correspond to the chalk markings.

A stretcher, which will be hidden under the seat liner, should next be cut to the width and length required. The stretcher should be wide enough to permit tacking it to the top side of the seat rails.

The seam of the channel nearest the center of the back should be lock-stitched along the seam of the corresponding line on the work. This channel is then ready for stuffing. Fig. 210A.

Prepare a quantity of hair or moss for use as stuffing, making sure that it is free of lumps and foreign matter. Tear a piece of cotton to the width and length of the channel and lay it under the cover. Start placing the loose stuffing under the cotton at the bottom and pin the seam of the channel with skewers along the line next to the seam already sewn in place. Pin the seam in place as the stuffing progresses to the top of the channel. Fig. 210B. Be sure that the channel center is stuffed full and firm. Use the dull point of the regulator under the cotton to adjust the stuffing. A stuffing iron can be used to aid in placing the stuffing evenly.

When the channel is smoothly filled to its top, sew the seam marked on the piece.

Repeat this procedure on all the

channels. The seams of the channels are always sewn down so that they face toward the outside of the work. The inside corners and ends of the channel covers are handled as if they were ordinary flat covers.

Slip-tack the stretcher in place along the top of the seat rails. Take care to avoid pulling the channel cover out of line as you tack the stretcher.

Now fill the tops of the channels, starting with the channel first stuffed. Pull the cover over the top and tack it down directly behind the top center of each channel. Here again be sure that the channel is not pulled out of line. Tack down the rest of the channels as shown in Fig. 211, making a pleat on each side of the channel. Make these pleats face the outside edge of the piece, away from the center on the back, and toward the back on the arms. Trim away any surplus fabric.

If there is show wood above the channels, turn the covers under and tack them down with gimp tacks. Trim the cover to allow only ⅝ of an inch for the turn under. Cover the gimp tacks with gimp or decorative nails set head on head.

Muslin-Covered Channels are made in the same way as described above except that the muslin cover should be cut long enough at the bottom of the channels to permit tacking it to the back side of the liner at the bottom. *Do not place cotton under muslin channel covers.*

Cut and sew the final cover as described previously. Cut lengths of back twine 10 or 12 inches longer than the channels. Sew this twine in between the seams with a second row of stitches. While these stitches must in-

case the twine, they should not bind it so closely in the seam. This would cause the cover to wrinkle.

Mark the back side of the liner in line with each of the channel crevices. At these marks place slip tacks to which the back twines may be tied.

Starting at the center channel, place cotton over the muslin. Over that place the corresponding channel cover. Tie the twines to the slip tacks on the back of the liner and work the cover seams into the crevices on each side of the channel. At the top, slip-tack the twine in place temporarily. Cut the seams open at the bottom so that the twine will lie against the bottom side of the liner. Untie the twine, tighten and readjust it and tack it permanently in place. Tack the liner to the top side of the seat rail. Repeat this procedure with each channel, laying the channel-top pleats so that they face away from the center channel.

Tufting: The average person is often confused by references to *buttoning* and *tufting*. Buttoned pieces are those on which buttons have been placed and pulled down flush with the top of the cover. In tufting, the buttons not only assist in forming the tufts but also help to hold the cover in place.

Tufting buttons are small, are covered with the final cover fabric and should have tufted backs.

Tufting may be used on seats, arms and backs of upholstered pieces.

The positions of the buttons will be determined by the size of the area to be tufted, the design layout and the number of tufts to be made. The design layout is a matter of personal taste. Fig. 212 illustrates several tufting designs. Channeling is often com-

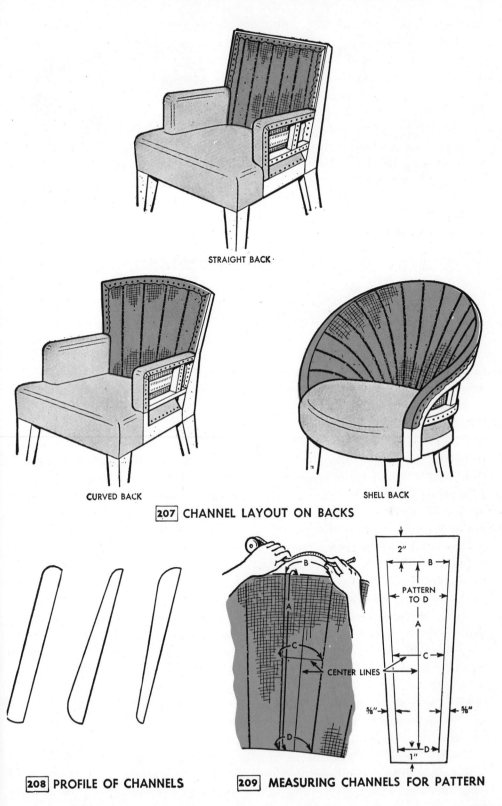

STRAIGHT BACK

CURVED BACK

SHELL BACK

207 CHANNEL LAYOUT ON BACKS

208 PROFILE OF CHANNELS

209 MEASURING CHANNELS FOR PATTERN

2"

B

PATTERN
TO D

A

C

CENTER LINES

⅝"

⅝"

D

1"

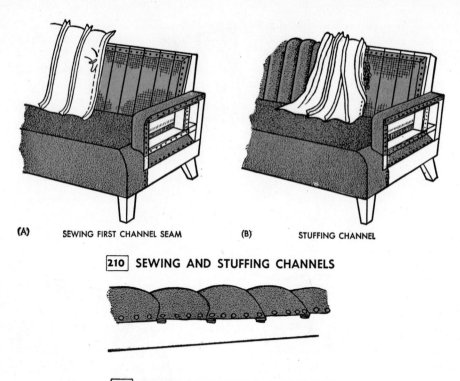

(A)   SEWING FIRST CHANNEL SEAM   (B)   STUFFING CHANNEL

210 SEWING AND STUFFING CHANNELS

211 PLEATING CHANNELS AT THE TOP

bined with tufting. The light lines in the illustration indicate the layout, while the dark lines show the tufting and buttons. The bottom or front row of buttons is usually parallel to the bottom or front of the piece with the top or back row of buttons parallel to the top or back of the piece. The other buttons should be equally spaced between these rows. If channels are to be used at the top or bottom, bring the top and bottom rows of buttons in closer to the center.

Lay out the button positions on the burlap and on the back side of the cover, allowing extra fullness for each tuft on the cover. Chalk mark the button positions and draw lines indicating how the tufts connect them.

To determine the amount of fullness that should be allowed for the tufts, make a few typical tufts and channels in muslin to the desired size and shape. Measure across the buttons over the tufts and channels and transfer the height and width measurements to the back of the cover.

Sew the first row of buttons in place on the face side of the cover through the burlap and webbing and tie the twine down to the webbing with a wad of cotton between the button twines. Lay in pleats as each button is sewn down. Tufting pleats should be placed so that they face down on the back and arms, to the front on the seat and to the outside of the work over the arms and back. The pleats are placed in this way so that the upholstery can be cleaned without brushing the dirt into the pleats.

Prepare a quantity of hair or moss for use as stuffing. Tear a piece of cotton to the size and shape of each

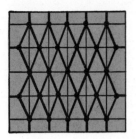
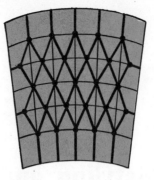
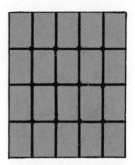

212 TUFTING LAYOUTS

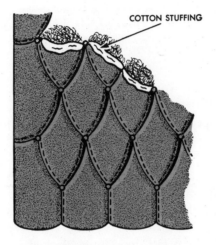

COTTON STUFFING

213 STUFFING TUFTS

tuft or channel, allowing for fullness, and place these cotton pieces under the cover. Starting at the center tuft or channel, place loose stuffing under the cotton until the cover is very firmly filled. Use the blunt end of a regulator to press the stuffing into the corners and sides. Fig. 213. Do this to each tuft or channel in the first row. Take care to stuff each tuft or channel to the same fullness as its neighbor.

Fasten the second row of buttons in place, laying the pleats in the proper direction. Fill this second row and all subsequent rows as you did the first.

Fill the edges of all the channels and tufts and fasten down the cover as you would on flat-surface work.

PART FIVE

Repairing, Restyling and Slipcovering

Lesson One — REPAIRING FURNITURE

REPAIRS MADE in slightly worn upholstery will often be all that is needed to improve the appearance and lengthen the life of an upholstered piece.

Loose, sagging or worn covers, sagging cushions, broken webbing, bent spring bars, loose springs, loose arms, loose wings, some frame weaknesses and marred show wood may all be repaired without stripping and reupholstering the entire piece. The same cover may be replaced unless the entire piece is to be re-covered.

Stripping, reconditioning and repairing the frame as well as re-covering and reupholstering the piece will be discussed in the next lesson.

Removing Covers: Unless you need only repair an open back, arm or wing, the dust panel must be removed from the bottom of the piece. Discard this panel and replace it with a new piece of cambric when the repairs are done.

Take great care as you remove the tacks over the covers so that no cuts or tears are made in them. It is best to use a ripping tool assisted by blows with a light mallet. Make sure that the flat side of the ripping tool lies flat to the covers. Cut any stitching loose with a razor blade.

Loose Covers: Broken webbing, bent spring bars and loose springs are the chief causes of loose or sagging covers. Their repair will be considered later. Packed-down stuffing and badly stretched cover fabric are other conditions often found in pieces with loose covers. Here is the remedy for these failures.

First remove the dust panel, outside back and outside arm covers from the piece. If chip board or burlap was used in the outside back or arm covering, remove this. Loosen the inside back and arm covers over the seat rails and the seat cover at the front. The seat cover should also be loosened at the top of the side and back seat rails if it needs tightening.

Start at the center on each side of the seat and, pulling the cover taut, slip-tack the seat cover. Work from the four centers to the corners, keeping the cover straight and free of wrinkles. The cover will be short. Use webbing pliers or ordinary household pliers to hold it taut. When the cover is neatly placed, drive the tacks in permanently. If the cover is weak or raveling along the edges, reinforce it by placing a 1-inch-wide strip of adhesive tape on each side of the cover edge. Always use tacks a size larger than those originally used for tacking the cover in place and try to avoid placing the tacks in the old tack holes. This is especially true if the tacks have pulled out of the frame through use.

Avoid disturbing the stuffing while the covers are loose. If the arm or back covers are sagging, loosen them around the top and side. Stretch the fabric and retack it. Replace the outside back covering and dust panel.

Sagging Cushions: Open the cushion by cutting the stitches along the back. Remove the stuffing and marshall unit. Discard the marshall unit.

Refill the cushion cover as described in Part 3, Lesson 7. The old cotton can be reused but an additional layer of new cotton should be added at the top and bottom of the cushion.

Worn Covers: Well-built upholstery will usually outlast two or three covers. The piece can be re-covered or slip-covered when the original cover wears out. Follow the instructions in the next chapter and those in Part 4, Lesson 2, if you plan to re-cover the piece. See Part 6 if you plan to use slip covers.

Loose Webbing: Since the webbing is under constant strain when the upholstered piece is in use, it is usually the first part to wear out.

Remove the dust panel from the bottom of the seat. Remove the outside covers when the back or arm webbing is broken.

If the webbing is in good condition it may be retacked and reinforced with steel band webbing. Before retacking the webbing, check to see that the springs are properly tied at the top of the coil. (See *Loose Springs* in this lesson.)

Cut a band of steel webbing to go over each jute band, and cut these bands 3 inches longer than the distance across the frame. Center the front-to-back bands of steel webbing over the jute bands and tack them to the front rail.

Cut two pieces of 1-by-2-inch wood as long as the front-to-back measurement of the frame. Drill holes at both ends of these pieces so that they may be screwed temporarily in place between the front and back rails. These pieces are used to compress the springs. Use 1¼-inch-long wood screws to hold the wood in place over the jute webbing. Stretch the steel band webbing taut on the back side of the frame and nail it in place. Fig. 214A. To stretch this webbing, insert the loose end through the slot in the webbing stretcher—which should be held 1½ inches away from the outside of the frame—making sure that the webbing is lined up over the center of the springs; draw the handle of the stretcher back and down and keep the steel band against the edge of the rail. This will draw the round head of the tool up against the side of the frame and tighten the webbing. Fig. 214B. Nail the band in place and remove the wood pieces. Repeat this operation on all the front-to-back steel webbing bands. Finally trim off the ends of surplus webbing.

Interlace the cross bands of steel webbing through the front-to-back bands, centering each band over the jute webbing and nailing the cross bands down on one side. Stretch these and nail them at the other side. Fig. 214C. The springs need not be compressed when cross-band webbing is installed. Finally trim off the surplus banding, adjust the springs and stitch them in place.

Broken Webbing: When the webbing is badly worn or broken and the springs are loose it is best to replace the entire webbing foundation.

If you are working on a badly worn commercially upholstered piece with springs mounted on heavy-weight burlap or canvas reinforced with spring wire, remove this foundation, make any necessary spring repairs and apply jute webbing.

If the piece was upholstered over jute webbing, be sure to mark the original placement of the webbing before removing it. The new webbing must be installed in the same places. After removing the webbing, fill any large nail holes with plastic wood and glue down or remove splinters. Glue and clamp all wood splits and breaks that might weaken the rails. The rail edges may be strengthened by coating them with glue, which should be allowed to dry thoroughly before any further work is done on the frame.

Before rewebbing the frame be sure to inspect the springs. If any of the twines at the coil tops have come loose or broken, retie these before starting to place the webbing.

Push the springs aside when stretching the new webbing in place and proceed to web the piece as described in Part 3, Lesson 1. After each webbing band has been stretched and nailed in place, push the springs back into position before placing the next strip of webbing.

Inspect the work to see if any of the springs have been forced up. If they are not level, tie them down to the proper height with a twine tied to each side of the coil at the top of the spring. Fasten the twines down at the bottom of the spring. Finally retack the covers on the rails and place the dust panel.

If you need to repair the webbing on pad-type upholstering, one of two processes may be used. You will have to either remove all the upholstering and reupholster the piece from the webbing up, or you may cut a ¼-inch panel of plywood or hardboard and fit it into the cavity of the frame. If the frame has corner blocks the panel will have to be cut off to fit around these blocks. This will not affect the support given to the padding by the panel. Cut strips of wood to be screwed to the rails to hold the panel against the padding. Fig. 215. The seat will not be quite as resilient as one built on a webbing foundation, but it will be comfortable and serviceable.

Bent Spring Bars may be straightened as follows: first remove the dust panel; clamp a 1¾-inch-thick piece of hardwood to one side of the bent spring bar; fasten another clamp to the hardwood and spring bar on the other side of the bend, placing a small block of wood directly under the bend; tighten the clamps on each side of the bend and the bar will straighten. Fig. 216A.

Cut a length of ¾-by-1¾-inch hardwood to fit between the rails. To each end of these pieces glue and screw a 4-inch length of ¾-by-¾-inch hardwood. Fold a piece of webbing double and tack it along the length of the hardwood cross bar. Fig. 216B. Then glue and screw the assembly to the rail, centering it and bringing it up against the lower side of the spring bar. Fig. 216C. Replace the dust panel.

Loose Springs may be found to have come loose from the webbing, or they may result from breakage of the cross ties at their tops. If the twines are broken in many places, or if they have broken away from the frame or have frayed badly, the cover and padding will have to be removed. These should also be removed if the spring edge wire is loose or broken. In this case, after the covers, padding and loose twine are removed the piece should be reworked as though it were new.

When only a few twines are broken these may usually be repaired by removing only a few strips of webbing in the area where the twines need to be retied. Tie the broken twine ends to the nearest coil and tie the loose coils with new twines. Tie these new twines to the nearest coils, working across the spring row. When all the broken twines have been tied off and replaced, retack the webbing and dust panel. Be sure that the coils have been tied to their original distance apart.

Loose or Broken Arms and Wings can be repaired quite easily. On all frame-repair work the joints and pieces should be reglued and clamped. Remove the old glue and fit dowels in the holes, reinforce the joints with glue blocks or corner blocks and hold the joint together with wood screws.

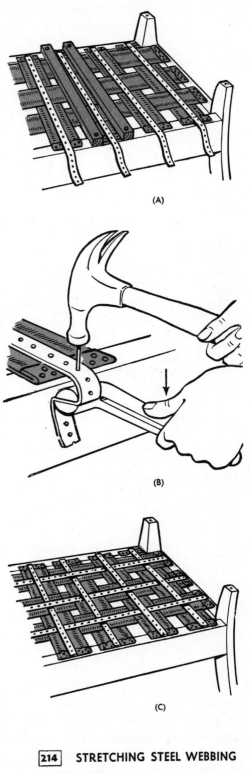

(A)

(B)

(C)

214 STRETCHING STEEL WEBBING

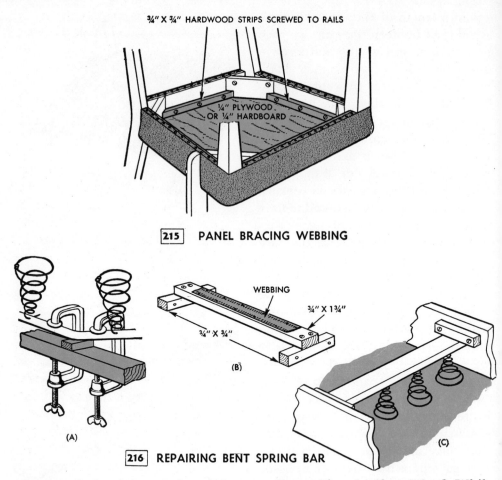

3/4" X 3/4" HARDWOOD STRIPS SCREWED TO RAILS

1/4" PLYWOOD OR 1/4" HARDBOARD

215 PANEL BRACING WEBBING

WEBBING

3/4" X 1 3/4"

3/4" X 3/4"

(B)

(A)

(C)

216 REPAIRING BENT SPRING BAR

Metal angle brackets may be used to strengthen the corners when it is not possible to use blocks.

If you find long splits running the length of the wood grain in a frame member, remove the upholstery around the split before attempting to repair it. These splits should be glued and clamped and, wherever possible, reinforced with another piece of wood glued over or under the split where it will not interfere.

Replace frame members that are broken across the grain or are so badly split that no repair would be durable enough to make it worth while. Be sure to let all glued repairs dry thoroughly before re-covering.

Retouching the Show Wood: While a total refinishing job should not be attempted on show wood while the final cover is still in place, defects of a minor nature can be successfully retouched without damaging the cover.

Scuff marks, minor scratches and cigarette scorches can be covered or rubbed out by two methods. A dab of toothpaste on a small damp cloth may be briskly rubbed over the area, or shoe polish matching the wood color may be burnished into the affected area.

Stick shellac of the wood color should be burned into deep cuts and bruises. This is best done by a professional finisher but may be done at home if you have had some previous experience with stick shellac.

Worn spots can be touched up with white shellac applied with a small soft brush. Be careful not to let the shellac spill or run onto the cover.

Finally polish the show wood with paste wax to bring out the luster.

Lesson Two — REUPHOLSTERING AND RESTYLING

AN AMATEUR UPHOLSTERER can learn more by reupholstering an old piece of furniture than by performing any other upholstery process. Carefully built frames made of choice cabinet woods are the only frames recommended for reupholstering, however, for if the original frame of a piece was not well made it would be impractical to try to renovate the piece. It would be better to buy or build a new frame and place the usable parts of the old upholstery over the new frame.

As you strip off the old upholstery you will be able to observe its construction and application, its good and faulty parts. Reupholstering is the same as upholstering a new piece, but many changes in the frame, padding and cover can be made to enhance and improve the original work.

STRIPPING THE FRAME

When stripping a frame take care to remove the cover carefully. It will guide you in figuring out the amount of new cover-fabric yardage needed. Do not use the old cover as a pattern for cutting out the new cover, for its shape has been distorted through use, and the necessary margins to allow for handling the cover during its application have been trimmed away.

If the cover is not too badly worn, it may be used for stretchers.

As you strip the frame, discard the old muslin, cambric, cotton padding, twine, burlap and webbing. Salvage springs, spring edge wire and any type ready-made edge rolls if these are in good condition. If the piece was stuffed with hair or moss save this stuffing. Other types of loose stuffing should be discarded.

Set the piece bottom up on trestles and begin the stripping process by loosening the covers from the bottom of the seat rails. Remove the outside back, outside arm, inside arm, inside back and seat covers in that order. The cotton padding and muslin covers should then be removed in the same order. Take out the loose stuffing, cutting loose any that was sewn down. Remove the understuffing, spring edge rolls, edge rolls and burlap from the back, seat and arms. Finally take out the spring ties and springs and the webbing.

RESTYLING THE FRAME

Frames may be altered to bring the style up to date or improve the appearance and comfort of the piece. Be sure to carefully plan any intended alterations so that seating height, depth and width will not be changed for the worse.

See Part 2, Lesson 3, for a discussion of the various woods to use in building or altering frames.

Glue and clamp the additional parts to the frame. Whenever possible these parts should be joined to the frame with two dowels. Where dowel unions cannot be made use screws to hold the joints together. Hide, casein or plastic resin glue should be used on all frame repairs and alterations.

If frame parts need to be removed for alterations but will be reused later, cut them away from the frame with a backsaw along the joints. Carved show wood can be eliminated by sawing off the carved surface or planing it down. These surfaces may then be covered.

Without actually changing the frame construction, you can change the appearance of the piece by varying the upholstery. Channels or tufting may be added or removed, borders can be placed and edge rolls and spring edges can be added.

Altering the Seat means building an entirely new frame unless the alteration consists solely of making a pad seat into a spring seat. This change may be effected as follows: glue a strip of wood to the top edges of the seat rails (Fig. 217) to make the seat rail 3 inches high; place No. 0 springs and note the seat chart, Fig. 99, before cutting off the legs of the piece to adjust the seating height.

If the piece was built with closed arms and back, raise the liners so that the bottom of the liners will be even with the top of the springs.

Altering the Back of a piece is relatively simple. Curved or serpentine top rails can be cut straight and then brought back to the proper height by gluing a flat strip of wood to the top. Fig. 218A. Wings or wing blocks can be removed or added to the sides of the back posts. Fig. 218, details B and

C. Pieces that were originally designed with round or knife-top back edges can be made into cushion or box-type backs by cutting the top rail flat and adding a strip of wood over the top rail so that the rail projects in front of the one already there. Fig. 218D. In completing this alteration, add a strip of wood to the front side of the posts and slats so that they will come even with the edge of the top rail. Scroll-top backs can also be made into cushion or box-type backs by removing the original top back rail, cutting down its width and replacing it as illustrated in Fig. 218E. To complete this alteration cut the top and back sides of the back posts flush with the top of the top rail and the back side of the post. Open backs can be closed by placing a liner at the top of the planned seat height. Fig. 219A. It is best to remove the original bottom back rails after the liner is glued in place and the glue is dry. If the top back rail and the back seat rail are curved, be sure to fit in a curved liner that will be compatible with the existing lines of the piece. Fig. 219B.

Altering the Arms of a piece can give it an entirely new look. Open arms may be closed very easily by removing them and building a new arm frame on the seat sides. Fig. 220, details A and B. If the seat rail is curved or rounded at the sides the arms must curve with the seat. Fig. 220C. The arm boards and liners will have to sweep in a wider curve at the back so they will meet the back posts and flow in line with the curve of the back. Fig. 220D. There should be a minimum space of 20 inches between the arms of a closed arm chair, and on larger chairs it is well to plan a 22 or

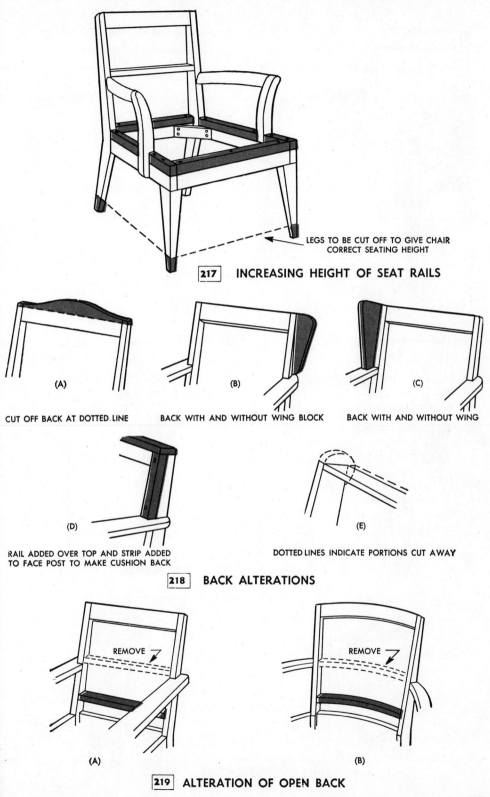

LEGS TO BE CUT OFF TO GIVE CHAIR
CORRECT SEATING HEIGHT

217 **INCREASING HEIGHT OF SEAT RAILS**

(A)

CUT OFF BACK AT DOTTED LINE

(B)

BACK WITH AND WITHOUT WING BLOCK

(C)

BACK WITH AND WITHOUT WING

(D)

RAIL ADDED OVER TOP AND STRIP ADDED
TO FACE POST TO MAKE CUSHION BACK

(E)

DOTTED LINES INDICATE PORTIONS CUT AWAY

218 **BACK ALTERATIONS**

REMOVE

REMOVE

(A)

(B)

219 **ALTERATION OF OPEN BACK**

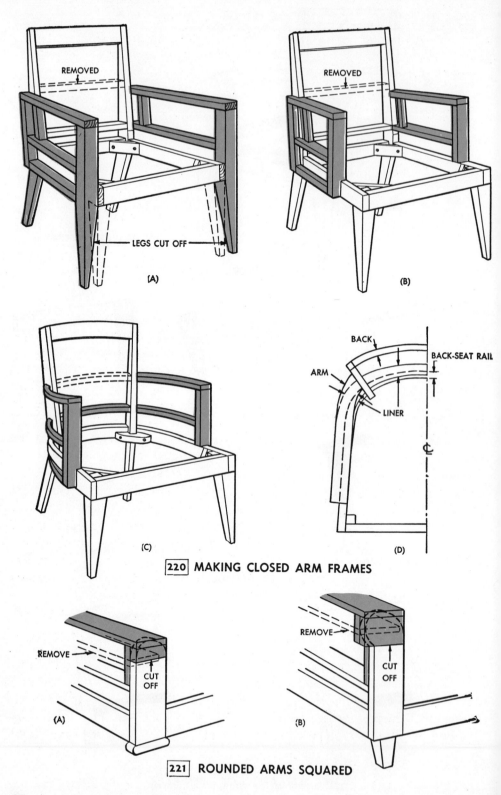

REMOVED

LEGS CUT OFF

(A)

REMOVED

(B)

(C)

BACK

BACK-SEAT RAIL

ARM

LINER

℄

(D)

220 MAKING CLOSED ARM FRAMES

REMOVE

CUT
OFF

(A)

REMOVE

CUT
OFF

(B)

221 ROUNDED ARMS SQUARED

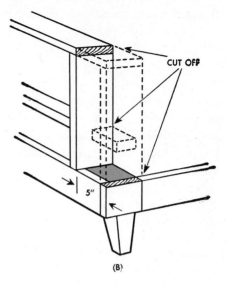

CUT OFF

DOWEL

(A)

CUT OFF

5"

(B)

222 RECEDED ARMS

24-inch space. The wider space will permit placing a 1-inch layer of cotton padding on the insides of the arms. Place the arm liners and slats so that they close the opening between the arms, seat and backs when the seat is upholstered to the correct height. Refer to the seating chart, Fig. 99, for correct seating proportions.

The height of the arms must always remain in constant proportion to the height of the finished seat. The top of the arm board should be about 5 inches over the planned height of the cushion on seats with built-in secondary springs or a loose cushion. On pull-up, occasional, boudoir and wing chairs the top of the arm board should be 8 or 10 inches over the planned height of the seat upholstery.

It is often possible to make wide arms narrower without impairing the strength of the arm. Move the seat rails in when making arms narrower.

Round or round-lawson-type pieces can be built square as shown in Fig. 221.

Fig. 222A shows how a receded arm can be brought forward and Fig. 222B shows how it may be moved back.

If the seat is to have springs or a loose cushion, the front of the arm stump should be placed 5 inches in back of the front seat rail. Place a board between the seat rails and the arm stump so that the corner spring can be mounted on it.

Note: After the frame has been stripped, inspect it carefully to see whether any repairs are necessary. If you find open or loose joints or broken or split frame members, follow the instructions given in the preceding chapter on "Repairing."

Refinishing Show Wood may entail a great deal of work or merely the application of a fresh top coat of varnish. If the finish is not badly scratched or dented, varnish will give it a pleasing fresh look. If, however, you wish to make the show wood a different color, or need to make major repairs in the wood, the old finish should be removed.

Liquid, semipaste or paste-type paint or varnish remover should be used to take off the old finish. Follow the directions given on the container for using the remover. Once the finish has been removed, neutralize the surface by wiping it with a soft cloth soaked with benzine or white gasoline. Always work in a well-ventilated area away from any flame or heat and dispose of the cloths and residue immediately, for these solutions are highly inflammable.

If you wish to lighten the color of the show wood you will need to bleach it with one of the various chemical solutions available. The two-solution bleach consisting of concentrated hydrogen peroxide and an alkaline liquid is generally considered most effective. One application of this bleach will produce almost white tones on walnut and mahogany as well as the lighter woods. Most finishers find it good practice to premix the solutions immediately before applying them, rather than applying one after the other. The mixed solution is corrosive and should be kept in a glass or porcelain container. Wear rubber gloves and a rubber apron while using this bleach. About an hour after it has been applied, the bleach will have completed its action and may be reapplied if necessary. The No. 2 solution alone is an effective second coat. After the surface is dry, sponge it off with water to remove any residue which might affect the finish. Let the wood dry for at least 24 hours before proceeding with the finish.

Bleaching will raise the grain of the wood and so make it necessary to sand the surface lightly. This grain raising may be partially eliminated by following the practice used in applying water stains. This entails applying water or a coat of thin glue sizing on the wood, sanding it smooth, letting it dry thoroughly and finally applying the bleach. It is well to avoid doing anything to the wood that will make additional sanding necessary, for too much sanding may expose unbleached wood. Another good practice is to make a test strip on the wood to see how it will react to the bleaching before applying the bleach to the entire surface.

Most dents and bruises can be restored by placing a damp cloth over the bruised area and applying a hot iron over the cloth covering the bruise. Take care to avoid scorching the wood. If the dents are deep you may have to repeat this restoring process several times.

Once the bleaching and restoring processes have been completed, use 4/0 sandpaper to polish the show wood to satiny smoothness and finish it as directed in Part 2, Lesson 3.

Place the upholstery, final cover and trim as you would on a new piece.

Lesson Three — SLIPCOVERING

USED TO PROTECT newly upholstered furniture or conceal badly worn coverings, slip covers are perhaps most often used to brighten up the furnishings in a home whose budget cannot include the purchase of new furniture. The economy thereby effected is, of course, even greater when the slip covers are tailored at home.

If you are planning to reupholster a piece of furniture, consider the possibility of upholstering the piece in muslin to be covered by slip covers. Enough fabric for two slip covers can be purchased for the cost of one cover-fabric piece. With two sets of slip covers you can change the color scheme and mood of a room to suit the seasons. Through fall and winter solid colors or fabrics patterned with geometric designs are appropriate. In spring and summer floral prints are attractive.

SELECTING MATERIAL

A wide range of fabrics, patterns and colors are available for use as slip covers. As with upholstery cover fabrics, the choice of color or pattern is a matter of personal taste. Here again, however, subdued patterns and colors are usually more pleasing over a period of time than bright or showy patterns and colors. No matter what you select, be sure that the slip cover will blend well with the other colors and decorations in the room.

Some slip-cover fabrics must be dry cleaned, while others may be laundered. If you choose a washable fabric, be sure to preshrink the material and check it for washfast coloring. To do this, soak the cloth in cold water for several hours and then *squeeze* the water out. Never wring these fabrics. Dry and steam-press the cloth before starting to cut it. Most washable slip-cover fabrics will shrink from 1 to 3 inches per yard.

Slip-cover fabrics that are best for home laundering are pebble texture, pebble cloth, twill, sail cloth and glazed and unglazed chintz, all of which are made of cotton.

Damask, tapestry, rep, boucle, nubby textures and other fabrics made of cotton in combination with yarns of other types should be dry cleaned.

PLANNING AND CUTTING

Before the fabric is purchased, an estimate must be made of the yardage required. Take the measurements across the widest and deepest part of each unit needed and make an allowance for seams and tuck-ins or slips. Fig. 223. Allow 1 inch on each of the pieces for seams and 4 inches extra for tuck-ins.

When all the measurements have been taken, lay out a scale plan as shown in Fig. 224. This plan applies to either 36 or 48-inch-wide fabrics.

Divide by 36 the total number of inches in length. The resulting figure is the number of yards of cloth you will need to buy. If the fabric has a large repeat design it is best to plan to cut only one slip-cover piece from each width of fabric. If you are covering a chair, allow 1 yard extra so that you will be able to center large patterns or figures correctly on the piece. Allow 2 yards extra for a double seat and 3 yards extra for a sofa.

To determine the yardage needed for welts or brush edging, measure along the welt lines as illustrated in Fig. 223. If the welts are to be made of the same material they should be cut 2 inches wide. One square yard of fabric will make 18 yards of welts. Cut the welts long enough to avoid having to piece them together to go around each part they will enclose.

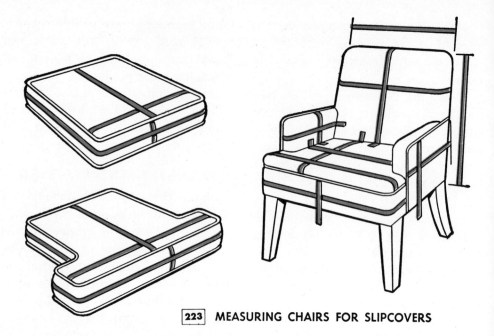

223 MEASURING CHAIRS FOR SLIPCOVERS

See Part 4, Lesson 1, for instructions on how to figure the width, length and seams for various skirt styles, and how to cut them.

Chalk mark the pieces on the slip-cover fabric and cut the material. Be sure to check each piece to see that the pattern is correctly centered and running in the right direction.

TRIM

Welts, brush edging and boucle edgings are used to conceal the exposed slip-cover seams.

Welts may be purchased ready-made or made as shown in Fig. 170. See Part 4, Lesson 1, for welt-sewing instructions. Cotton brush edging can be used instead of welts on slip covers that are to be laundered. Boucle edging may be used on slip covers that will be dry cleaned. This edging is more attractive and durable than brush edging but must be dry cleaned. Boucle edging shrinks and often fades when washed.

SEWING COVERS

On straight edges the welts or edgings are sewn in place while the two cover pieces are being joined. Fig. 225A. If the seams are curved or require hand-sewn corners, stitch the welts or brush edgings to either of the cover pieces before joining them. Fig. 225B. Baste or pin the pieces together around curves or where corners will be hand-sewn. This will assure neat seams and well-fitting covers.

Use French seams to sew together the tuck-ins. Fig. 225C.

FITTING COVERS

It would be extremely difficult to describe the cutting and fitting of slip covers to suit the wide variety of furnishings annually slip-covered, but a study of this section should reveal solutions to most problems.

With slip covers, as with the final upholstered covers on sofas and other large pieces, the fabric will need to be pieced together. Make these needed

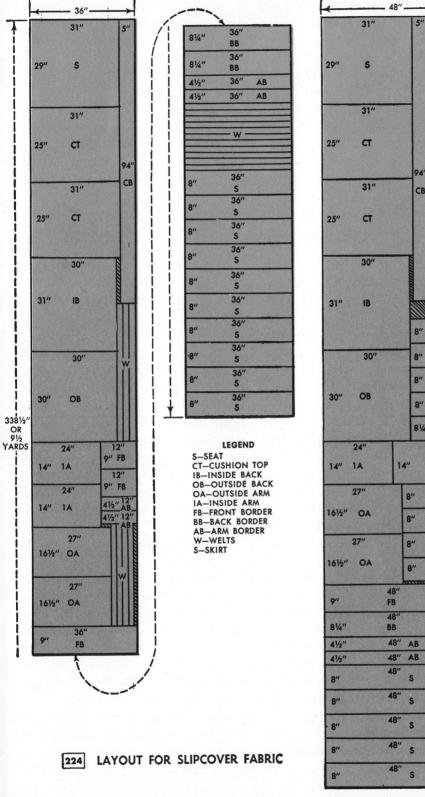

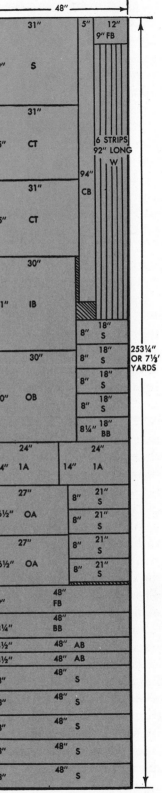

LEGEND

S—SEAT
CT—CUSHION TOP
IB—INSIDE BACK
OB—OUTSIDE BACK
OA—OUTSIDE ARM
IA—INSIDE ARM
FB—FRONT BORDER
BB—BACK BORDER
AB—ARM BORDER
W—WELTS
S—SKIRT

224 LAYOUT FOR SLIPCOVER FABRIC

joinings in line with the cushion and back divisions of the upholstered pieces. If the slip-cover fabric is patterned, center the pattern in each section and keep these in line with each other. Use a welt or an edging between the sections on the front seat borders and the inside back. Ordinary seams should be used in sewing the outside back and seat sections together. Do this sewing before fitting these parts of the cover to the adjoining parts. If a solid color or patternless fabric is used, however, the cover need not be pieced at all. It may be run straight across the width of the piece.

The same method of fitting and sewing is used for all slip-cover work. Pin the slip-cover fabric directly to the piece being covered, carefully centering the pattern over the large areas. Tailor the slip cover to fit snugly over the upholstered piece. Lay the first piece of the cover in place. Starting at the center of the edges and working toward the corners, place pins close to the edges of the fabric. The slip-cover seams should follow the lines and seams of the upholstered piece, and the pins should be placed parallel to the edges where the seams will be sewn.

Where necessary, make pleats to fit the contour of the upholstered piece. These pleats should be small, uniform in size, evenly spaced and laid down from the top to face the back at the sides. Pin or baste the pleats in place so that they will not be upset when the slip cover is removed for stitching.

Miter the fabric at the corners and trim away any surplus material. Leave ⅝ of an inch for seams, which should taper out to almost nothing at the inside of the miter.

Where needed, to relieve the tension between adjoining covers, cut notches in the fabric around curved and rounded areas. If these notches are not cut as needed the covers will tend to wrinkle and pull along the seams.

When pinning a piece of the fabric to one already in place, turn the raw edge of the fabric under and pin it close to the edges where the seams are to be made.

Fitting the Seat: (NOTE: Do not confuse the *seat* of the chair with its *loose cushion,* which will be mentioned later.) The seat, together with the front border below it, is the first part to be fitted and sewn. The seat cover should have a tuck-in at the back and along the sides at the arms. Fig. 226 shows cutting and fitting seats. When the seat and front border are pinned in proper order, chalk mark a line on the fabric along the planned seam. Remove the pieces from the chair and pin them together along the seam marking with a welt or edging between them. Sew the pieces together. Trim the seam to make it uniform. Replace the cover on the chair and pin it down.

Fitting the Arms: Pin the cover fabric in place over the inside of the arm, or, as the case may be, over the top and inside of the arm. Cover both arms at the same time, checking to see that the pattern of the slip-cover fabric is the same on the inside and face of both arms. The panels on the arm faces should be identical in size and shape.

Center and pin in place the outside arm slip-cover fabric. If the fabric is patterned, take care to place the pattern perpendicular to the floor.

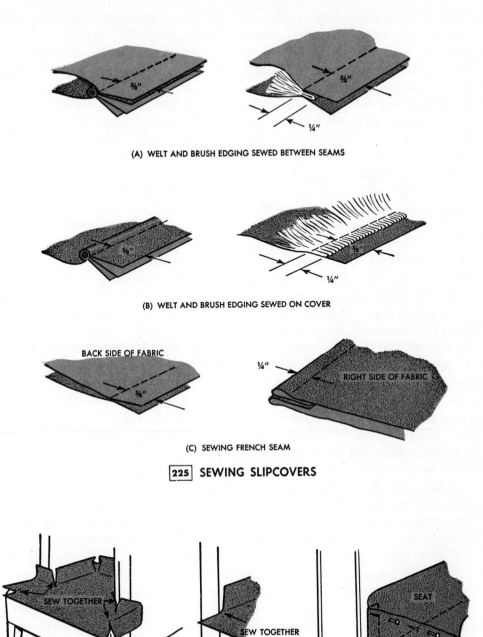

(A) WELT AND BRUSH EDGING SEWED BETWEEN SEAMS

(B) WELT AND BRUSH EDGING SEWED ON COVER

(C) SEWING FRENCH SEAM

225 SEWING SLIPCOVERS

226 CUTTING AND FITTING SEAT SLIPCOVER

When the outside arm covers are correctly placed and pinned, chalk mark the seam lines on the adjoining cover piece. Remove the cover pieces and sew them together with a welt or edging between the pieces. Place the cover on the chair again and pin it in place.

Make a tuck-in allowance at the seat. Mark the seam on the adjoining piece and sew the pieces together as shown in Fig. 227A. Use French seams.

The seams between the seat and arms are next marked and sewed together, allowing for a tuck-in between the arms and seat at the front. Fig. 227B. Trim the seams.

Fitting Wings: If the chair has wings they should be fitted next. First pin the cover fabric to the inside of the wings. If the fabric has a pattern, see that it is the same on the inside of each wing. If the wings are to have borders along their edges, pin the borders in place and chalk mark the seam on the adjoining edges. Remove the cover and sew the marked seams.

Replace the inside wing covers, pin them in place and pin on the outside wing covers. Chalk mark the seams, remove the cover and sew the seams with a welt or edging in them.

Once again return the cover to the chair, pin it in place, chalk mark the seams between the wing and arm covers, remove the covers and sew the seams. Trim seam edges.

Place the slip cover on the chair, adjust and pin it down and place the back cover.

Fitting the Back: Place the inside back cover. When the back is the box type or requires side panels, fit these panels in place. Mark the seams on the adjoining fabric, remove the cover and sew the seams with a welt or edging in them.

Trim the seams to uniformity, replace the cover on the back and chalk mark the seams between the arms and back. If you are covering a wing chair, mark the wing seams at this time. Be sure to allow sufficient material between the arms and back for tuck-ins. Remove the cover and sew all these seams with French seams.

Now put the cover on the chair again and pin the outside back cover in place. Mark the seams. An opening, usually on the right rear corner of the chair, must be left so that the finished slip cover may be removed from the chair. This opening should extend from the bottom of the slip cover up to about 3 to 7 inches above the top of the arm along the edge of the back post.

Remove the cover and sew the outside back cover in place with a welt or edging inside the seam. Continue the welt or edging around the whole outside back, sewing it along the outside of the arm covers and the underside of the outside back cover or, as the case may be, the underside of the back boxing, at the corner opening. Make a facing along the opening. Replace the slip cover and pin closed the open back.

Fitting the Skirt: Pin and steam-press the pleats in the skirt. Sew a welt along its top edge.

When the skirt and slip cover are completed except for the fasteners along the back opening, mark the cover for sewing on the skirt. The skirt bottom should be ½ inch above the floor. With a yardstick or wooden ruler chalk mark the top edge of the skirt around the chair. Fig. 228A.

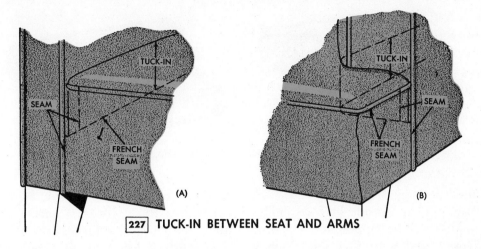

Starting at the back opening, pin the skirt in place. Lay the face of the skirt over the slip cover. This is perhaps most easily done by turning the chair upside down. Following the chalk marks, pin the skirt along the welt seam to the slip cover.

Sew the skirt along the welt cord over the seam of the welt. Fig. 228B. Trim the finished seam to uniformity.

FINISHING THE OPENING

Snap fasteners mounted on a tape, or a Zipper can be used to fasten the back opening. These should be stitched in place with a machine. Hooks and eyes or individual snap fasteners may be applied by hand.

If you do plan to use the hand-applied fasteners, sew them about ¼ inch in from the edge of the opening on the slip cover and skirt. Start 2 inches down from the top of the opening and place the fasteners about 2 inches apart.

If you plan to use a Zipper, place the open end of the closed Zipper about 2 inches below the top of the skirt. Pin the tape to the welt so that the stitches can be made about ¹⁄₁₆ of

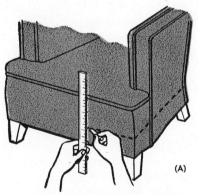

MARKING LINE OF SKIRT ON SLIPCOVER

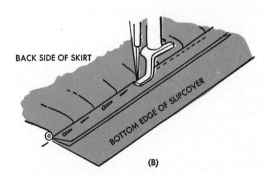

BACK SIDE OF SKIRT

BOTTOM EDGE OF SLIPCOVER

228 FITTING THE SKIRT

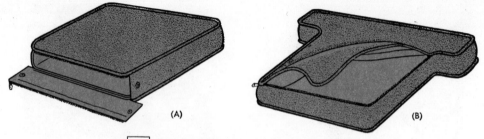

an inch away from the metal. Carefully pin the outside back cover into position on the Zipper tape. Open the Zipper, and with a cording foot attached to the sewing machine, sew the Zipper in place.

LOOSE CUSHIONS

Center the pattern of the slip-cover fabric over the top of the cushion and chalk mark the planned seams. Trim the fabric to allow a ⅝-inch seam. Lay this piece of the cover face to face on the material to be used for covering the other side of the cushion. Cut the second piece. Sew a welt around the edges of both the top and bottom of the cushion-cover pieces.

If the piece being slip covered requires more than one seat cushion, make sure that the pattern on each cushion fits the same.

Measure the height and length of the border or boxing. On straight-outline cushions, measure the length from the back corner around the sides and front to the opposite corner. Add to this length 1¼ inches for seams. A separate flap is made for the back side of the cushion. On T cushions or others made much larger at the front, measure all the way around the entire cushion and add 1¼ inches for seams.

The border should be as wide as the cushion is thick, plus 1¼ inches to allow for a ⅝-inch seam on each side. The border fabric may be pieced together except at the front of the cushion, where it should be one continuous piece.

If the cushion cover will have an open flap at the back, sew together the top, bottom and sides of the cover. Make a facing along one side and at the ends of the flap and sew the other side to the back of the cushion cover. Pin and then sew a Zipper or snap-tape to the loose sides of the flap and cover. Sew snap fasteners to the ends of the flap and the border at the corners. Fig. 229A.

On T cushions, sew the border closed and to it sew one side of the cushion cover. Then attach the other side of the cover to the unit, sewing it at one side, around the T and about halfway along the other side. Pin a Zipper in place and sew it along the rest of the opening to the cover and the border. Fig. 229B.

If any parts of the slip cover have become wrinkled during the sewing processes, remove the cover, steam-press it and finally put it on the piece, smoothing the tuck-ins in place and closing back and cushion openings.

BOOK II

PART VI – MODERN MATERIALS AND METHODS

Preface

NEW METHODS AND MATERIALS for upholstering furniture were developed as far back as the middle 1930's. However, because of their limited use and production, these materials were expensive at first. Then, with the outbreak of
World War II and the ensuing shortage of manpower and
imported materials, the new upholstering methods and materials came into their own. These innovations permitted
greater freedom in design and more rapid production.

The new materials—sagless-wire springs, foam rubber and
rubberized fibers—have made upholstering easier for the amateur. The resulting upholstered pieces, moreover, are lighter
in weight, more durable and just as comfortable as those upholstered with the traditional materials.

The newer materials can be used with the traditional
methods of upholstering with very satisfactory results. For example, loose stuffing may be applied over sagless-wire springs
in the same manner as it was applied over coil springs. Foam
rubber and rubberized fibers may be used over coil springs
in the same manner as these materials are applied over sagless-
wire springs.

The author wishes to thank the following firms for their
assistance in supplying information and photographs:

AMERICAN PAD AND TEXTILE CO.

AIRFOAM DIVISION OF GOODYEAR TIRE AND RUBBER CO.

FLEX-O-LATERS, INC.

ROBERT FLOESS AND CO.

HEWITT RESTFOAM DIVISION OF HEWITT-ROBBINS INC.

SPONGE RUBBER PRODUCTS CO.

U. S. KOLON FOAM DIVISION OF U. S. RUBBER CO.

NO-SAG SPRING CO.

Modern Materials and Methods

Lesson One — **TOOLS AND MATERIALS**

Tools: The tools used in working with sagless-wire springs, foam rubber and rubberized fiber are essentially the same as used when working with conventional upholstery materials.

If you are going to cut your own sagless-wire springs to length, it is best to have a bolt cutter. The springs may also be cut to length with a triangle file or a hacksaw having a blade with 24 to 32 teeth per inch.

The ends of the sagless-wire springs should be bent. This is accomplished best with a special bending tool. Fig. 230. The ends can also be bent by placing the wire in a vise and bending the end of the wire over by striking the end of the spring wire with a hammer. Fig. 232. Sagless-wire springs can be purchased cut to length with the ends already bent.

To cut foam rubber or rubberized fibers, a bandsaw may be used. It is best to use a special blade with a bread-knife edge in the bandsaw, though a regular 1/4-inch blade with little or no set can also be used in cutting foam rubber and rubberized fiber.

Sagless-Wire Springs and Accessories: Sagless-wire springs are sold under the trade names of No-Sag, and Zigger Wire. They are also called non-sagging springs and zigzag wire. These springs are made from a continuous piece of spring wire crimped into a zigzag form and into a circular coil. The wire does not actually become a spring until it is uncoiled from its original circular form and stretched and anchored to the frame of a seat or back at both ends. The spring then constantly pulls between the anchored ends, trying to regain its original circular form, thus giving the spring a permanent arc and flexibility.

Sagless-wire springs are sold in cut lengths and in coils from 111 to 160 feet long. The chart in Fig. 231 not only gives the number of feet in each coil but also the gauge of wire in which the springs are made. Springs from 8 to 11 gauge are recommended for use in seats. Springs from 10½ to 12½ gauge are used in backs.

Clips: There is a great variety of clips available for holding the sagless-wire springs to the frame. The following clips are most commonly used. All the clips are antisqueak lined.

K Clip: This is a two-nail clip for average back-and-seat construction wherever two nails are strong enough for permanent anchorage. The hole on the bottom lip of the clip is larger than the corresponding hole on the top lip so that the nail can be driven on a slant towards the center of the rail. Fig. 233.

E Clip: This is a three-nail clip for heavy-duty back-and-seat construction. It is best used with heavy-gauge springs and whenever springs are to be hung inside the rail. The larger holes in the bottom lip permit driving the nails on a slant towards the center of the rail or on a downward slant when used inside the rail. Fig. 233.

G Clip: With staggered nail holes for placing springs close to the outside edge of the frame, this clip is suggested (nail to outside and top surfaces). This clip can also be used to drop springs below the top of the rail (nail to top and inside rails). Fig. 233.

FIG. 230. Special bending tool

SAGLESS WIRE COIL SPECIFICATIONS			
Gauge	Feet	Gauge	Feet
8	111	10½	128
8½	111	11	140
9	120	11½	154
9½	120	12	154
10	127	12½	160

FIG. 231. Chart for sagless-wire coil specifications

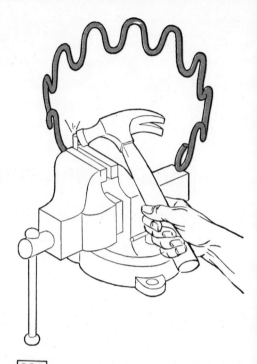

232 WIRING ENDS BENT IN VISE

C Clip: This clip is best for rear seat rails where the lower rail of the back liner interferes with nailing on the top side of the back seat rail. The long straight end is then bent around the rail for nailing to the outside vertical edge. Fig. 233.

For Nailing Down Clips: For best results use nails with solid, countersunk heads, barbed and cement-coated in ¾, ⅞ and 1-inch lengths. A ⅞-inch length is recommended for all standard installations.

When nailing clips to the frames, make certain that the looped end of the clip overhangs the inside edge of the rail by approximately ⅛ inch. Fig. 234. This will permit the sagless-wire springs to swivel freely within the clip, allowing maximum spring action and preventing noise that might otherwise result due to restricted movement of the springs

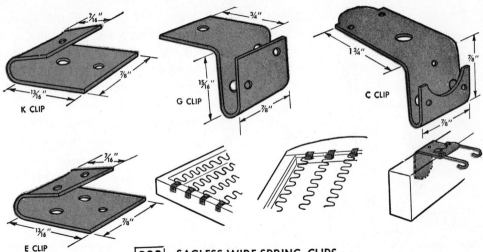

233 SAGLESS-WIRE-SPRING CLIPS

Retainer Plates: For anchoring seat helicals and extension springs to the side rails, retainer plates are used. Fig. 235. They allow a straight pull from the outside rows of the sagless-wire springs and maintain the crown shape or arc of the spring construction.

All crossties of seat helicals or extension springs must be taut for good spring action and the prevention of noise.

Hinge Links: Hinge links are used at the back seat rails. Fig. 236. The movable pivot makes a higher spring arc (up to 2¼ inches is possible), creating greater resiliency and comfort. If a normal arc is desired (1¾ inches), deduct up to 1 inch from the sagless-wire-spring length to allow for a hinge link (normally the distance between the inside of the front and back rails).

Seat Helicals: Seat helicals should be close bound for anchoring the outside rows of sagless-wire springs to the side rails of seats. They also may be used as ties between sagless-wire springs in seats, making them perform as a single unit with greater flexibility and support for upholstery filling. Fig. 237.

For best results use a 2-inch size for 4-inch spacing, a 3-inch size for 5-inch spacing, and a 4-inch size for 6-inch spacing of sagless-wire springs.

Extension Springs: Extension springs, open wound, are used as ties between sagless-wire springs in backs. This spring creates a flexible action and a support for upholstery filling. Fig. 237.

In back work, use the 2-inch size for 4-inch spacing, a 3-inch size for 5-inch spacing, and a 4-inch size for 6-inch spacing of sagless-wire springs.

Edge Springs: Edge springs for spring-edge constructions are used in pairs of two lengths and are alternated in assembling. They are clipped to the border wire by special edge clips on the spring-edge assembly.

Edge springs for seats are longer and of heavier gauge than edge springs for backs. Fig. 238.

Spring-Edge Wire or Border Wire: Edge wire for seats should be 9 or 12 gauge and for backs 12 to 14 gauge. Spring-edge wire is highly tempered

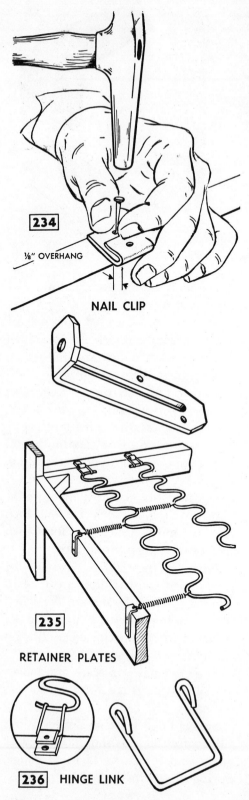

234

⅛" OVERHANG

NAIL CLIP

235

RETAINER PLATES

236 HINGE LINK

steel wire used to unite the spring edge and to shape and strengthen the exposed edges. It is also used to reinforce corners and top back-edge wire in backs. The wire comes in 5 to 10-foot lengths.

Spring-Edge Clip: The border wire is attached to the edge springs with spring-edge clips. The antisqueak lining holds the border wire securely to the springs. Edge clips for the seat are 1⅛ inches. Fig. 239. Edge clips for backs are ⅞ of an inch. Fig. 239.

These clips can be fastened to the border wire and the spring edges either with edge-clip pliers or ordinary household pliers.

Torsion Springs: Torsion springs are used to support spring edges where spring-edge springs cannot be used. Fig. 240. This spring is used in front of the arm stump on T-type seats and to support the top-edge wire of spring-edge backs. They are also used to support the spring-edge wire at the sides of seats that have exposed edges at the sides.

One leg of this spring is fastened to the frame with an A or K clip and the other leg is fastened to the spring-edge wire with a spring-edge clip.

Insulators: Insulators are sometimes used in place of burlap over springs to prevent the padding from pushing down into the springs. An insulator over springs also helps eliminate the feeling of the springs through the padding. Less padding is required over the springs when an insulator is used.

There are two types of insulators made that are used in place of burlap over spring work. They are called Perm-a-lators (trade name). One is a wire-mat construction consisting of piano wire woven through rope cords and has a strip of burlap attached to each side for tacking. Fig. 241. The piano wire in this insulator is spaced 1 inch apart. They can be purchased with 16, 19, and 21-inch-long wire: with 5 or 10-inch-wide burlap tacking strips on both sides. This insulator can be purchased in cut lengths or in 50-yard rolls. Rubberized fibers and cotton can be used directly over this insulator. Foam rubber can also be used over this insulator when it is used over coil springs.

The second type of insulator has piano wire woven through burlap. Fig. 242. The insulator can be purchased with the wires spaced 1, 1¼ and 1½ inches apart: with 12-inch-long wires woven in burlap from 14 to 40 inches wide, with 14-inch-long wires woven in burlap from 16 to 40 inches wide, with 16-inch-long wires woven in burlap from 18 to 40 inches wide and with 19-inch-long wires woven in burlap from 20 to 40 inches wide. This insulator can also be purchased in cut lengths and in 50-yard rolls. Any type of stuffing and padding can be placed over this insulator.

These insulators are installed in the same manner as burlap.

There is yet another type of insulator that is used over burlap to eliminate the spring feel and saves padding. This insulator is a sisal pad and has a heavy coating of latex on one side. This insulating pad can be attached to the burlap with hog rings along the edges or by coating the burlap with rubber cement, then setting the pad in over the burlap, thus welding the pad to the burlap.

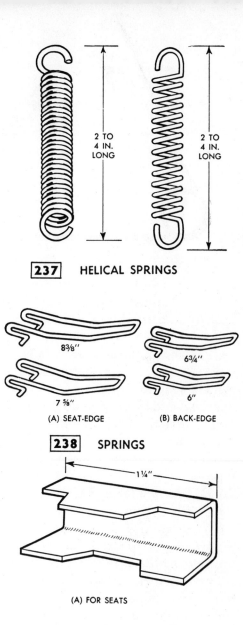

237 HELICAL SPRINGS

(A) SEAT-EDGE   (B) BACK-EDGE

238 SPRINGS

(A) FOR SEATS

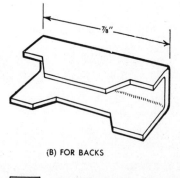

(B) FOR BACKS

239 SPRING EDGE CLIPS

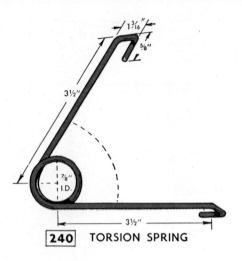

240 TORSION SPRING

Foam Rubber: Foam rubber is made from natural liquid latex of the rubber tree. With a few chemicals for catalytic and preservative action added, it is whipped into a fluffy frothlike foam in a mixing machine. It is immediately poured into a mold designed for the final size and shape of the product. Then it is vulcanized into permanent form. As a result, the foam rubber is about 85 percent air and the remainder is 15 percent latex. Foam rubber is completely porous, as all the air cells are connected. The air circulating through the foam carries away the body heat and maintains room temperature.

Foam rubber should not be confused with sponge rubber. They are entirely different products. Sponge rubber is made from dried sheets of

Fig. 241. Wire and rope insulator

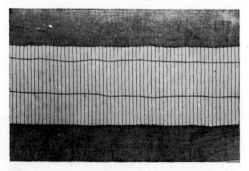

rubber by a kneading process. Its cells are nonporous as they are disconnected and unevenly distributed, unlike the cells of foam rubber which are connected and breathe air.

Foam rubber is made in three forms: slab stock, cored stock and in molded units. Fig. 243.

Slab stock is a thin comfortable pad used in covering the top and the inside of the arms, making cushions, fabricating over open-core holes, and as a top covering on seats and backs that have been padded with other materials. It is also used in padding slip seats and thin backs. The slab stock is available in four compression densities: the extra soft is 5 to 10 pounds, soft is 10 to 25 pounds, medium is 25 to 40 pounds, and the firm is 40 to 60 pounds. All these are available in 1/4, 3/8, 1/2, 3/4, 1 and 1 1/4-inch thicknesses. The width and length of the slab stock vary with different manufacturers.

Cored stock is open-cored on the underside to provide a deep-cushion effect and is used over spring work or on a solid base. Cored stock comes in five compression densities: extra soft is 5 to 10 pounds, soft is 10 to 25 pounds, medium is 25 to 40 pounds, firm is 40 to 60 pounds and extra firm is 60 to 85 pounds. This stock is available in 3/4, 1, 1 1/2, 2, 2 1/2, 3 and 4 1/2-inch thicknesses. The width and length of the cored stock vary with different manufacturers.

Molded foam rubber is used mostly in loose-cushion work. Molded foam rubber comes in many sizes and shapes and in five compression densities. Some hand fabrication work is usually required to make molded-foam-rubber cushions fit the individual pieces being upholstered.

Fig. 244 illustrates the tools and materials used in fabricating foam rubber. Foam rubber can be cut to the size and shape desired with scissors or it can be cut on a bandsaw.

When foam rubber cannot be purchased in the size and shape desired, it can be cemented together, making a piece of the size desired. Pieces of waste stock can also be cemented together. Foam rubber is best when applied over flat surfaces. It is difficult to apply foam rubber over severely curved surfaces, especially on surfaces that have compound curves. Foam rubber is never used as an understuff; loose stuffing should be used for this purpose before applying foam rubber.

Soapstone: In working with foam rubber it is a good practice to dust the work table with soapstone or talc so it can be handled more easily. Hand iron and cushion-filling machines should also be dusted to eliminate friction when filling the foam-rubber cushion into the cover.

Soapstone or talc should be dusted on seams that have been cemented together to prevent the foam rubber from sticking. The soapstone and talc absorb any excess cement which may have been applied. When cored stock has been cemented, dust the cores with soapstone or talc. This will eliminate the possibility of the core walls sticking together and collapsing.

Foam-Rubber Cement: It is advis-

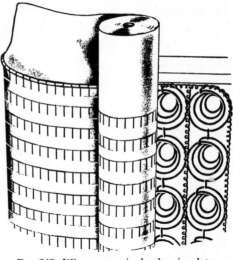

FIG. 242. Wire woven in burlap insulator

FIG. 243. Foam-rubber stock

FIG. 244. Tools and materials for fabricating foam rubber

able to purchase the cement made by the same manufacturer that made the foam rubber. This will assure satisfactory cementing results. Some cement is ready to use as it comes from the can; others need to have an activator added. Follow the instructions that are given on the container. The cement used in fabricating foam rubber is also used when working with rubberized-fiber stock.

The cement is used in fabricating foam rubber into a single unit and in cementing tacking tape to foam rubber. The cement is also used to attach the foam rubber firmly to the base on which it is to be placed.

Tacking Tape: Tacking tape is used to fasten foam rubber to the frame along the edges and to reinforce the edges of the foam rubber. The tape comes in 100-yard rolls in 2, 3, 5 and 6-inch widths. One inch of the width is adhesive-treated for application to foam rubber. Full-surface-adhesive tape can also be purchased.

Muslin can be cut into strips to the desired width and coated with cement and left to dry. When cement has dried on muslin it can be used in place of tacking tape.

Rubberized Fibers: Pads made of animal hair, vegetable fiber and minerals and bonded with latex are used in upholstery or furniture. The fibers are coated and felted into the thickness and density desired and are then vulcanized into pads.

Rubberized-fiber pads are made in three densities: soft, medium and firm. Pads of various densities are often cemented together, the firm pad at the bottom and the softer pad or pads on the top

Like foam rubber, rubberized-fiber pads are not suitable for understuffing and are difficult to install over curved surfaces, especially on surfaces that have compound curves.

All rubberized-fiber pads have to be covered with cotton or ½-inch foam rubber before applying the final cover. This prevents the fibers from working through the cover and silences a scratching sound between the cover and the fibers.

All rubberized-fiber pads can be cut to the size and shape desired with a scissors or a sharp knife. When cutting rubberized fibers with a scissors or a knife, be careful to cut a thin layer at a time.

Rubberized-fiber pads can be sewed; glued in place with rubber cement and placed on the piece being upholstered, or tacked to a wood base. In tacking rubberized-fiber pads, force a small hole three-quarters of the way through the pad and tack it down with a large upholstery tack. The hole is then closed over the tack with loose fibers.

Rubberized Hair: The hair used in making rubberized-hair pads comes from hogs, cattle tails and horse manes and tails. Horse manes and cattle tails produce the better-quality fibers. The density of the rubberized-hair pads varies with the quantity of hair that is used in making the pad. The more hair used, the firmer the pad. Rubberized-hair pads can easily be identified by the grey-black color.

Hair in rubberized pads is moth proof, durable and clean.

Rubberized-hair pads come in the following thicknesses: ¾, 1, 1⅛, 2 and 2½ inches. The size of the pad varies with different manufacturers.

FIG. 245. Rubberized hair

The back sides of rubberized-hair pads are meshed. Fig. 245. This back is the bottom side of the pad and placed there to prevent the stitching from pulling through the back, especially when the pad is stitched along the edge.

Rubberized Saran Fiber: Saran (trade name) fibers are extruded from vinylidene-chloride polymers as a plastic. Rubberized Saran fibers are sold under the trade name of Saraflex.

Saran pads are constructed of individual Saran fibers of various diameters, curled and coated with latex and formed into sheets of desired thicknesses. The firmness and load-bearing quality of Saran fibers can be controlled merely by using fibers of larger diameter.

Rubberized Saran-fiber pads can be identified by their multicolor fibers which are every color of the spectrum.

Rubberized Saran-fiber pads can be cemented and fabricated in the same manner as foam rubber.

Rubberized Tampico Fibers: Tampico fibers come from the tula-tampico plant and are shredded, permanently curled and then bonded with rubber latex into pads. The trade name of this product is Tulatex. Fig. 246.

Rubberized tampico is a straw color and is sterilized, vermin and moth proof. It can be purchased in 24 x 72 and 84 x 72-inch-size pads, and in 1, 1½, 2, 2½, 3½ and 4-inch thicknesses.

Frames: Most frames do not require a radical change in order to accommo-

FIG. 246. Rubberized tampico

247 RAISING SEAT LEVEL

SIDE-SEAT
RAIL

FRONT-SEAT
RAIL

248 SIDE RAIL IN BACK
OF FRONT RAIL

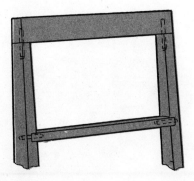

249 BACK FRAME CONSTRUCTION

date sagless-wire springs. However, all frames must be strong enough to withstand the "live pull" of sagless-wire springs. The seat rails must be at least 1 inch thick. One should keep in mind that all the pull of the springs is between the front and back rails of the seat, and on the top back rail and liner on the back.

Some alterations and reinforcements will have to be made in frames that were intended to be upholstered with coil springs and are now to have a sagless-wire spring construction.

In order to retain the seating height it may be necessary to raise the height of the seat rail at the front and back. Fig. 247. To determine how much the rails have to be raised, subtract the height of the spring arc from the distance between the top of the front and back seat rails to the bottom side of the arm liner. This will give the height that front and back rails are to be raised. For example, if the arc height of the sagless-wire spring is to be 1¾ inches and the distance between the top of the front and back seat rails and the bottom of the arm liner is 3 inches, the rails are raised 1¼ inches.

On seats without arms or back liners, raise front, back and side seat rails according to the following formula: subtract from the desired seat height the distance between the front seat rail from the floor plus the height of the spring arc. Therefore, if the desired seat height is 17½ inches, the distance from the floor to the front seat rail is 14½ inches and the spring arc is 1½ inches high, the rails should be raised 1½ inches.

On seats that are to have spring edges, the spring edge should be 3 to 5 inches above the rail. Usually, no alteration need be made in frames that formerly had coil springs when spring edges are made with sagless-wire springs.

Select hardwood that is clear and free of defects. The width of the existing rail should be used in making the strips for raising the seat rails. These strips should be screwed and glued firmly to the top of the seat rails, and then glue-blocked into place wherever it is possible. This is done because the pull of the sagless-wire springs will be on top of these rails.

When new frames are to be built and the sagless-wire spring construction is to be used, it is best to have the side rails fit between the front rail and the back posts. Fig. 248.

When sagless-wire springs are used in the back, it is best to notch the back liner into the posts and fasten the top back rail on top of the posts. Fig. 249.

All frames must be corner-blocked. Instead of placing corner blocks at the bottom of the rails, they should be set no farther than 1 inch from the top of the rails. Fig. 250.

It is also important where the dowels in the back and front rails are placed—one near the top and one near the bottom of each rail. These precautions will prevent the turning of the rails under the pull of sagless-wire springs.

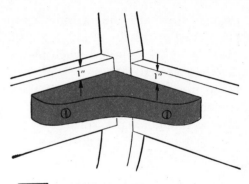

250 CORNER BLOCK

In addition to the proper corner blocking, seat slats or braces are needed on long front and back seat rails of love seats and sofas. There can be either a shaped brace with at least a 2½-inch dip, Fig. 251, or a regular slat with triangular blocks placed against the front and back rails on top of the slat. Fig. 251. The triangle blocks should reach the top of the rails and must have a base of 6 inches. The slats and braces should be spaced no more than 24 inches apart and should be doweled and glued in place. The triangular blocks should be glued and screwed in place.

The backs of love seats and sofas should also have slats placed between the top back rail and the back liner. Fig. 251.

Solid bases that are to be padded with foam rubber or rubberized fibers should have ⅜ or ½-inch holes drilled

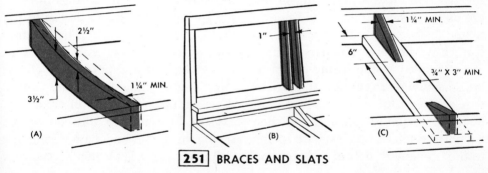

251 BRACES AND SLATS

through them at frequent intervals to allow for the passage of air. Fig. 252. More holes are required when plastic sheeting, coated fabric or leather is to be used as a final cover. If these precautions are taken, the frame will wear well under sagless springs.

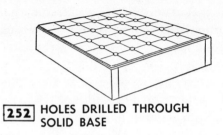

Lesson Two — SPRINGING WITH SAGLESS-WIRE SPRINGS

SAGLESS-WIRE SPRINGS are simple to install if the instructions given in this lesson are followed. Webbing is not needed when installing sagless-wire springs. The use of sagless-wire springs also eliminates stitching down and tying down of the springs to the desired height. It is also much easier to make a flat regular surface with sagless-wire springs.

The comfort and resiliency of the sagless-wire springs will depend entirely on the correct arc, gauge of the wire and length of the springs. The greater the arc the more resilient the seat. Never make the arc greater than 2 inches high without using a back seat link. The arc should not be over 2½ inches high when using the back seat link.

There will be less upholstery breakdown when using a sagless-wire spring construction than when coil springs are used; however, one should not attempt to save material by using less springs in the seats and back than is recommended in the spring charts. It is also advisable to connect the sagless-wire springs with at least two rows of helical or extension springs and then anchor the outside sagless-wire spring to the frame with helical or extension

springs. A poor sagless-wire spring installation will not stand up under severe use any better than a poor coil spring installation.

Measuring Length: To measure sagless-wire springs, place one end of the sagless-wire spring on one end of a yardstick. Then roll back the other end until the spring lies flat on the yardstick. Fig. 253. The distance between the extreme outside of each bent end is the correct length of the spring. Never use a flexible tape around the curve of the sagless-wire springs as this will not give the correct measurement of the springs. Springs that are sold already cut to length have been measured by this method.

Cutting and Bending Ends: Sagless-wire springs can be purchased either cut to length or in coils. When one purchases sagless-wire springs in coils, the springs will have to be cut to the desired length. Fig. 254. The bending back of the end is necessary to prevent the spring from slipping out of the clip. The bending of the ends can be done with a special bending tool, Fig. 230, or by clamping the end of the spring in a vise and hammering the end over. Fig. 231. When sagless-wire springs are purchased cut to length, they are furnished with the ends already bent.

Installation of Springs: The clips are fastened on the frame first. The chart in Fig. 255 gives the number of sagless-wire springs needed in the seats and backs and the spacing of the clips. Mark the location of the clips on the rails of the frame. When the seat tapers to the back, the outside clips on the back rail should be installed the same distance in from the sides as they are at the front. The other clips for the back seat rail are then spaced equally between the outside clips. On large seats, the second clip from the outside on the back rail is spaced evenly between the outside clip and the normal position of the third clip. The springs are always installed between the front and back seat rails, on the seats and from the top back rail to the back liner on the back. The only exception is when the back and seat are upholstered together in one continuous form. The springs are then installed between the side seat rails and between the back posts.

The type of clip to use will depend upon the job, but whenever possible use an E clip. When installing clips, be sure the clip overhangs the inside edge of the frame by at least ⅛ of an inch. Fig. 234. This will permit the sagless-wire springs to swivel freely within the clip, allowing maximum spring action and preventing any noise that might result from restricted spring movement. It is best to install all the clips in their place with one nail before fastening sagless-wire springs in place.

In all sagless-wire spring installations, it is important to alternate the

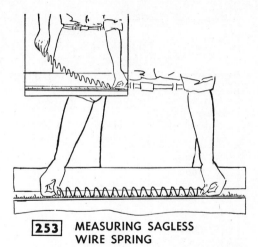

253 MEASURING SAGLESS WIRE SPRING

direction of the bent ends. Fig. 256. If the bent end of the first spring points to the right, the bent end of the next spring should point to the left. This alternating of the direction of the bent ends of the springs provides closed loops opposite each other, permitting helical and retainer springs to be applied in a straight line. Alternating the direction of the bent ends is also necessary in order to install edge springs.

Installing Springs in Seat: When the clips have been installed the seat is ready for the installation of sagless-wire springs. To determine the gauge and length of the springs needed, measure the frame from the inside of the front rail to the inside of the back rail. Fig. 257. When the distance be-

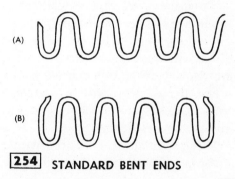

(A)

(B)

254 STANDARD BENT ENDS

TABLE FOR DETERMINING
NUMBER OF SAGLESS STRANDS, PROPER
SPACING OF CLIPS AND CORRECT SIZE OF SEAT
HELICALS, EXTENSION SPRINGS FOR CHAIR AND SOFA SEATS

Distance Between Arms Along Front Rail	Number of Sagless Strand	Center to Center Spacing for Clips	Center Spacing of Two Outside Clips From Inside Arm Posts	Seat Helical and Extension Spring Size
21" Chair	5	4¼"	2"	2"
22" Chair	5	4½"	2"	2"
23" Chair	5	4¾"	2"	3"
24" Chair	5	5"	2"	3"
24" Chair	6	4"	2"	2"
25" Chair	6	4¼"	1⅞"	2"
58" Sofa	12	5"	1½"	3"
59" Sofa	12	5"	2"	3"
60" Sofa	13	4¾"	1½"	3"
61" Sofa	13	4¾"	2"	3"
62" Sofa	13	4¾"	2½"	3"
63" Sofa	13	5"	1½"	3"
63" Sofa	14	4½"	2¼"	2"
64" Sofa	14	4½"	2¾"	2"
65" Sofa	14	4¾"	1⅝"	3"
66" Sofa	14	4¾"	2⅛"	3"
67" Sofa	15	4½"	2"	2"

Where distance between arms is in half inches use table for next smaller or larger size and set each outside clip ¼" farther away from arm post (if table for smaller size is used) or ¼" closer to arm post (if table for larger size is used).

Fig. 255.

tween the front and back seat rails and the height of the arc desired is determined, refer to the chart in Fig. 258 to find the length and the gauge of the sagless wire of the springs needed. Whenever possible use as high an arc as possible; up to 2 inches is preferred as the seat will then be most resilient.

To make a seat more resilient, a link hinge can be installed on the back side of the seat. The use of a link hinge will increase the height of the arc ¼ of an inch. When using a link hinge, the arc thus will be increased from 2 inches to 2¼ inches and will give greater resiliency.

If the normal arc is desired with a link-hinge installation, deduct 1 inch from the length of the sagless-wire spring.

When installing springs to the frame, fasten and nail the clip closed on the back rail first. Be sure the bent ends are alternated. The springs are then pulled to the front and hooked onto the front clips and the clip is then nailed closed. Be sure you have a good hold on the spring when stretching the springs over the frame, because you must exert a good deal of energy when stretching the springs.

The springs should then be connected together with seat helical springs. See the chart in Fig. 255 for the size of the helical springs required. Helical springs are used to connect the sagless-wire springs so they will function as a unit and spread the seating load over all the sagless-wire springs. The connecting of the springs will also form a better base for the padding that is to follow. When installing helical or retainer springs, be sure the open hook of the coil is faced down or away from the spring surface. If this is not done, the open hooks of the helical spring may snag the burlap and padding. The sagless-wire springs should be connected with two or three rows of helical springs. Fig. 256. The more rows of helical springs that are used, the firmer the seat.

Two helical retainer plates should be installed on each side rail. The retainer plates should be installed at an equal distance from the center of the sagless-wire spring (from three to five loops apart) along the sagless-wire coil. The retainer plates are nailed perpendicular to the side seat rail. This should be done as high as possible in order to provide a straight pull against the outside row of sagless-wire springs. A helical spring should then be connected between the retainer plates and the loop of the sagless-wire spring opposite the retainer plate. Using retainer plates eliminates the side-to-side sway in the seat. Fig. 259 shows two typical sagless-wire spring seats.

Springing Backs: Whenever possible install the same number of rows of springs in the back as there are in the seat. It is a good practice to keep all back springs in the same line as the seat springs. If a softer back is desired, one less sagless-wire spring may be installed. When this is done the back springs are spaced in between the rows of the seat springs.

First nail the spring clips in place

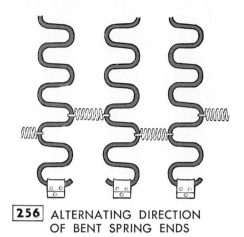

256 ALTERNATING DIRECTION OF BENT SPRING ENDS

with one nail to the back liner and to the top back rail.

The chart in Fig. 260 gives the gauge of sagless-wire springs for back installations. Back installations vary too much to specify definite sizes in a table. One method to find the length of the sagless spring needed is to place a 30-inch sample length of the sagless-wire spring in a clip nail on the back liner. Then form the desired arc while holding the spring in place over the top of the top back rail. The length of the sagless-wire spring needed is then measured. Cut the number of springs needed to the size desired. When the springs are cut to length, bend the ends.

Next, springs are fastened and clips nailed closed to the back liner. They are then pulled up and hooked to the clips installed along the top back rail. The top clips are then closed, securing the sagless-wire springs in place.

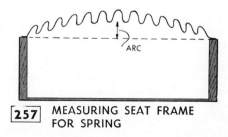

257 MEASURING SEAT FRAME FOR SPRING

Two or three rows of extension springs are then installed across the back. The extension springs anchoring the last rows of the springs to the frame are held to the frame with staples. See the chart in Fig. 255 to determine the size of the extension spring to use. Fig. 261 illustrates a typical back installation.

When a back finishes over an arm and a spring must be installed to fill out the contour, a short length of sagless-wire spring is installed. Fig. 262. A clip is installed on top of the arm so it is in line with the other sagless-wire spring at the height of the arm. First fasten the sagless-wire spring to arm clip, then hook it to the clip on the top rail and nail the clip closed.

Building a Spring-Edge Seat: A spring-edge seat makes a much more resilient seat than one without a spring edge. When a loose cushion is to be used, it is necessary to build a spring edge in order to retain the cushion.

The clips and sagless-wire springs are first installed in the seat as previously described.

Fig. 263 illustrates how the spring edge is hooked on the sagless-wire springs, one arm being hooked on to the closed side of the sagless-wire spring loop F. The other faces, or is parallel to, the closed loop of the adjacent sagless spring G. In order to get facing or parallel closed loops, it is necessary to attach the sagless-wire springs with open ends in an alternating direction. Because it is impossible to get all the closed sides of the sagless-wire spring loops facing or parallel throughout the construction, it is necessary to use edge springs, Fig. 264 A. These edge springs are made in two

FIG. 258. Sagless-springs chart

TABLE OF GAUGES AND SIZES OF SAGLESS SPRINGS FOR SEATS

Inside Seat Dimension	Gauge	1¼" Arc	1½" Arc	1¾" Arc	2" Arc
12"	11	11¾"	12"	12½"	
13"	11	12¾"	13"	13½"	
14"	10½	13¾"	14"	14½"	
15"	10½	14¾"	15"	15¼"	
16"	10	15¾"	16"	16¼"	
17"	10	16¼"	16½"	16¾"	
18"	9½	17"	17½"	18"	
19"	9½	18¼"	18½"	18¾"	
20"	9	19"	19½"	19¾"	20"
21"	9	20"	20½"	20¾"	21"
22"	8½	21"	21¼"	21¾"	22"
23"	8½	22"	22½"	22¾"	23"
24"	8½	23"	23¼"	23½"	24"
25"	8	24"	24¼"	24½"	25"
26"	8	25"	25¼"	25½"	26"
27"	8	26"	26¼"	26½"	27"

Inside seat dimension is the distance between the inside of the front and back rails. Sagless springs cut to this exact length will give you the normal arc. It varies from 1¼" to 2" increasing with the length of the spring as shown above. When clip is not attached to inside edges of frame, clip-to-clip dimensions can be used instead of inside dimensions.

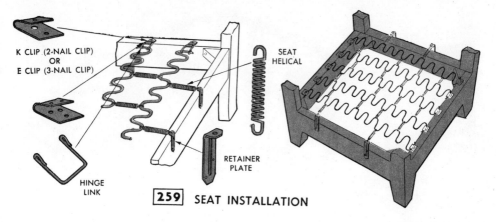

K CLIP (2-NAIL CLIP)
OR
E CLIP (3-NAIL CLIP)

SEAT HELICAL

RETAINER PLATE

HINGE LINK

259 SEAT INSTALLATION

sizes and the two are successively alternated in assembling.

On the two outside springs, both arms of the spring-edge unit are hooked to the same outside loop to create a stiffer corner than is generally desired in spring-edge construction, as shown in Fig. 266. To obtain a still stiffer corner and greater leverage, both loops of the two outside spring-edge units may be opened slightly with pliers. Fig. 264B.

The edge springs are hooked far enough back on the sagless-wire spring so that when the border wire is clipped on and pulled down, the front edge of the border wire will be in line with the outside edge of the front rail.

The assembling of the border wire to the edge springs is similar to the coil-spring spring-edge construction. It is done with clips and pliers.

A 9 or 10-gauge border wire is used for forming the spring edge on the seat. The border wire should be bent to the shape of the outside edge of the frame before being attached to the edge of the springs. The border wire can be held and bent with two pairs of pliers, but it is simpler and easier to make sharp bends by running the wire

through a ½-inch-dia. pipe about 8 inches long. Bend the wire over the inside edge of the pipe. Fig. 124A. When the border wire has to be bent to a curve, lay the edge wire on a block of wood and strike with a hammer until the wire has been formed to the shape desired. Fig. 124B. The ends of the border wire should be bent down to prevent them from making holes in the burlap and padding over the springs. The border wire should then be straightened so that it lies flat.

Figs. 265 and 266 illustrate how border wire is attached to the edge springs and fastened at the ends. After the border wire has been attached, the edge is pulled down to the desired height with a twine. For the most

Fig. 260		BACK-SPRING SIZES	
Inside Back Dimension	Arc	Gauge	Length
16″	1½″	12 or 13	16″
17″	1⅝″	12 or 13	17″
18″	1¾″	12 or 13	18¼″
19″	1⅞″	12	19¼″
20″	2″	12	20¼″
21″	2″	12	21¼″
22″	2″	12	22¼″
23″	2¼″	11½ or 12	23½″
24″	2¼″	11½	24½″
25″	2½″	11	25½″
26″	2½″	11	26½″

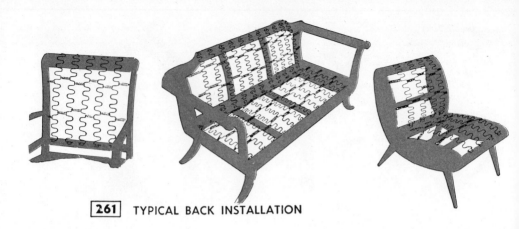

261 TYPICAL BACK INSTALLATION

resiliency, the edge should be left as high as possible. Under no circumstances should it be tied down lower than 3 inches above the front rail. So the twine will not make lumps on the border wire, it is looped around the wire between the edge springs. Figs. 265 and 266. Tacks are slip-tacked into position along the rail directly under the clips. They are made to face outward at an angle so that when the twine has been looped around the tacks, they can be driven permanently in place without the border wire in-

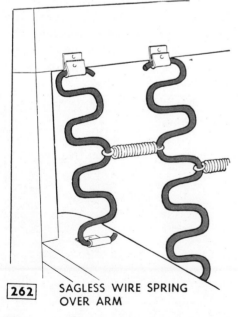

262 SAGLESS WIRE SPRING OVER ARM

terfering with the head of the hammer. There is no strain on the twine after the burlap or wire-type insulator has been attached over the springs.

When a spring edge is desired on two or three sides of the seat, the wire is fastened to the back post, Fig. 267A, then placed around the side and fastened to edge spring at front. Two torsion springs are placed on each side where border wire is installed. Fig. 267B. The border wire is tied down along the side edges in the same manner as the front edge. The side border wires are then connected by helical springs to the outer sagless-wire springs.

To install a border wire on four sides of a seat, edge springs are installed along the back as well as the front side of the seat. No hinge links should be installed at the back rail when the seat is to have a spring edge on the four sides. Two torsion springs are installed on each side. Fig. 267B. The border wire is then tied down to the height desired.

Making a Spring-Edge Back: There are two methods of making spring-edge backs. One method is the same as when making the spring seat, except that 12 or 14-gauge border wire and smaller and lighter-gauge edge springs

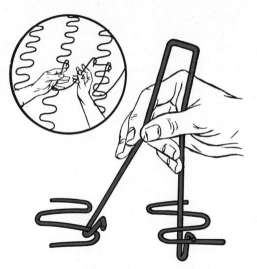

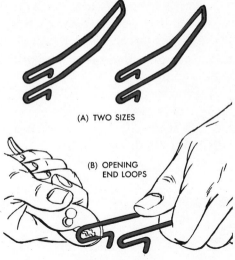

(A) TWO SIZES

(B) OPENING END LOOPS

263	INSTALLING EDGE SPRING

264	EDGE SPRINGS

are used to support the border wire. Torsion springs are not needed to support the border wire at the sides.

When the back overhangs the arms, the border wire is installed. Fig. 268. The ends of the border wire are fastened to the outside sagless-wire springs. A short sagless-wire spring is then fastened to the border with clips.

The second method of installing a spring-edge back is shown in Fig. 269. When this method is used, the border wire should be 9 or 10 gauge. The border wire is first bent to the shape desired and fastened to the top side of the back liners. Corner braces made of border wire should then be installed to brace the corners. Notice the top corner brace is bent slightly back at the top so it will not interfere with the sagless-wire spring. A brace to support the top border wire is then formed and attached to the back edge of the top side of the back liner at the center. The ends of the brace wire are then attached to the top edge of the border wire to prevent the sagless-wire springs

from pulling the top edge of the border wire out of line. Care must be taken that braces will not interfere with the installing of sagless-wire springs.

The sagless-wire springs are then fastened in place to the back liner and pulled up and attached to the top edge of the border wire. If the back runs over the arm, a short length of the sagless-wire spring is attached to the border wire over the arm and then fastened to the top border wire.

265	SPRING EDGE ON SEAT BETWEEN ARMS

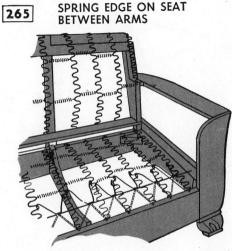

It may be necessary to make adjustments in the top border-wire brace when the springs are fastened in place to make certain the top of the border will be straight.

Torsion springs are then fastened to the top rail and to the top border wire. Fig. 270 illustrates the torsion spring fastened to the back and border wire; this figure also gives a clear view of the top border-wire brace. Torsion springs should be installed from 12 to 14 inches apart on the backs. Two torsion springs are enough on backs 22 inches wide or less.

The border wire is then tied down to the height desired. Two or three rows of extension springs are then installed across the back. The sagless-wire springs are then covered with burlap or an insulator in the same manner as coiled springs.

Fig. 266. Spring edge on T seat

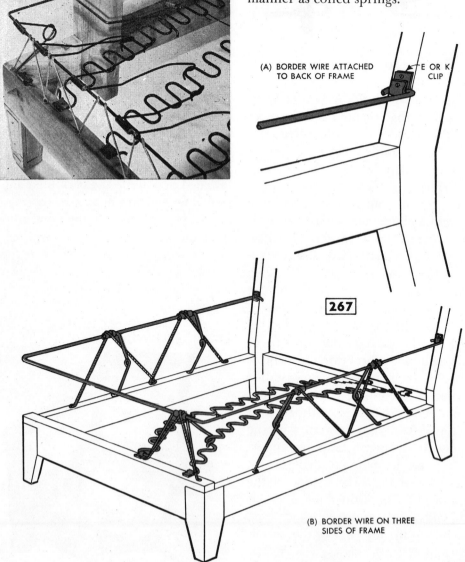

(A) BORDER WIRE ATTACHED TO BACK OF FRAME

E OR K CLIP

267

(B) BORDER WIRE ON THREE SIDES OF FRAME

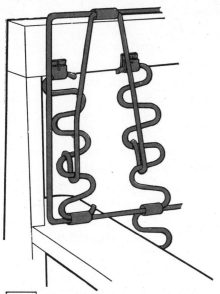

268 SPRING EDGE BACK OVER ARM

Fig. 269. Spring edge back

Fig. 270. Torsion spring attached to border wire

Loose Stuffing: When loose stuffing is to be placed over sagless-wire springs, burlap should be tacked over the spring work in the same manner as over coil springs. Edge rolls should be made along all exposed edges in order to prevent the loose stuffing from working over the edges. The edge rolls on sagless-wire spring construction should not be more than ¾ of an inch in diameter. The loose stuffing is then placed over the burlap as on coil-spring work. Care should be taken when stitching the stuffing in place that the stitching twine does not enclose the sagless-wire spring. This would cause the stitching twine to wear through and the stuffing to work loose.

Lesson Three — **PADDING WITH FOAM RUBBER AND RUBBERIZED FIBERS**

UPHOLSTERING with foam rubber and rubberized fibers is much simpler than when working with loose stuffing because the pad will be of a uniform thickness and density. Foam rubber and rubberized fibers also make a more comfortable and durable pad than loose stuffing. They are usually more resilient and retain their shape.

Selection of Slab Stock: Foam rubber and rubberized fibers are often used together with very good results. Fig. 271. Rubberized fibers are less expensive than foam rubber. A rubberized-fiber pad is always placed under the foam rubber. On seats use firm-density, rubberized-fiber slab stock both on pad work and over springs. The rubberized-fiber pad is then covered with soft-density, foam-rubber slab stock. For back work use medium-density, rubberized-fiber slab stock on both the pad and over the springs, and then cover the rubberized-fiber pad with extra-soft-density, rubber slab stock. Arms are padded with soft-density, rubberized-fiber slab stock and then covered with extra-soft-density, foam-rubber slab stock.

When working with foam rubber, use only soft or medium-density slab stock for padding tops and insides of arms, slip seats, benches, shaped seats and thin-padded chair backs. Soft and medium-density slab stocks are also used as edging strips in fabrication work, in forming edge rolls and in border work.

Cored foam-rubber stock is used in the following work: (extra-soft density) on the back for topping over springs, (soft density) on the seat or back for topping over springs, (medium density) for soft seats with or without springs, (firm density) for a firm seat with or without springs.

Base for Padding: Foam rubber and rubberized fiber can be applied over a solid base, a semiflexible base or a flexible base.

The solid base may be solid wood, plywood, hardboard, metal or expanded metal. The solid base should have ⅜-inch or ½-inch holes drilled through it at frequent intervals. With cored stock, a hole should be drilled in the base for each core to assure the free movement of air through the foam rubber or rubberized fiber.

The semiflexible base offers more comfort than a solid base. Webbing is used most often with a semiflexible base. Proper ventilation should be provided by spacing at least a ½-inch opening between the webbing strips.

A flexible base is a spring base that can be either of coil springs or sagless-wire springs. This is the most comfortable seating base. The springs must first be covered with burlap or an insulator before the foam rubber or rubberized fibers can be placed over the springs. The burlap should be stitched to the springs in the same manner as when loose stuffing is used.

When the padding is of foam rubber and burlap is used over the springs, it is best to apply a rubberized-sisal pad, a plain sisal pad or cotton between burlap and springs to reduce the friction between the springs and the foam rubber. The insulator between the burlap and the foam rubber is not required if the foam rubber is cemented to the burlap. Thinner foam rubber or rubberized-fiber stock can be used over the spring work when an insulator has been installed.

Upholstery Allowances: Foam rubber and rubberized fibers are very resilient. That is, they give easily when subjected to any pressure, and spring back to their normal shape when the pressure is removed. Therefore, when covering foam rubber or rubberized fiber, the cover should fit snugly and surface lines should be smooth and flowing. To assure that the cover will fit snugly, the foam rubber or rubberized fiber should be cut slightly larger than the surface being padded. Use the chart in Fig. 272 for upholstery allowances.

When making cutouts for the arms and posts, make the cutouts ¼-inch smaller at each edge for upholstery allowances. Fig. 273. This will assure a snug fit around the arms and post. Other upholstering allowances will be given later in this chapter.

Cutting Pads: A paper pattern should be made of all the parts that are being padded with foam rubber or rubberized fiber. The pattern can then be drawn on foam rubber with an indelible pencil, ball-point pen or colored pencil. When marking a pattern on foam rubber, make the upholstery allowance on all sides of the pattern and cutouts for the frame parts. The pattern will have to be pinned on the rubberized fiber and kept in place while the stock is being cut around the pattern, making the proper upholstery allowance. Fig. 274.

Any thickness of solid-slab foam rubber can be cut clear through with scissors. The same applies to cored stock up to 2 inches in thickness. For heavier stock it is best to make the first cut through the smooth top surface deep enough to separate the top of each core. This leaves only the core separations joined. Then cut through each core well to complete the separation. This will assure a true vertical

FIG. 271. Rubberized fiber used under foam rubber

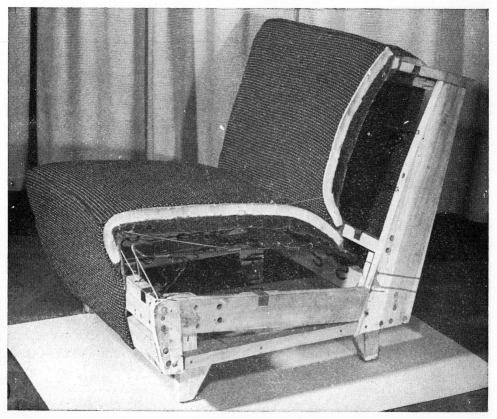

UPHOLSTERY ALLOWANCE	
0 to 6" — Allow ¼" overall	36 to 48" — Allow 1¼" overall
6 to 12" — Allow ½" overall	48 to 60" — Allow 1½" overall
12 to 24" — Allow 1" overall	60 to 72" — Allow 2" overall

These allowances can be varied slightly when extra soft or very firm foam rubber or rubberized fiber is used. When using extra soft stock add more to these allowances and when using very firm stock less allowance can be made.

FIG. 272. Upholstery allowance chart

cut. Fig. 275. Any rough surfaces are trimmed smooth. The scissors should be dipped in water frequently for lubrication when cutting heavy or firm foam-rubber stock.

When a beveled or slanted edge is desired, it is best to make the first cut vertical. Then the edge can be trimmed to the contour desired. Fig. 276. With a little practice one will be able to get a perfect round edge by trimming away the sharp edges of the bevel cut. First cut with scissors, then finish by buffing the cut edge smooth with sandpaper.

When cutting rubberized fibers, cut through a thin layer at a time until the pad has been cut through. Rubberized fiber can be cut at a slant, beveled or rounded off in the same manner as foam rubber; however, rubberized fiber cannot be sanded smooth.

A 14-inch vertical bandsaw with a ¼-inch blade that has little set to the teeth can be used for cutting most

FIG. 273. Allowance for arm and post cutouts

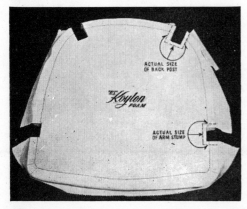

foam-rubber and rubberized-fiber pads. Wider work will require a larger bandsaw. Material can be cut wider than the bandsaw clearance by rolling up a portion of the material. When cutting foam rubber with a bandsaw, dust the table of the saw with talc or soapstone so that the material will slide more easily. With a tilting table on the saw one can cut foam-rubber or rubberized-fiber pads to the desired angle or bevel.

Cementing Foam Rubber: Cement for fabricating foam rubber varies with different manufacturers. Some cements can be used directly from the can, others require the adding of an activator. It is best to follow the instructions given on the container and also to purchase the cement made by the same manufacturer that made the foam rubber. This will assure you that the cement will be compatible with the foam rubber. All rubber cements can be thinned with lead-free gasoline when they become too thick.

When cementing foam rubber to foam rubber, make sure the pieces are cut to the proper size and shape that is required. The surfaces should be free of lumps and loose particles.

In fabricating foam rubber, one should have a clean flat surface upon which to work. This surface should be dusted with talc or soapstone.

The meeting surfaces of the pieces to be bonded should be given a light coat of rubber cement. Fig. 277. Allow the surfaces to become tacky. The cement will usually become tacky in three to five minutes. The pieces are then brought together, lightly at first, making sure they are in the proper relation to each other. Fig. 278. When the pieces are in exact alignment, press

FIG. 274. Cutting rubberized-fiber pad

them together firmly for a few seconds. In a few minutes the joint will be sufficiently bonded to work with the material. Dust the joint with talc or soapstone. If it is cored stock, the cores should also be dusted. Severe handling or assembly of cemented parts should not be attempted for several hours. But, when set, the bonded seam will be stronger than the foam rubber.

Foam rubber and rubberized fibers are bonded to wood, burlap and metal in the same manner. First, coat the surface to which the pad will apply and then the pad itself. The cement should be allowed to become tacky. The pad is then set in place with a little pressure and allowed to dry for several hours before any more work is done. The cores of cored stock and rubber-

FIG. 275. Cutting cored foam rubber

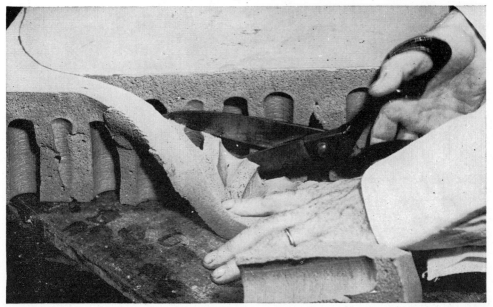

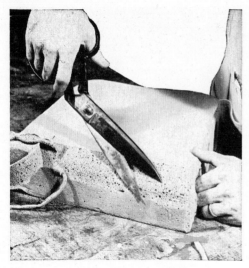

FIG. 276. Cutting a bevel

FIG. 277. Coating cement on foam rubber

FIG. 278. Cementing foam rubber together

ized fiber should be dusted with talc or soapstone before applying cement to the stock. This prevents the cores or fibers from sticking together.

When cementing rubberized-fiber pads together, dust them thoroughly before applying rubber cement. They then are cemented together in the same manner as foam rubber.

Cementing Tacking Tape to Foam Rubber: Tacking tape plays an important part in fabricating foam rubber. It should always be used when the edges of the foam rubber are to be secured to the frame. The foam rubber itself should never be tacked to the frame directly.

In order to fasten down foam rubber along the edges of a frame, a tacking strip is cemented to the edges of the foam rubber. The tacking tape comes with a 1-inch-wide coating of adhesive. A strip of muslin can be prepared with a 1-inch width along an edge coated with rubber cement. This should be allowed to dry. Then apply a thin coat of rubber cement along the edges of the foam rubber where the tacking tape is to be applied. Allow the cement to dry for a minute or two. Then apply the tacking tape. Fig. 279.

The tacking strip is also used to reinforce the edges of the foam rubber and the cemented seams that are subject to severe strain. The tacking tape gives extra protection along the front edges and also helps in keeping a sharp, clearly defined edge.

The tape should be completely coated with cement for use in reinforcing edges. The cement and tape are applied in the same manner as when applying tacking tape. Fig. 280.

When working the reinforcing tape

around the curves and the round corners, the tape should be notched where surplus tape accumulates or becomes too taut. The surplus should be cut away after the tape has been applied. Notches will have to be cut in the tape as the strain occurs. This is done when applying the tape.

Forming Edges: Cushion, feathered or contoured edges can be formed with the aid of tacking tape.

To make a cushion edge, cut the cored-stock foam rubber so it will overhang the edge ¾ of an inch on each side. This ¾ of an inch includes upholstery allowance. Cement the tacking tape 1 inch along the top edges of the cored foam-rubber stock where the cushion edges are to be formed. Fig. 281A. Then tuck in the bottom edge of the cored foam rubber so as to collapse the core holes. This prevents excessive bunching and wrinkling of the foam rubber. Fig. 281B. Allow the fingers to slide back to the tape, leaving the tucked-in portion of the foam rubber resting on the base. The tape is then tacked to the underside of the base or the frame. Fig. 281C.

When working with solid foam-rubber slab stock, allow ¼-inch upholstery allowance along each edge. Then cement the tacking tape 1 inch in along the top edge of the foam rubber. Draw the tape down to a tacking position taut enough to round off the edge to the desired shape. Fig. 282.

Feathered or contoured edges differ from cushion edges in that the curvature of the edges is more gradual. The bevel of the cut will determine the degree of the curvature. To get a long taper, the bevel should be long. To get a rounded curvature the bevel should be short.

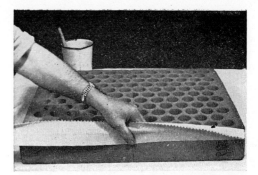

Fig. 279. Cementing tacking tape to foam rubber

First cut the foam rubber to the size and shape desired, making the normal upholstery allowance on all sides. Then cut the bevel to get the desired shape. Cement tacking tape to the top edge of the foam rubber with a 1-inch lap. Next, position the foam-rubber pad in place and pull the tacking tape down until the beveled edge meets the base. Fig. 283. The tacking tape is then tacked in place.

To make a square edge, cut the foam rubber to the size and shape desired, making the normal upholstery allowance on all sides. Cement the tacking tape to the vertical edge. Fig. 284. Tack the tape to the bottom side of the base or frame.

Fig. 280. Reinforcing foam-rubber edges

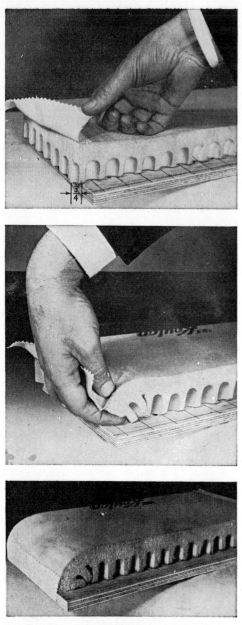

Fig. 281A, B and C. Making cushion edge

Fig. 282. Making rounded edge

To shape the edges on rubberized-fiber stock, the edges have to be cut with scissors along the top edge. Fig. 285. Cushion and square edges cannot be made using rubberized-fiber stock.

Making a Crowned Surface: There are two methods by which crowned surfaces can be built. The two methods will work equally well with both foam rubber and rubberized fiber.

First, one must determine the thickness of the pad desired at the edges and then the amount and shape of the crown desired. One method to achieve a crowned surface is as follows. Select a piece of stock having the thickness desired at the top of the crowned surface. Then cut the stock to the size and shape of the surface to be padded, making the upholstery allowance. Next mark a line around the slab stock along the edges where the taper is wanted. Fig. 286. Then mark a line along the bottom side of the slab stock, 6 inches in from the edges, where the crowned effect is desired. Next cut away the tapered wedge shape with a scissors, taking care to follow the guide lines when cutting. Trim a little at a time rather than making big cuts that may go too deep. Fig. 287. Do the same to the other edges. Foam rubber can be sanded smooth. The cushion is then placed on the surface being upholstered and cemented along the bottom where the taper area occurs. Rubberized-fiber pads can be stitched or tacked to the base instead of being cemented in place.

The same cushion contour can be achieved by the following method. Select a pad that is the thickness of the edge desired. Cut this stock to the size and shape of the surface to be padded,

FIG. 283. Forming feathered or contoured edge

making upholstery allowances. Then select a soft-density slab stock the height of which is one half the difference between the height of the crown and the height of the pad along the edge. For instance, if the crown is to be 6 inches high and the height of the pad along the edge is 4 inches, then stock 1 inch thick should be used.

Cut a piece 3 inches smaller in size along the edges where the taper is desired and cement this pad to the bottom side of the first pad. Cut a second piece from the same stock. This should be 3 inches smaller than the second pad along the edges where the taper is desired.

The third pad will then be cut 6 inches smaller along the edges where the taper is desired than the top pad.

For example, if the crown of the pad is to be 5 inches high and the pad is to be 2½ inches high along the edge, the top stock will be 2½ inches thick and the second and third-pad stock will each be 1¼ inches thick.

The three pads are then cemented together in the proper position to form the desired crown. If needed, trim the lower edges of each pad to help the contour of the crown. The completed pad is then cemented on the surface that is being padded. Fig. 288. Rubberized-fiber pads can be stitched together and then stitched or tacked in place to the surface being padded.

When the cushion is to be crowned in all directions, the taper will have to be built on four sides. With tight seat cushions, it is best to keep the

FIG. 284. Forming squared edge

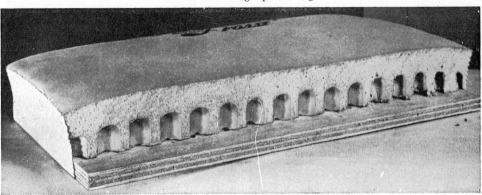

FIG. 285. Trimming edge on rubberized fiber

front edge as high as possible. This edge is subject to a great deal of flexing. Keeping the front edge high will prevent a seated person from feeling the frame.

Under Stuffing: To apply slab padding stock, the surface must be regular in contour. Surfaces that are irregular or have deep hollows should have loose stuffing sewed or tacked in place so as to make the surface uniform. The stuffing then is covered with burlap. Depressions between the edge roll and springs must be understuffed as well as on the rounded backs and arms. Fig. 289.

Application: The base that is padded with foam rubber and rubberized fibers is built onto the frame in the same manner as when padding with loose stuffing except that edge rolls are

FIG. 286. Marking slab stock for crown

not required to prevent stuffing from working over the edges. But edge rolls are required at times when coil springs are used as a base to help build a flat surface.

Slip Seats: Use ¾ or 1-inch-thick firm-density foam-rubber stock or firm ¾ or 1-inch-thick rubberized-fiber stock cut to the shape of the slip seat, making the necessary upholstery allowances. Cement the pad to the base. If a crown is desired, cut a ¾-inch-thick soft-density slab 3 inches smaller along each side and cement this pad to the center of the top slab. Then cement this assembly to the base.

Pad Seats and Backs: If the frame being upholstered is open, it must first be webbed. See Part III, Lesson One. The webbing should be kept at least ½ inch apart when padding with foam rubber or rubberized fiber. Fig. 290.

If a more resilient seat is desired, the webbing may be applied to the bottom of the frame. The cavity in the frame is then filled with an extra-firm-density pad, cored foam rubber or rubberized fiber that has been cut to the size and shape of the cavity. This stock should project from ½ to 1 inch above the frame rails and is cemented to the webbing.

The seat and back are now padded to the thickness and shape that is desired, with medium-density foam rubber or rubberized fiber. Fig. 290.

Spring Seats and Backs: The springs should be covered with burlap or a wire-type insulator before padding. The seat and back are then padded with a thickness of foam rubber or rubberized fiber to the shape desired. Fig. 291A-B. If a wire-type insulator or a rubberized-back sisal pad has been used over the springs, a pad of

FIG. 287. Cutting slab stock for crown

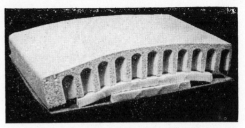

FIG. 288. Crowned pad

thinner or softer density can be used over the springs.

Platform Seats: A platform seat is a seat that is to have a loose cushion. Burlap should first be applied over the springs. A spring-edge roll is then applied along the edges so the platform will retain a loose cushion.

The edge roll can either be built of loose stuffing or a ready-made spring-edge roll can be stitched to the platform. A spring-edge roll can also be made from 1¼-inch-thick, extra-firm-density foam rubber cut 3 to 4 inches wide and cut to a taper along the back edge of the foam-rubber roll. The back edge of the roll should be ¼ inch high and the taper cut 2 inches in from the back edge. The foam-rubber roll is then cemented to the burlap, allowing the front of the foam rubber to overhang the edge ½ of an inch.

A rubberized-back sisal pad is ideal to use over the springs in back of the spring-edge roll, but an extra-firm ¾-inch solid-foam-rubber stock or rubberized fiber can also be used. A layer of cotton should be placed over a rubberized-back sisal pad or rubberized fiber before applying muslin or the final cover. Fig. 292.

Arms: The cavities on the inside of the arms that are to be upholstered should first be webbed and then covered with burlap. The arms are then padded with soft slab stock to the thickness and shape desired. As with loose stuffing, the arms should be upholstered together so they will match each other.

Tacking strips should be cemented to all sides of the foam-rubber pads so the edges may be tacked to the front of the arm stump, along the top of the arm, along the arm liner, at the bottom and to the arm slat on the back.

Rubberized-fiber pads are held in place by tacking the pad to the wood

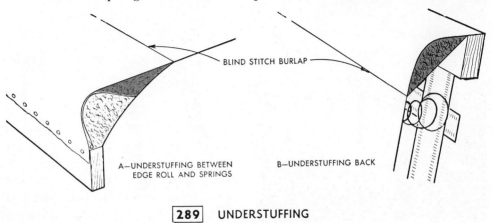

BLIND STITCH BURLAP

A—UNDERSTUFFING BETWEEN EDGE ROLL AND SPRINGS

B—UNDERSTUFFING BACK

289 UNDERSTUFFING

FIG. 290. Padding over webbing

before a final cover or muslin is applied. This will prevent a scratching sound between the cover and the rubberized fiber and will also prevent fibers from working through the final cover.

As a rule, cotton does not need to be applied over foam rubber, but if the final cover is to be unsupported, plastic-sheeting cotton should be placed over the foam rubber. There have been instances where a chemical reaction between the plastic sheeting and the foam rubber caused the plastic sheeting to discolor.

Muslin Cover: As a rule, a muslin cover is not required on upholstery work that has been done in foam rubber, but a muslin cover is recommended when the final-cover fabric is a pile fabric. This especially applies to cut velour. The pile is made of individual threads hooked into a cloth base. When in direct contact with foam rubber, these fabrics rub back

of the arm with large upholstery tacks.

Fig. 293 illustrates the application of slab stock to the arms.

Cotton: When a piece has been upholstered with rubberized-fiber stock, cotton should be placed over the stock

FIG. 291. Padding over springs

and forth as flexing occurs, and in time, the pile will pull loose from the base.

A muslin cover is recommended over cotton and rubberized fiber. The muslin cover should be applied just tight enough to compress the cotton slightly and hold the padding in place.

Applying Final Cover: The final cover is sewed and applied in the same manner as over loose stuffing. See Part IV, Lessons One and Two.

The final cover should be drawn down just enough to compress the foam rubber or rubberized-fiber padding slightly. Applying the final cover too tightly will compress the foam rubber or rubberized fibers and cause the pad to lose some of its resiliency. The padding, if compressed too tightly, will also put too much strain on the cover and cause excessive cover

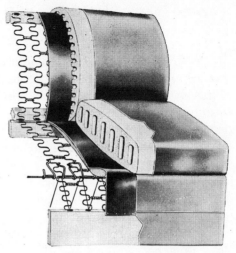

Fig. 292. Padding platform seat

wear. Too loose a cover will produce a wrinkled job.

Straightness in cover welts and seams, and neatness in making small pleats, will do much to give the work a well-tailored appearance.

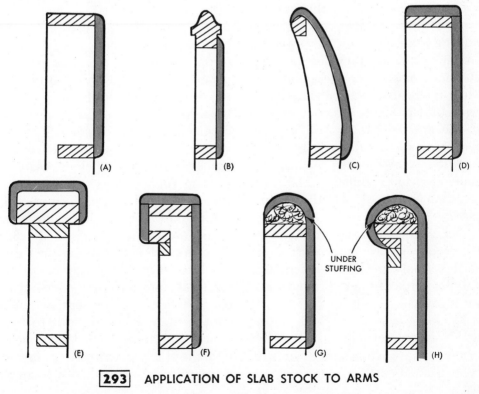

293 APPLICATION OF SLAB STOCK TO ARMS

CHANNELS AND TUFTS are much simpler to make when one uses foam-rubber or rubberized-fiber stock. The advantages are numerous: the material is of uniform thickness; it comes in one piece and eliminates all the laborious effort of stuffing and equalizing that is necessary with loose stuffing. A pattern must still be made, the cover material must be cut and sewed in the same manner and fitted to the base. But the tedious operations of shredding, prodding into place, adjusting and holding the loose stuffing in place while the work progresses are eliminated when working with foam rubber or rubberized fiber. With foam rubber or rubberized fiber, one can be sure that the channels and tufts are of uniform density and the lines one builds into the work are there to stay.

As with loose stuffing, the channels and tufts are built directly over the burlap with no previous padding. Rounded or scrolled backs and arms must first be understuffed and covered with burlap before proceeding with the channels and tufts. Also, any surfaces that are irregular or have hollows should be built to an even contour with loose stuffing. The loose understuffing should be stitched into place.

One should select either a cover that has no pattern or a cover with a very small over-all indistinct pattern that will not detract from the channel and tufting work.

Making the channels and tufting with foam rubber requires a different method than when making them with rubberized fiber.

When working with foam rubber or rubberized fiber, the laying out of the channels and tufting on the frame is the same as for loose stuffing.

Review Part IV, Lesson Three for designing and laying out channels and tufts.

Making Channels With Foam Rubber: Cored foam-rubber stock should be used in making channels for the best results. The cored stock gives the needed softness and yet hugs close to the confining cover. The chart in Fig. 294 will be helpful in selecting the foam-rubber stock to use.

When the surface to be channeled is laid out, a pattern should be made for cutting the cored foam rubber and fabric. To do this take a steel tape and curve it to the thickness of the stock being used. Fig. 209. The length from top to bottom for the cored foam-rubber stock will depend upon the type of the finished top edge that you are planning. If it rolls generously over the top edge and feathers down the back, you will need to take these measurements into consideration. Start the measurement at the very bottom of the frame where the channels originate.

Foam rubber offers the most resiliency when it is slightly compressed. Allow an inch or so in length in order to achieve this resiliency in the finished channel. If there is too much material, the surplus stock can be cut off the top before the cover is tacked in place. These dimensions are then transposed on paper. A paper pattern is made for each channel that varies from the others. These patterns should be saved for the cutting of the cover.

THICKNESS AND COMPRESSION OF STOCK USED TO MAKE CHANNELS			
Channel Size	Thickness of Stock	Stock Compression	
		Over Springs	Over Webbing
up to 4"	1½"	extra soft	soft
4 to 5½"	2"	extra soft	soft
5½ to 8"	2½"	extra soft	soft
8" & over	3"	extra soft	soft

FIG. 294. Stock for channels chart

Tapered channels can be cut to follow the pattern or they can be cut with straight parallel sides, using the widest dimension for the width. This method means that more foam rubber will be compressed at the lower end of the channel, making the channel firmer at the bottom. This will give the occupant of the seat greater support at the small of the back.

If the foam rubber is to be cut at a taper, it will be more economical to reverse the pattern of the adjacent pieces when cutting them. Fig. 295.

When constructing individual channels, the foam rubber should be rolled to the desired curve and cemented to a backing strip of muslin, so there will be no chance of the material shifting.

The muslin backing strips should be cut to conform to each channel as it is laid out on the work. Fig. 296.

When the channels are shallow or when thick stock has been used, there may be too much fullness at the center area of the channel. This can be reduced by cutting a bevel along the sides of the channels at the bottom. Fig. 297.

Coat each piece of muslin with cement and allow to dry. Then apply cement to one edge of the foam rubber and to the cement side of the muslin backing. When in proper order, press the muslin to the edge of the foam rubber. Fig. 298.

Upon completing these steps, coat the free edge of the muslin and the other edge of the channel with cement and allow them to become tacky; then pull the muslin backing in place against the edge of the foam rubber. This will pull the foam rubber into a half-round contour. When the foam rubber is in proper position along the entire edge, hold it there for a few minutes, applying pressure gently. Fig. 299.

All the channels should be fabricated before starting to apply channels to the work.

Making Channels with Rubberized Fiber: Use the chart in Fig. 294 to determine the thickness and compression of the rubberized-fiber stock.

When the channels have been laid out on the work, make paper patterns of them. Pin the patterns to the rubberized-fiber stock and cut out the channels to the size of the patterns, making an upholstery allowance at the top and bottom.

When all the channels have been cut, trim round the side edges with scissors. Fig. 300. When all the channels have had their edges trimmed, they are ready to be installed.

Cotton must be applied over the rubberized-fiber channels and under the cover when they are installed on the work.

Cutting and Sewing Covers: If the channels were made of foam rubber, the patterns that were used to cut the foam rubber can be used for cutting the cover fabric.

If no patterns have been made, make them according to the following method. Measure each channel as shown in Fig. 209 and transpose these full-size dimensions to a piece of paper. At the top side, 2 inches are

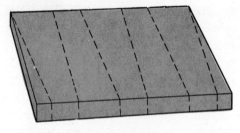

added for handling of the cover, ⅝ inch is added to each side for seams and 1 inch is added to the bottom for the sewing of the cover stretcher. At the corners and ends, an allowance must be made so that the cover can be pulled around the frame members and tacked. A paper pattern should be made for each channel that varies from the others.

The paper patterns are then laid on the cover fabric and the covers are cut to size. Cut as many covers as needed. The paper pattern should be centered over the cover so that the pattern or weave of the fabric is vertical to the center of the channel.

The channel covers are then sewed together, allowing a ⅝-inch seam. When the different covers are sewed together in the proper order, they will correspond to those marked on the work.

A stretcher is cut to the width and length needed and then sewn to the

bottom of the channels. The stretcher should be wide enough to be tacked to the top side of the back seat rail.

The seam of the channel nearest the center is then sewn with a lock stitch along the corresponding line of the work. The channel cover is then ready for filling. Fig. 210. Place the channel made for this spot under the cover and pin the seam in place along the line marked on the work. When the cover is in satisfactory order, the seam is then stitched in place. Repeat this operation until all the channels are in place. At the inside corners and end, the channel covers are handled in the same manner as when covering flat work.

The stretcher is then slip-tacked in place along the top of the seat rail. Care should be taken that the covers over the channels are not pulled out of line when tacking the stretcher in place. It will be necessary to pleat the stretcher in order to gather the surplus from the fullness of the channels.

The cover is then tacked in place over the top of the channels. The cover is pulled over and tacked down directly on the center of each channel. One should take care that the channel is not pulled out of line. If there is too much material at the top of the channel, it should first be cut away before tacking down the cover. The

FIG. 296. Cutting muslin backing

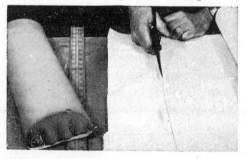

FIG. 297. Cutting bevel along sides of channel

FIG. 298. Cementing muslin to edge of foam rubber

FIG. 299. Cementing muslin to other edge of pad

channels are then tacked along the top. Fig. 211. Make a pleat on each side of each channel, facing the pleats to the outside of the work away from the center of the back—except on arms, where pleats should lay to the back.

Tufting: Tufting with foam rubber or rubberized fiber is much simpler than when working with loose stuffing because only one pad is used. One can use either extra-soft or soft-compression cored foam rubber, or rubberized fiber. The thickness of the stock should be at least 1½ inches. For most work, the stock should never be over 3 inches thick. For large pieces, such as club chairs and large sofas, it is sometimes advisable to use stock as thick as 4 inches.

Draw the tufting pattern desired on the piece that is to be tufted first. Fig. 301A. See Part IV, Lesson Three for designing and the laying out of tufts.

Cut the cored foam rubber or rubberized stock to the size and shape desired, making an upholstery allowance. Then draw the pattern on the foam rubber or rubberized fiber in the same position as it is on the work.

It is best to cut or punch ¾-inch holes through the foam rubber or rub-

berized fiber where the buttons are to be placed.

The pleats will lay better if the foam rubber or rubberized fiber is cut from hole to hole, the cuts outlining the shape of the tufts or channels. One should use a knife or scissors and make the cuts ½ inch deep or to the points where the cores begin on the foam rubber. Fig. 301B.

Fasten the foam-rubber stock in place either by using tape or cementing the pad directly to the work.

Measure the tufts for the laying out of the button positions on the fabric. Starting at one edge and using a steel tape, measure over each tuft from hole to hole, laying out these measurements on the cover fabric with chalk. Work across the area in this manner to the

FIG. 300. Trimming edges round

opposite edge. Follow the same method for vertical measurements. Apply tension to the steel tape as it is drawn from hole to hole so the pad stock assumes a round form.

As the tufting work progresses, tear pieces of cotton to the shape of each tuft and channel being covered. Then apply cotton over the rubberized fiber under the cover.

The buttons used in tufting should be covered with the cover fabric. The first row of buttons is then stitched in place on the face side of the cover through the burlap and webbing. The twine is tied down to the webbing with a wad of cotton placed between the twines. This holds the buttons and the cover to the burlap. This is done to each tuft or channel in the first row.

The second row of buttons is then fastened in place, with the pleats lying in proper direction. Fig. 301C. Each row of tufts and channels is then fastened in place until all the rows of the tufts and channels are completed.

The cover is then tacked around the sides, top and bottom—as in flat-sur-

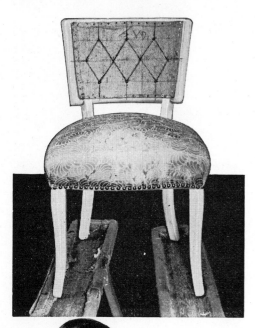

Fig. 301. Tufting layout, making cuts for pleats, buttoning tufts

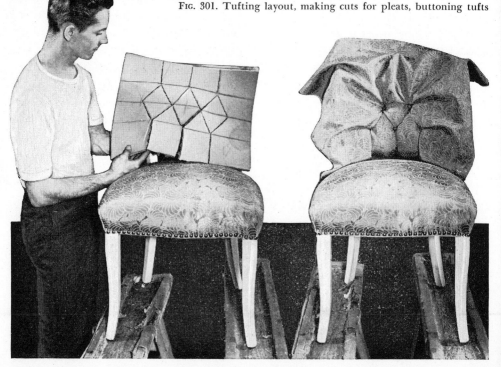

face work—except that each channel or tuft is pleated when the cover is tacked in place.

In tufting work the pleats should be placed so they face down on the back and arms. On seats the pleats are laid to face the front. Pleats on channels over the arms and back are laid so they face the outside of the work. Fig. 213.

Lesson Five — MAKING LOOSE CUSHIONS WITH FOAM RUBBER

WITH FOAM RUBBER, one can fabricate a luxuriously comfortable and durable loose reversible cushion to any size or shape desired.

The covers are cut and sewed in the same manner as when making an innerspring-filled loose cushion. Refer to Part III, Lesson Seven for measuring, cutting and sewing cushion covers.

Fabricated foam cushions can be placed in the cover with hand irons, a filling machine or by hand.

There are two standard cushion heights. One has a 5½-inch crown and is 3 inches high around the edges. The other size has a 6½-inch crown and is 3½ inches high around the edges. The thinner cushion is used on small pieces and period furniture. The thicker cushion is used on large pieces and modern furniture. There are several methods of fabricating an all-foam-rubber reversible cushion, but the method given here is the best way to make the loose cushion.

Fig. 302 illustrates the stock used in fabricating a loose reversible cushion. Cored stock (A) is used for the top and bottom of the cushion. Solid-slab stock (B) is used for the border of the cushion. Cored stock (C) is used for the inner core of the cushion.

Extra-soft cored stock should be used in making cushions for the backs. Soft cored stock should be used for making seat cushions that are placed over springs. Medium cored stock should be used for seats over a solid base or webbing and on cushions where the final cover is of plastic sheeting even if it is supported with leather covers. The border stock should be of soft foam rubber for all cushion work.

First a paper pattern must be made of the cushion. This pattern must conform to the size and shape of the seat. The pattern can also be used in cutting the top and bottom of the cushion covers.

An upholstery allowance of ⅜ inch

Fig. 302. Stock for fabricating loose reversible cushion

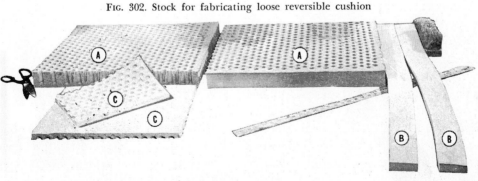

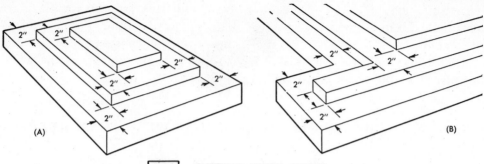

should be made on all sides of a foam-rubber cushion except on the T of a T-cushion. In this case, the allowance is ³⁄₁₆ inch on the back of the T and ⁹⁄₁₆ inch at the end of the T. See Fig. 304A.

On a cushion with a 3-inch-high edge and a 5½-inch crown, use the following foam-rubber stock: 1 by 3-inch soft slab stock for border; 2-inch-thick cored stock for top and bottom; 1-inch-thick soft cored stock for center cores.

On a cushion with a 3½-inch-high edge and a 6½-inch crown, the following foam-rubber stock is used: 1 by 3½-inch soft slab stock for border; 2½-inch-thick cored stock for top and bottom; ¾-inch-thick soft cored stock for center cores.

Cut the bottom and top foam rubber first; it should be ⅝ inch smaller on each side of the pattern. On T-cushions, however, the foam rubber should be cut ¹³⁄₁₆ inch smaller than the pattern at the back of the T and ⁷⁄₁₆ inch smaller at the end of the T. Fig. 304B.

One inner core is then cut 2 inches smaller on each side than the top and bottom of the cushion. The second inner core is cut 2 inches smaller on each side than the first core. In other words, it is 4 inches smaller than the

top and bottom of the cushion. Fig. 304. These inner cores will give the cushion a crowned effect.

The larger inner core is then cemented in place on one side of the top or bottom stock, allowing 2 inches on all sides. The smaller inner core is then cemented to the larger inner core, allowing 2 inches on all sides. Fig. 305. When cementing, be sure that the cement does not reach the 2-inch-wide exposed area along the edge of the top and bottom pieces. To prevent this, dust talc or soapstone liberally in the open cores and surfaces in this area. Then place the other side of the cushion over the thinner cores and cement it to the inner core. Fig. 306. The top and bottom stock should not be cemented together along the 2 inches of the outer edges.

Next cut the boxing to the length of each side and to the width desired. Apply cement to one side of the top and bottom pieces of the cushion and to the border stock of the corresponding side. Allow the cement to become tacky and then register the border in place along the edge of the cushion. Fig. 307. On cushions that have 3 inches of edge and a 5½-inch crown, the top and bottom stock is 2 inches thick, making the total thickness along the edges of the cushion 4

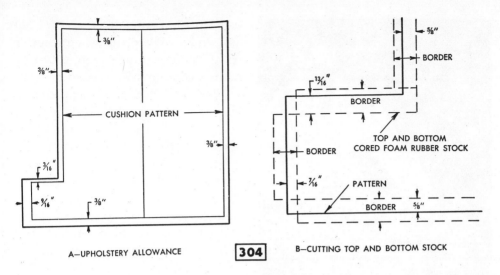

A—UPHOLSTERY ALLOWANCE | 304 | B—CUTTING TOP AND BOTTOM STOCK

(Diagram A labels: 3/8", 3/8", CUSHION PATTERN, 3/8", 3/16", 3/16", 3/8")

(Diagram B labels: 5/8", BORDER, 13/16", BORDER, TOP AND BOTTOM CORED FOAM RUBBER STOCK, BORDER, 7/16", PATTERN, BORDER 5/8")

inches. The border is only 3 inches wide. When applying the border to the edge of the cushion, center it on the edge, leaving ½ inch of the cushion edge exposed at the top and bottom. On cushions that have a 3½-inch edge and a 6½-inch crown, the top and bottom stock is 2½ inches thick, making the total thickness along the edges of the cushion 5 inches. The border is only 3½ inches wide. So, when applying the border to the edge of the cushion, center the border on the edge of the cushion, leaving ¾ of an inch of the cushion edge exposed at the top and bottom.

When the borders have been ce-

mented to all the edges, the top edge of the border is then cemented to the exposed edge at the top of the cushion. These edges are brought together to form a crown. Apply cement to the edge and allow it to become tacky. Fig. 308. The edges are then pressed together gently, giving a fully rounded contour. Fig. 309. When the edges on one side of the cushion are completed; the cushion is turned over and the edges are then cemented together in the same manner.

The same procedure is followed when cementing the edges of the border together at the corners. Fig. 312. The corners should be left full so as

FIG. 305. Cementing cushion cores

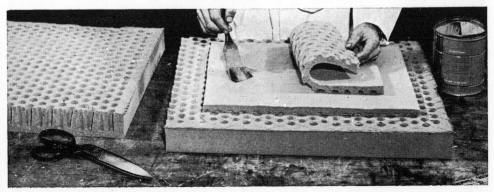

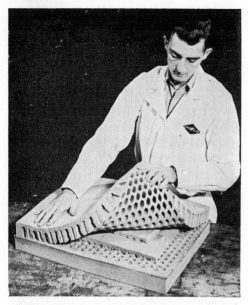

FIG. 306. Cementing top and inner core

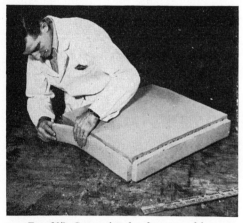

FIG. 307. Cementing border to cushion

to keep the corners of the cover full and plump. If too full when completed, the corner can be trimmed to the desired contour with scissors.

The cushion is now complete and ready for covering. When the cushion has a 3-inch edge, the boxing of the cover should be 3 inches between welts or the brush edging. When cushions have a 3½-inch edge, the boxing of the cover should be 3½ inches between welts or the brush edging. Let the cement dry thoroughly for several hours before stuffing the cushion into the cover. The cushion can be placed in the cover by hand or with the aid of hand irons or a cushion-filling machine. When you use hand irons or a cushion-filling machine, dust these tools thoroughly with talc or soapstone to avoid friction. This is not necessary if the foam-rubber cushion is first covered in muslin. A muslin cover should be used if the cover is a pile fabric.

Foam Rubber over Marshall Unit: Extra comfort can be built into an innerspring cushion by placing a layer of cored foam-rubber stock on the top and bottom of the marshall unit. A cushion of this type can be made by hand or in a filling machine.

First make up a marshall unit to the

FIG. 308. Cementing edge of border and edge of cushion

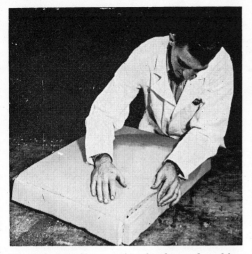

FIG. 309. Pressing together border and cushion

FIG. 311. Placing foam rubber over marshall unit

FIG. 310. Padding cushion with cotton

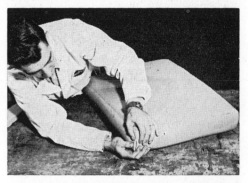

FIG. 312. Cementing corners together

size needed. See Part III, Lesson Seven. Then place a 1-inch slab of soft cored foam-rubber stock on the top and bottom of the marshall unit. Fig. 311.

The marshall unit and the foam rubber are then placed over a layer of cotton and the edges are filled out with cotton so it will fill out the cover. Be sure the corners are filled out full and plump. Fig. 310. A layer of cotton is then placed over the top. The cushion is then stuffed into the cover in the conventional manner.

Rubberized-fiber pads alone do not build into satisfactory loose cushions. However, rubberized-fiber pads work well over marshall units, eliminating the feel of springs and giving added comfort to the cushion.

INDEX